To Leo Blakely, with best wish, service to the greatest country in the world

Sincerely
Hubert "Herb" Marlow
CW 3, USA (Ret.)
23 May 2008

CID

ARMY DETECTIVES IN PEACE AND WAR

all the best Leo. It was good to see you again in Tampa, Carlo

BY

HUBERT "HERB" MARLOW
SPECIAL AGENT (RET.) U.S. ARMY CID

with contributions by the USMC Marine Corps CID

RoseDog ❧ Books
PITTSBURGH, PENNSYLVANIA 15222

ISBN # 0-8059-9595-1
Printed in the United States of America

First Printing

For additional information or to order additional books,
please write:
RoseDog Publishing
701 Smithfield Street
Pittsburgh, Pennsylvania 15222
U.S.A.
1-800-834-1803
Or visit our web site and on-line bookstore at
www.rosedogbookstore.com

This book is dedicated to the memory of United States Army CID Special Agent Leroy Halbert Jr., a fellow agent at the Cam Ranh Bay Field Office, Detachment B, 8th Military Police Group (Criminal Investigation), 18th Military Police Brigade, Vietnam, who lost his life in the line of duty on 31 Dec 1970. To CID Special Agent James T. Abbott, 101st MP Co, 101st Airborne Division (Ambl) Camp Evans, Thua Thien Province, Vietnam, who lost his life in the line of duty, on 11 January 1971, and to German Police Officer, and member of the Drug Suppression Team, Volker Walliser, murdered by a drug dealer during an undercover drug operation with CID and other law enforcement officers during Dec 1991, and last but not least to my wife, Monika.

ABOUT THE BOOK COVER

The book cover was re-created by Lue Gregg from a 1980 photo by retired CID Special Agent Henry H. G. Mungle, which captures the essence of what it means to be a CID special agent. The "King down" signifies "capture," or a successful investigation through deductive reasoning. The "handcuffs & gun" represent "strength & commitment," while the "badge" displays the "authority" necessary to perform the job of a CID Special Agent. I am indebted to Lue Gregg for reconstructing the photo image, and to Henry Mungle the designer and photographer for his kind permission to permit me to use his photo design as my book cover.

"*Kudos to Herb Marlow for producing a very readable, informative and, at times, humorous book. It provides a concise history of US Army criminal investigative organizations, summaries of actual cases from around the world during the WWII/cold war eras, and Herb's experiences as a child in WWII Germany through decades of investigative experience. As a career Military Police officer and one of Herb's former commanders, he has brought back many memories to me. Many thanks, Chief!*"

James D. Smith, Colonel, MPC USA, Retired

"*This book contains all of the hard hitting drama of a detective on the job in any city. Thirty four years of law enforcement experience, civilian and military, tells me this is a must read for any police officer who has carried a badge in either the military or civilian worlds.*"

John K. Groves, Lieutenant Colonel. MPC, Retired

"*The collection is an interesting selection of stories which trace the author's life experiences. They also truly convey the heart and soul of CID Special Agents and the tremendous job they do for the Army and all soldiers. It was a source of great pride to me that the US Army Criminal Investigative Command reputation was among the highest of all investigative agencies throughout the world. This was possible only because of the outstanding performance by all Special Agents. They truly "lived" by the motto "Do What Has To Be Done". Please accept my heartiest congratulations for your effort in writing these stories which truly honor all past, present and future Special Agents and Investigators. Please, also keep up the good work you do for the CID Agents Association. Thanks for the memories.*"

Respectfully
Paul M. Timmerberg, Major General, MPC, USA, Retired

As a one time commander of Herb Marlow, I can thoroughly attest to his expertise in the field of criminal investigation. Herb was a "Top Gun" CID Agent during his many years of service in the US Army. In his book, CID: Army Detectives in Peace and War, Herb has offered a unique collection of investigative vignettes never before available to true crime readers inside or outside of the military. His vivid recollections of CID personalities and investigations around the globe, by CID agents, will keep the reader interested from the cover to the very end of the book. As a bonus, Herb has included many photographs which add a further dimension into the inner-world of the US Army's Criminal Investigation Division. Finally, Herb's contribution adds to the proud legacy of the Army's Detective Force and I, for one found it to be a fascinating read.

Robert K. Ressler, Colonel, MPC, AUS, Retired
and Special Agent, FBI, Retired

Contents

Acknowledgments

The author wishes to thank the following persons for their help, advice, review, and stories or photographic contributions. Without the assistance of these persons, this book could not have been written.

Thanks to – Franz Stigler; Criminal Investigators: Werner Loewenstein; Virgil V. Becker; Anthony F. "Tony" Correri; Alvin P. Fackerell; Carl C. Craig; James E. Mercer; Walter F. Junkins; Shel F. Miller, and Oscar Michaud; Tony Schneider; Peter Dedijer; Skhugeshi "Shug" Madokoro; William C. Ward; Russell M. Dunn; and Robert R. Meier. Special Agents Alfred L. "Al" Cummings; Courtland D. "Court" Bradbury; Robert L. Cherry; Martin W. Quattlebaum; Steven C. Volk; Daniel E. "Danno" White; Russell M. Dunn; Jearl E. "Buck" Ballow; Bunyan Johnson; Richard A. Denoo; Robert F. Coucoules; Henry H. G. Mungle; Weeden R. Nichols; Robert N. "Bob" Zaza; Robert J. Woods; Albert F. "Al" Kaan; Arcy W. Lyle; Donald E. Riffe; Richard W. Smith; Robert A. Cappuccio; Frank A. Chiusano; Henry Kuhn, and Andrew A. Jackson.

Criminal Investigators (Ret.) of the USMC CID

James B. Benson; Barton E. "Bart" Immings; Roy M. Winters and Robert L. Ruble who, using the pen name of Bobby Ruble wrote the books *Have no Mercy* and *The Mysterious Farm Girl*.

A special thanks to my former commanding officer, Colonel (Retired) James D. Smith for his thorough review of my draft book.

INTRODUCTION

When I retired from the U. S. Army Criminal Investigation Division I did not plan to write a book about the CID, it never entered my mind. Then I worked for Munford, Inc as an investigator and attended Munford Institute of Polygraphy in Augusta, Georgia, and finally finished my working career by working for the Defense Investigative Service now called the Defense Security Service for twenty and one half years and still had no thoughts of writing a book.

I joined the CID Agents Association in 1984, and pretty soon I was one of the directors for four years, followed by six and one half years as chairman of the Ways and Means Committee. In February 1998, I wrote an article for the CIDAA, which I titled "Someone You Should Know." The article featured the history of Rev. Charles F. Grieco (deceased), who was the chaplain of the CIDAA at the time. I had gotten to know Father Grieco pretty well, and thought his story should be shared. Father Grieco was a CID agent for eight years and had then decided to become a priest.

Paul Haubner, the newsletter editor of the CIDAA liked the article and asked me if I would be willing to make it a regular feature of the newsletter, and I agreed. By writing the "Someone You Should Know" feature articles I collected many stories from different agents and one day I thought this would make a good book and should be shared.

You might wonder why I included the story of the bombing and sinking of the ocean liner *Cap Arcona* and the story about the Me=109 fighter and the B=17 bomber. The story about the *Cap Arcona* was something I witnessed during WWII. Since it reflects the horrors of war, I thought it might be nice to also reflect a true account that shows chivalry and honor still existed during WWII.

CID agents serve in peacetime and during wars and they are the hardest working bunch of people you will ever meet. The life of a CID agent, both United States Army and USMC is not only in danger of hostile forces, during time of war, but is also in danger from criminal elements within the military during both time of peace and time of war. This book then is the record of true accounts, investigations conducted by U.S Army Criminal Investigators/Special Agents and Criminal Investigators of the United States Marine Corps, to whom I dedicate one Chapter.

Army CID investigators had the title of Criminal Investigator prior to the creation of the U.S. Army Criminal Investigation Command (USACIDC) in 1971. Since the creation of USACIDC, CID investigators have the title of Special Agent.

CHAPTER ONE

The Pre-through Post WWII Years in Germany

The Childhood Days

I was born one of two identical twins, on 27 August 1935, as Hubert Kluenter, in Hamburg, Germany. The early growing up years in Germany were pleasant because on weekends my dad would take us down to the harbor. There we would see all the ocean liners, including the *Cap Arcona* later sunk in the bay of Lubbock (Luebeck), by the British Air Force, with a loss of over five thousand lives, mostly concentration camp inmates from the concentration camp Neuen Gamme, near Hamburg, but more about that later.

Peacetime, as I remember it, did not last very long. With the beginning of war also came the first air raids on Hamburg. I remember running to the big concrete air raid bunkers, and as a kid this was exciting in the beginning. Often we would emerge from the bunker, at the end of the air raid and buildings would be burning in various locations. I recall a big lumberyard, across from where we lived and a little down the street, being an ocean of flames and the post office burning. We would go around and collect bomb splinters, like someone else would collect postage stamps. The bomb splinters would have different shapes and colors as a result of the extreme heat the blast caused.

Early in 1943 the British Air Force began heavy bombing of Hamburg and so our entire first grade class, with teacher (Charlotte

Kuehl), was evacuated to Bavaria and spread out to different farms surrounding the town of Schesslitz (twelve miles from Bamberg). My brother and I ended up at Zeckendorf and were there when on 23 July 1943 the big bombing raid on Hamburg occurred, in which my maternal grandfather was killed. Living on the farm was kind of exciting for us kids. We had a ruin of an old castle, the Giech Burg only about one half mile up the hill from us and we, with our classmates, would go to the castle and play games.

A yearly event, which some might find unusual, is that since 1950, Dr. Juergen and Charlotte Kuehl have held a reunion of our first class, I have attended about four of the reunions, the last one in April 2001. Our class was the first class that Mrs. Kuehl taught, and Dr. and Mrs. Kuehl never had children of their own, so our class became their children.

Another experience was watching a B-17 get hit by anti-aircraft guns and burn and crash only about five miles from the farm. So the next day a bunch of us kids went to see where the bomber had crashed and found all kinds of debris on the ground. One kid was very dumb and tapped a bomb with a stick, causing it to blow up and rip off all the fingers on his hand. He was lucky he did not get killed. What a way to grow up as a kid.

The big bombing raid on Hamburg, on 23 July 1943, left only about two houses standing in the section of the city, called Hamm, where we had lived. My mother, grandmother, and sister still resided there. My brother and I had been moved to Zeckendorf already. The bombing raid, by a force of one thousand bombers, resulted in 50 percent of Hamburg being completely destroyed and another 25 percent being heavily damaged.

The basements of the apartment buildings in Hamburg were used as air-raid shelters, including the one in which my family lived, because you did not always have time to make it to the big air-raid shelter. A soft spot had been created between each adjoining basement, so if one building collapsed you could escape into the next one and eventually to the outside. This was exactly how my mother, sister, and grandmother escaped the inferno and were left homeless. My mother told us that had we (my twin and I) remained in Hamburg we might well have perished. Very often these basement shelters would become the grave of those seeking safety in them. Initially my mother, sister, and grandmother came to us in Bavaria; however, there was not enough room on the farm for our entire family and so we moved from Bavaria to a little fishing village by the name of Haffkrug, on the Baltic Sea and at the Bay of Luebeck.

My grandmother had grown up at Haffkrug, and we resided in a two-room apartment in a small house, next door to the little house she grew up in. At that time it was occupied by one of her sisters and her family, including our cousin, Horst Kelling. For us kids those were happy times.

Horst was sixteen or seventeen years of age at the time, and working at one of the German Air Force Research Centers. One day Horst came home and had some signal flare ammo that he had swiped from his job. We all promptly created an artillery piece, consisting of two wheels with a metal pipe mounted on it (the gun barrel) and a shield in the front to make it look like the real thing. Next Horst inserted one of the flares, with the fuse line pulled through a little hole in the pipe and he lit it. It left the pipe like a true artillery shell and promptly flew over a farmer's head. He did not appreciate what we kids considered fun and got real angry at us kids.

Then came the day, during the Summer of 1944, when we were supposed to go to the *Gau* Seat (County Seat) in the city of Eutin, to register for the Hitler Youth. Five of us boys got the day off from school, an idea we really liked, and started to proceed to Eutin. It was a beautiful day and as we walked along and came close to a railway station, we suddenly heard the sound of aircraft. Since the German Air Force was pretty much no longer in existence, we knew right away that this meant bad news, and sure enough the aircraft started to strafe a train and the train station. The five of us dove into a nearby forest to take cover. After that we lost all interest in registering for the Hitler Youth. We all returned home and told the teacher we couldn't find the place. We did not try again to register for the Hitler Youth. It was to our benefit that we resided in the little fishing village of Haffkrug, because the Nazi authorities were not as strict as those in the big cities, such as my home town Hamburg.

My mother, a beautician by trade, was forced by the Nazis to work in the aircraft factory and the famous shipbuilding yard of Blohm & Voss in Hamburg; they told my mother "we don't need beauticians."

I will now tell you about a famous German ocean liner. You might wonder why I'm telling you about this ocean liner, but at the end you will understand why. I will follow up with a story about a German fighter aircraft escorting a B-17 bomber to the North Sea and this is to show you the good and the bad that can happen during a war.

Peacetime travels of the *Cap Arcona*

The *Cap Arcona* - "The Queen of the South Atlantic"- A German Luxury Liner. The Hamburg South American Steamship Line's *Cap Arcona*, known as "The Queen of the South Atlantic," traveled between Hamburg, Germany, and many South American ports.

The ship, a three-stacker with 27 561 gross tons, was launched on 14 May 1927 at the shipyard of Blohm & Voss, Hamburg. This ocean-going vessel was turbine-driven and had a speed of 20 knots, a crew of 630, and room for 1315 passengers. The ship went on her maiden voyage on 19 November 1927, from Hamburg to Rio de Janeiro, Brazil, Buenos Aires, Argentina and other ports of call. The trip from Hamburg to Rio de Janeiro took twelve days, and to Buenos Aires fifteen days. The liner had many innovations other ships of that time did not have, and only a total of four captains had been at the helm during her existence. During her time as a luxury liner she made ninety one trips, transporting approximately 200,000 passengers and traveling 750,000 nautical miles, all without incident.

At the end of June 1939, the *Cap Arcona* left Hamburg on its ninety first journey to South America, with a return date, to Hamburg, of 25 August 1939. The ship had hardly tied up, when the youngest of the crew were confronted with the fact that they had been drafted, most into the German Navy.

Wartime role of the *Cap Arcona*

On 1 September 1939, the *Cap Arcona* became an auxiliary ship of the Germany Navy and during Nov. was moved to Gotenhafen, Germany, where she served as a crew accommodation ship, mostly for German submarine crews.

On 9 October 1944, three hundred seventy eighth bombers of the 8th United States Air Force attacked the harbor and sank the fully loaded Red Cross ship *Stuttgart*, however the *Cap Arcona* escaped unscathed. Two hundred and fifty Soviet divisions were ready to move on Berlin, and the Eastern Provinces of Germany had been cut off by the Soviets. The only way to escape was by ship across the Baltic Sea, and so began the mass evacuation of two and one half million refugees. Only approximately twenty five thousand refugees died as a result of the sinking of ships. That was quite an accomplishment that a collection of war ships, ocean liners, and small fishing boats performed. The largest loss of life, which makes the loss of the 1503 from the *Titanic* seem small, occurred on the 25 484 gross tons ocean liner *Wilhelm Gustloff*, with six thousand one hundred refugees on board. The *Wilhelm Gustloff* was sunk by the Soviet submarine S-13 with a loss of life of 5196 lives (estimates put the loss at over 9000 lives, because several thousand had boarded without being recorded in the passenger list). Such is war.

On 24 January 1945, work began to get the engines, which had been idle and neglected for years, ready for travel. The first refugees came on board and by 3 February 1945, the number had reached 12000 to 13000 (No one kept an accurate account). So began the first trip with refugees, consisting of old men, women, children and wounded, across the Baltic Sea to Neustadt, in the bay of Luebeck, which would end up as the grave of this beautiful ship and the tragic end for many concentration camp inmates. The *Cap Arcona* made three trips, rescuing a total of 25795 people and she was by far the largest ocean liner on the Baltic at that time. The 21 046 gross tons ship *Deutschland* made a total of seven trips and became the record breaker on the number of people saved with 69379. More about the *Deutschland* later.

The *Cap Arcona* was still at anchor in the bay at Neustadt and Captain Gerdts, master of the *Cap Arcona*, refused to make another trip to Gotenhaven because, in his opinion, the ship was no longer seaworthy. On 20 February 1945, Captain Mende (also of the South American Shipping Line) arrived and had a private conversation with Captain Gerdts. Gerdts had known of rumors to make the *Cap Arcona* a floating concentration camp; however the subject matter of his conversation with Captain Mende was never determined.

Mende left Gerdts's cabin, shortly before 2200 hours, leaving his overcoat and pistol behind. Ten minutes later, the captain's steward entered the cabin and found Captain Gerdts's dead on the floor with the pistol next to him. It was never determined why he had committed suicide but your guess is as good as mine.

The ship did make another trip to Gotenhafen, leaving Neustadt on 23 March 1945, but then due to the lack of fuel and the closeness of Soviet troops made no additional trips. The last load of 9,000 wounded and 2000 refugees was unloaded on 3 April 1945, at Copenhagen, Denmark, at that time under German occupation. Captain Bertram, who had been a first officer on board during peacetime, received orders to use the remaining fuel and move the ship to Neustadt, which was the beginning of a great tragedy that could have been averted.

On 14 April 1945, the *Cap Arcona* lay at anchor in the Bay of Neustadt, and Captain Bertram wondered why she could not have stayed in Copenhagen to wait for the end of the war. He would not have to wait too long for an answer.

During 1938, the Nazis had established the Concentration Camp Neuengamme, near Hamburg, which contained 12536 male inmates. Not wanting the approaching British troops to find the inmates, on 20 April 1945 the Nazis, less than one month before the end of the war, moved all but 500 German inmates who were left behind to clean up. The other inmates were moved, in railway cattle cars and by forced marches, to Luebeck, and placed on board ships. By noon, 20 April 1945, the first officer of the *Cap Arcona* was notified that the ship would become a floating concentration camp. Captain Bertram was not on board but was notified by telephone by his first officer. Bertram refused to allow any inmates to be placed on board and for the next few days attempted to keep inmates from being placed on board. During the morning of 26 April 1945, an SS man, with two other armed SS men, informed Bertram that inmates would be placed on the ship, and if he refused he would be shot on the spot. Over 7000 concentration inmates were placed on board, along with 500 Navy guards, 50 SS troops, and a crew of 70.

From among the inmates, a group of eleven Soviet sailors, who were in fairly good physical condition, slipped into the icy water hoping to swim the four to five kilometers to the coast. They wanted to notify the approaching British troops of the confined concentration camp inmates on board the *Cap Arcona*, and request they rescue them. One Russian sailor was fished out of the water by a German coastal boat, returned to the ship, and shot. Three others were found dead in the water, and the others were never found.

The Tragedy

During the early morning hours of 3 May 1945, the staff at HQ, 2nd Tactical Air Force, RAF, made the decision to initiate one last large offensive against ships in the western Baltic, to include the Bay of Luebeck, and to attack troops, vehicles, and refugees, even though Grand Admiral Doenitz, who had become the leader of Germany after Hitler's suicide on 30 April 1945, was negotiating with the British for the capitulation of all German forces.

At 1135 hours, under the leadership of Martin T. Rumbold, a squadron of the RAF departed the airbase at Ahlhorn, Germany, with the destination of the Bay of Luebeck. At 1205 hours, four Typhoon aircraft, led by Lieutenant Stevenson, arrived and started to attack the empty 21 000 ton *Deutschland*, which was to be converted to a hospital ship and had one of its two smokestacks painted white with a red cross on it. My stepfather served on the *Deutschland* during peacetime, more about that later.

Four rockets had been fired at the *Deutschland* when Stevenson spotted the Red Cross and aborted the attack. The captain of the *Deutschland* ordered a white flag to be flown on the ship and that the entire crew was to leave the ship and go ashore in the lifeboats, thereby saving their lives. Shortly thereafter, eight additional aircraft arrived and fired rockets at the *Deutschland*, which then burned from bow to stern.

At 1212 hours, Rumbold's squadron arrived with eight aircraft and encountered heavy antiaircraft fire. Low on fuel, Rumbold ordered that they return to base. At 1400 hours, the 198th Squadron, 84th Group, RAF, under the leadership of Jonny Baldwin, commander of the 123rd Wing, the same individual who had led the aircraft that wounded Field Marshall Rommel, started with nine Typhoon fighter-bomber aircraft, all equipped with newly developed rockets with more explosive power. Upon arrival at the Bay of

Luebeck, at 1425 hours, the aircraft attacked the *Cap Arcona*, firing their rockets and cannon. Forty rockets struck the ship from the stern to midship, and the once beautiful liner soon was an ocean of flames, killing several hundred inmates in the first few minutes.

Again, the British aircraft came and attacked the *Deutschland* with five hundred-pound bombs. Seeing the three-stacker (*Cap Arcona*) was burning and showing signs of capsizing, they now attacked the few lifeboats that had been launched (most had been shot to pieces on board), and other rescue vessels at the scene. About one thousand of those on board the *Cap Arcona* jumped into the cold water of the Baltic Sea; the majority burned to death. Of those who made it to land, approximately one hundred inmates, including women and children, were shot by fanatical SS troops only a few hours before the arrival of British troops. Only about five hundred of those on board the *Cap Arcona* survived, including the ship's captain.

The inmates consisted of German, French, Danish, Dutch, and others, and Russian POW's who represented the largest group. The Nazis hated the Russians the most, so they ended up in the engine room and the lowest parts of the ship without light and fresh air. The *Cap Arcona, Deutschland, Thielbek* (a smaller ship) and another small ship all burned for three days and capsized. Why did I write about the ships? Because my twin brother and I stood on the beach and watched as these ships were attacked and burned, and we saw the bodies in the water after the attack, and the holes in the lifeboats of the *Deutschland,* used by the crew to escape the inferno, who were then attacked by the British aircraft. My twin Carlo and I returned to Haffkrug during April 2001, and as I looked out over the Bay of Luebeck I could clearly visualize, first the smoke, then the masts and finally the superstructure of the arriving *Cap Arcona* during April 1945. We also paid a visit to the Honor Cemetery for the victims of the *Cap Arcona* and *Thielbek* catastrophe. I thought to myself, how peaceful it now is for these poor victims and the hell they had gone through at the concentration camp Neuengamme and then on board the *Cap Arcona* and *Thielbek*.

Now that I have told you about the horrors of war and the cruel actions taken by military men, let me now relate a true story of WWII, which showed that compassion and chivalry were not dead.

The Ultimate Honor
An Act of Chivalry during WWII

On December 20, 1943 the U.S. 8th Bomber Command attacked targets in the Bremen, Germany complex. B-17-F aircraft No. 42-3167, of the 379th Bomb Group (H), marked with a large triangle K, was severely damaged by flak and Luftwaffe fighters, with the engagement lasting between thirteen and twenty two minutes.

It took two miracles for WWII B-17 pilot Charlie Brown and Luftwaffe fighter pilot Franz Stigler to meet and become close friends! The first miracle was when the German Air Force ace could have blown Brown's crippled bomber into oblivion in 1943 and didn't! The second miracle was that both survived the war and met forty six years later -on friendlier terms! Since that meeting in 1989, the onetime mortal enemies have welded a strong friendship. Now older and mellowed by the passing of time, their deadly duels in the skies over war=torn Europe are gone, but not forgotten.

It was December 20, 1943, when Lieutenant Charles Brown guided his B-17 *Ye Olde Pub* toward the target, a German aircraft factory in Bremen. Brown, now sixty nine, originally from Weston, West Virginia, and now living in Miami, Florida, gave this account of his miraculous escape from death: "Suddenly, the nose of the B-17 was mangled by flak. Then three of the four engines were damaged; the entire left stabilizer and left elevator were gone; 90 percent of the rudder was gone; and part of the top of the vertical stabilizer was gone. I quickly pulled out of formation. It didn't take long for the Germans to pounce on us," Brown went on.

"Eight fighters came at us from the front and seven more from the rear and we were in no condition to fight them off. I headed straight at one of them. I had given up. I really didn't think we would get through this one. I had the plane in a tightening circle when I blacked out. Our oxygen system had been shot up."

Brown had no recollection of the plane's plunge from twenty five thousand feet. When he regained consciousness the crippled B-17 was two hundred feet above the ground. Incredibly, *Ye Olde Pub* was flying straight and level directly over a German airfield! And that's when Oberleutnant (First Lieutenant) Franz Stigler, on the ground reloading his guns, spotted Brown's mortally wounded plane. He leaped into his ME-109 and took off in pursuit. Eager to score the kill, Stigler closed in from the rear to within ten feet of the B-17. This is how he described the encounter:

The B-17 was like a sieve. There was blood everywhere. I could see the crew trying to help their wounded. The tail gunner was slumped over his gun, his blood streaming down its barrel. Through the gaping hole in the fuselage, I could see crewmen working frantically to save a comrade whose leg was blown off. I thought to myself, *How can I shoot something like that? It would be like shooting at a parachute.* When I was flying in North Africa, my commander had said, 'You are fighter pilots. If I ever hear of you shooting someone in a parachute I'll shoot you myself.'

Stigler then flew wingtip-to-wingtip with the crippled bomber, close enough for the two enemies to see each other clearly. The German ace escorted the struggling B-17 to the North Sea. Then, to Brown's amazement, he saluted, put his plane into a crisp roll and flew away, allowing Brown to make it back to a British airfield.

Brown had nine other crewmembers. On this ill-fated mission four were wounded and one was dead. Brown had a bullet in his right shoulder but it was not discovered until forty years later.

Stigler, who was shot down seventeen times, is one of only 1,200 of Germany's 30,000 fighter pilots to survive the war. Stigler originally from Regensburg, Bavaria, is seventy seven and now lives in Canada. During WWII Stigler had twenty eight confirmed shot-down enemy aircraft. Only five are needed to become an ace.

The two old warriors had a chance to rehash that wartime memory when they attended a ball in Miami, Florida, celebrating the forty fifth anniversary of the USAF as a separate branch of the armed forces. How did they find each other? Brown, while attending a meeting of the American Pilots Association, was asked if anything interesting ever happened to him during WWII, and he replied, "I think I was saluted by a German Luftwaffe pilot one time."

Brown had not thought too much about the incident for years but now started to gather files and after five years had sufficient information to publish a letter, with the assistance of General Leutnant (Major General) Adolf Galland, another German fighter ace, in the German Fighter Pilots Association newsletter.

Stigler, who received this newsletter on a quarterly basis, read the article and said, "that could have been only me." Stigler wrote a letter to Brown and they both met in Seattle, Washington. After discussing the WWII encounter they both knew, based on knowledge that only those present could have had, that they indeed were the two pilots who had met in the skies over Germany on 20 December 1943. Stigler, who had shot down two B-17 bombers that day, would automatically have been awarded the Knight's Cross had he shot down Brown's B-17. Had the German military found out he had let the B-17 go, he would have been court-martialed and shot.

Now, you might ask where I got the information on Stigler and Brown. I received the information from my twin brother, Carlo, who is a friend of Stigler and who also has the largest collection of autographed photos of aces from all nations in the world. He is getting ready to turn the collection over to the USAF museum, and has recently been visited by two officers and one civilian from the Pentagon, who surveyed and logged the collection. I have personally talked with Stigler when he called my brother and have received an autographed copy of the painting called The Ultimate Honor. The painting was done by the intelligence officer of Brown's squadron, who also assisted in removing some of the wounded from Brown's heavily damaged B-17 after it returned to its airbase in England.

The war ended on 8 May 1945, and while the ships were still burning, the British Army arrived and disarmed what was left of the German Army in that area. There were many Russian, French, and other POW's in the area. The French POW's would work the fields for the farmers and run the horse and wagon for the farmer. They were not guarded and none of them wanted to leave during the war, because on the farm they had plenty to eat. After the British occupied the area they gave all POW's, including survivors of the *Cap Arcona* and *Thielbek* three days of freedom, where they could do pretty much anything they wanted (except murder) in the area. They chased all the Germans out of their homes and commenced to tear them apart. We also had to leave, but only for a brief period. Since my sister was born in Chicago, Illinois, and thereby had U.S. citizenship, this came in handy and we were permitted to return to our residence. During that time it was not safe to ride a bike, should you own one, because the former Russian POW's would push you off the bike and take it. This happened to one of our friends.

By now there was a British Area commandant and the British established a food distribution system for all foreign nationals. Once again my sister's U.S. citizenship came in handy because she was entitled to rations. Not only did the British commandant authorize rations for my sister, but he also authorized it for our entire family. That meant five rations of butter, eggs, milk, meat, and potatoes, something we had not seen for some time.

During the spring of 1946, we moved back to Hamburg since there was no employment for my mother in the fishing village of Haffkrug or the surrounding area. During 1946, it was very difficult to move because there were very few moving trucks available and if you found a truck, you also had to supply the gasoline.

Acts of Kindness of the Occupation Military Forces

I have already reflected part of this when I told you of the kind actions by the area commandant, but there were additional acts of kindness. My mother, who had resided in the U.S. before the war, was fluent in English and again British soldiers had compassion. They dropped off five gallons of gasoline at a time for a few nights, until we had a sufficient amount to enable the moving truck to take us to Hamburg.

In Hamburg the British had taken over a merchant marine school on the banks of the Elbe River, which they used as a barracks for their troops. My brother and I befriended a British soldier (at the time we could not speak English) who showed extreme kindness to two hungry German kids, and he was soon joined by one of his buddies. I don't recall their rank and names, but they went through the chow line and ate their meal, then went through the line again and handed us their filled mess kits. You can't imagine what a feast this was for my brother and me. Over a period of several months, prior to their being sent back to England, they would do this again and again when we visited them.

On another occasion a Willys station wagon, containing four officers (I believe they were American) stopped and called a group of us over to the vehicle, then gave all of the kids a Hershey bar. What a treat! We had not seen chocolate in years.

One particular incident has stayed with me through the years, seemingly insignificant now, but of great importance at the time it happened. At 2000 hours the air raid sirens would go off, indicating curfew was in effect. The British military police patrolled in a jeep accompanied by a German policeman who thought he was important and had a need to show it. On this particular evening our British soldier friend, who happened to be a barber, gave my brother and me a haircut. My mother had worried about us because it was almost curfew time. We lived only three blocks from the merchant marine school, and she came to get us. Just as she arrived the siren went off.

We had to cross a major thoroughfare to get to our apartment. As luck would have it, when we attempted to cross this street, the military police showed up followed by a British Army truck. If you were caught out after curfew you were loaded on the truck and detained to chop wood for three days. As soon as the jeep stopped next to us the German policeman started shouting at us, mainly at my mother, to get on the truck. My mother ignored him, turned to the British military police officer in the jeep and started to converse with him in American style English. He then called her "Yank". They had a nice conversation and we went home without having to chop wood.

Were there any negative incidents? Yes, but even the negative was made positive. The British Army had confiscated a grade school which the used as barracks for the troops. A British sergeant, who had been wounded by a German soldier during the war, had developed extreme hatred for all Germans. Whenever we walked past the school the sergeant, who was on the second floor, would throw rocks at us. But even this negative act produced a positive reaction from some of his fellow soldiers who would pull him away from the window whenever they caught him throwing rocks.

From all of this I learned that there are kind people in every army, and as one who lived under a military occupation I will never forget the acts of kindness the British soldiers showed us. Yes, folks, count your blessings, the United States of America is still the greatest country in the world.

In Hamburg we moved into a basement apartment of an uncle, who at the time was a POW of the Russians. He returned in 1947 and we moved into one room (five persons), of an apartment on the fourth floor, as all available living spaces were regulated by the

German authorities. While living there a fire broke out and one neighbor was killed, the fire department was ready to extract us from the fourth floor but then got the fire under control.

The last year of the war and even after the war until the money reform in 1948, were difficult years. The British had removed all the potatoes and wheat from Germany to England and we were left eating bread made from feed corn (very bitter) and would take slices of turnip to school in lieu of a real sandwich because there was no bread, no butter, and no milk. Standing in line for hours to purchase some food was nothing unusual, and then there was no coal to heat the homes. We kids would often go to the train yard and steal some coal or to the fish market to steal some fish, and would be chased by the fish dealer with a fishhook in his hand which he would use on us if he caught us. One time one of my friends, twelve years of age at the time, ran after a horse-drawn butcher wagon, with curtains on the side. He grabbed a sausage and started to run with a whole chain of sausages dragging behind him. The driver of the horse and buggy was afraid to chase him too far because then he would run the danger of having his entire wagon emptied. Needless to say we kids had a feast.

School was a regular thing for us, and since some of our generation had missed a lot of school, due to the war, we were required to attend nine grades of school. In school my twin brother and I would often get into trouble for playing tricks. In those days we still used inkwells and pens and many girls wore their hair in pigtails, so my brother and I would at times raise the inkwell and dip the pigtail of the girl seated in front of us in the ink. Often the teacher would not know which of the two of us had done it and so we both had to bend over and get whacked with a bamboo stick. It hurt, believe me. The teacher would also make use of the bamboo stick on any member of the class who could not recite a poem, which had been part of the homework. Oh yes, discipline was still big in those days.

My parents had resided in the United States before WWII, but had returned to Germany during the depression. My father was a sign painter by trade and in either 1939 or 1940 my parents had divorced. My stepfather, William Malchow had also been in the U.S. before the war, but illegally. He was a Merchant Marine sailor on the *Deutschland* and when the ship came into New York, a regular stop

14

for its transatlantic run, he got off the ship on liberty and failed to return. He remained in the United States for eight years in the San Diego area. One day he and some of his friends decided to go to Mexico, and they did. However, upon their return he was caught and promptly deported. He was told he could return to the U.S. legally after one year. He returned to Germany, where Adolf Hitler had established the draft and was promptly drafted into the German Navy. During 1944, while along the coast of Norway, his Navy ship was attacked by British aircraft and sunk. He survived, eight crewmen did not. He ended up as a POW of the Yugoslav partisans and worked several years in the copper mines. He returned to Germany in December 1949 and married my mother in 1950.

Dumb Things Kids Will Do

My grandmother had a plot of land along the railroad embankment, with a little hut on it, big enough to sit around and have coffee and cake and get out of the rain. The little hut was not hit during the bombing raids, although entire apartment houses only about three hundred yards from the hut were burned out. As a result of the bomb blasts, however, the hut was blown off its foundation and was a total loss. Along the street we had streetlights and so my twin and I would play "lead the blind man," which meant that he (or I) would close our eyes and the other twin would lead him. One day I was leading my brother and thought it might be exciting to lead him into one of those lamp posts, which I did. My brother of course ended up with a big lump on his forehead, which turned black and blue, and I ended up with a sore butt after the beating I got from my grandmother.

In those days we had a lot of burned-out buildings, that had collapsed, so there were plenty of bricks around. One apartment building, still intact, had a bottom floor apartment which was accessible from the street, and had a recessed door with about four steps leading up to it. So one evening all of us neighborhood kids picked up a bunch of bricks from a nearby ruin and piled them up, completely blocking the entry or let's say exit way. We left a square hole in the middle, so we could knock on the door with the aid of a stick. The tenant had never liked us kids anyway and when he ripped open his door and came storming out he ran right into the brick wall.

15

Chapter Two

The New World

The beginning of a new life in the United States

My parents always had the desire to return to the United States and so in December 1950, we left Hamburg on board the *U.S.S. Washington* for New York. My stepfather's sister, who owned a small factory, vouched for us. The trip on the *U.S.S. Washington*, sister ship of the *U.S.S. Manhattan*, was exciting for my brother, sister, and I, and we were on board over Christmas. I remember an individual playing the accordion and all of us following him through the gangways singing Christmas carols. The ship stopped at Southampton, England, and Halifax, Canada, and then pulled into New York. Seeing the skyscrapers was new and exiting. We then rode the train to Chicago, Illinois, where our aunt picked us up in her Cadillac, another new luxury for us, and that was the first time I ate a banana split.

My twin and I could not speak English, so my father was trying hard to find a school with someone who spoke German. No public school had anyone who spoke German, but Emmanuel Lutheran School, in Elmhurst, Illinois had a principal, Mr. Bertram, who also taught classes and was fluent in German. Mr. Bertram spoke German to my brother and me for the first two months, and thereafter told us that he would only speak German if we really got stuck. My brother and I learned how to converse in English in five months, well enough to enter York Community High School (YCHS) in September 1951.

We both graduated from YCHS in June 1955. My stepfather was having problems with his name being misspelled and mispronounced and so he had it changed by court order, at the same time he also changed my brother's and my name to Marlow.

Joining the U.S Army

After graduating from high school, my brother joined the army (Ordnance Corps) and got out after three years. I had a job with International Harvester on the outside loading dock, and a co-worker who was a master sergeant in the Army Reserve, which kind of impressed me. So on 23 August 1955, I joined the 878th Engineer Aviation Battalion, a SCARWAF unit (Special Category Army Personnel with Air Force), of the Illinois Army National Guard, O'Hare Air Base, Chicago, Illinois. At the time I was working as a loader on the dock for International Harvester Co. On 4 April 1956, I was discharged from the 878th Aviation. Engineer Battalion, which at that time was deactivated. Since the draft was still in effect I decided to join the army. I had intentions of joining a unit which would train me in heating and air conditioning, but a friend talked me into joining the Military Police. I did not know it at the time but he did me a big favor.

I was going to serve three years in the army, but made a career of it

On 16 April 56, I joined the U.S. Army, as a Private (E2), and was assigned to Company D, 2nd Battalion, 1st Basic Training Regiment, Fort Leonard Wood, Missouri. The commanding officer was First Lieutenant Theodore D. Wilson, a black gentleman and a great commanding officer. Next I went to Fort Gordon, Georgia, for military police training. Jerry Hale, who had talked me into joining the MPs, was constantly in trouble. One day he was mad at the cooks for making him work hard at KP, and so Jerry decided he was going to get even. He took a small portion of the picket fence and applied a nice new coat of white paint to it, figuring the cooks would have to finish the job after our class departed the next day. The cooks figured out who did it and he spent all evening painting the entire fence.

The Return to Germany as a U.S. soldier

I graduated from MP school, and on 19 September 1956, a group of approximately twelve of us were assigned to the newly re-activated 142nd Military Police Company (Service), Detachment A, Schwaebisch Hall, Germany. We all boarded the *General Gallahan* for Bremerhaven, Germany. After arriving in Germany, I was placed in charge of the Group because I was fluent in German and we all boarded a train from Bremerhaven to Schwaebisch Hall, Germany. The Commanding Officer of the 142nd Military Police Company (Service), was Captain Earl J. Martin. I was promoted to Private First Class on 30 October 1956, and reassigned to the Crailsheim Detachment during November 1956. On 30 April 1957, I was promoted to Specialist 3 (it was a blood stripe, two members of the 142nd had been reduced in grade and in those days the Commanding Officer could give the stripes to other members in his unit).

While in Schwaebisch Hall, Germany, a detail of us used to have to go to the Stuttgart area, to the quartermaster laundry, in a two and a half ton truck (or duce and a half as we called it) to drop off and pick up laundry and when we initially arrived all of us, since we were MPs, were issued one extra class A uniform. So we went to the quartermaster store and one of two German ladies working behind the counter, asked my buddy. "What size jacket do you wear?" He replied, "I don't know," and she said in German to the other lady "*Ist der aber bloede, weiss nicht mal seine Jacken Groesse,*" which I immediately translated into English by loudly saying to my friend "She said, boy is he stupid, he doesn't even know his own jacket size." Needless to say, she got a red face and disappeared. On the way to the QM laundry we used to pass some apple orchards a farmer owned. They were right along the road, so we would pull the duce and a half under the tree, shake the branches and let the apples fall on the truck bed. One time the old farmer came out with his shotgun and chased us away.

I enjoyed my assignment at Crailsheim and a couple of funny things occurred while I was there. I got off the midnight shift one day, and awoke in the morning because it was a little moist and cool and I noticed that my bed was outside in front of the barracks, facing Highway 2, for all to see me. My dear fellow detachment MPs had carried my bed outside, I did not think it was funny at the time.

While on patrol one evening, my partner and I made our rounds and part of it was to drive down Highway 2, turn right on another major highway and then go through a forest. Now the forest had a dirt road only wide enough for one car and various parcels of forest were owned by individual farmers. At the location of each parcel of forest there would be something like a littledrive way to pull the farm wagon in and off the road. The Forest also contained a training area for the prisoners of the stockade at Crailsheim. My partner and I drove down the dirt road and spotted a car with U.S. Forces Europe license plates. The forest was off limits to all U.S. Forces members after 2200 hours. We pulled up in back of the car and I walked up on the driver's side while my partner checked the passenger side. In the car were a black sergeant and his German girlfriend, both naked as Jay Birds.

Unfortunately the sergeant made the mistake of opening the car door, activating the inside light and exposing both himself and his girlfriend in their glory. His girlfriend did not know what to do, first she folded her arms across her breasts, then she placed them over her private parts and finally decided to cover and hide her face, it was a funny scene. The sergeant said to me "Do you mind?" indicating he wanted to close the door and turn the lights off, so they could get dressed. I had asked him for his ID card and I said "no, go ahead," and they both put on some clothing. The rule of the day was that anyone who got caught in the Forest after 2200 hours, was reduced one grade. Had we reported the sergeant, we would have had a brand new corporal. My partner and I decided to give him a break and did not report him. He was forever grateful and was friendly towards the MPs after that.

During July 1957, the 142nd Military Police Company was reassigned to Garmisch Partenkirchen, with detachments in Murnau, Fuessen, and Oberammergau, Germany. This involved the rotation of three units. Company D, 508th Military Police battalion, was in the Garmisch Area, and Company C of the 793rd Military Police battalion was in Nuernberg, Germany. Since the battalions were combat MP's and spent a considerable amount of time in the field, it always required placing MP's from other units on TDY (Temporary Duty) in the areas covered by Company D, 508th Military Police Battalion, while they were in the field. That was the reason the 142nd Military

Police Company (Svc) had been transferred. Garmisch was also one of three U.S. Forces Recreational Areas in Germany, which required having a stable MP unit there. I was initially assigned to Garmisch (Company HQ) and then to Oberammergau.

While at Oberammergau, we also had the responsibility of checking ID cards for individuals entering the Atomic and Special Weapons Building, which had a tall wire mesh fence around it, inside the Caserne. One day one of those big conferences attended by high=ranking NATO officials occurred and I drew the lot of checking the ID cards at the Atomic and Special Weapons Building. As the conference ended a big sedan pulled up and then General Hans Speidel came out of the building (he was Field Marshall Erwin Rommel's Chief of Staff – Rommel having been famous as the "Desert Fox"). As the general passed by me I said, "Guten Morgen, Herr General" (Good morning, General), he continued to walk and after he had taken about six or eight steps, turned around and came back to me. He had not realized that I had said it in German until he took a few steps. We talked for about five minutes about Hamburg, my hometown, which he knew well and he asked me how I liked it in the American Army.

After about four months, I was reassigned to Garmisch because one interpreter was on vacation and another became ill, so I performed duties as an interpreter on the MP Desk until the interpreter returned from vacation. The CID members at Garmisch, Norm Land, Bill Hurst and a Chief Warrant Officer (W4) Peterson (can't recall the names of the others assigned) tried their best to have me join them in CID as a Provost Marshal Investigator. At the time I was young and a little apprehensive about taking such a big step.

One incident that occurred in Garmisch that stuck to me was the apprehension of a full USMC colonel. While on the swing shift from 1600 to 2400 hrs, on patrol with my partner, a really tall black MP, we went to the *Dackel Bar* for a routine check. Once we entered the bar we noticed one of our MPs present whom we knew to be on restriction. To prevent him from getting in deeper trouble we intended to just take him back to the barracks. A gentleman at the bar told me "I'm a full colonel in the USMC and I'm talking to this gentleman so you are not going to take him anywhere." I politely reminded the colonel that my MP brassard (I then pointed to it) told me I would take the individual with me. The good colonel kept on interfering with my patrol and so I told him if he did not stop interfering, I would take him into custody and that is exactly what happened. We were driving 1957 Chevy's for patrol cars at the time and when I attempted to seat the Colonel in the back of the sedan, he raised his head just as my partner and I were trying to put him in the car. Of course he banged his head on the doorframe. After we got into the car the good colonel was calling us "mother f.....s" and all kinds of choice names. As it happend our commanding officer, Captain George M. Schneider, was the MPOD (Military Police Duty Officer) and when we arrived at the MP station the good colonel told Captain Schneider that we had called him the names he had called us. Captain Schneider turned to me, looked me straight in the eyes and said "Marlow, did you guys call the colonel those names?" and I replied "No sir, but that is exactly what the colonel called us." Captain Schneider looked at the colonel and said "Coming from this man I know what he said is the truth." The colonel had to see the area commander the next day and a letter was forwarded to his command. Knowing the Marine Corps, I doubt he ever made general.

Captain Schneider was well liked, and when he left the 142nd Military Police Company the entire company was at the train station lined up on the ramp and he walked down the line and shook each man's hand with tears in his eyes. Captain Smith was a little more on the strict side, but he was a fair man and looked out for his men, at times this would cause him grief.

One man was due to depart the 142nd Military Police Company and apparently had done something that required a little last minute disciplinary action. When the guys found out the good Captain and First Sergeant were looking for this individual, one of the MP patrols put him in the squad car and drove him to the train station in Murnau out of reach of the good Captain. Captain Smith did well, he retired as a Colonel (O6), and now resides in Texas.

I remained in Garmisch and was married to Monika in the chapel, Sheridan Caserne, on 08 November 1958. First Lieutenant James D. Smith (shortly before his promotion to Captain) gave away the bride. I re-enlisted for the Army Ordnance School, Aberdeen Proving Grounds (APG), Maryland, because there were no promotions to Sergeant in the MP's, and my family was growing making it difficult to live on the pay of an Specialist Four (E4), which was not that great at that time.

I was very happy about having been assigned to Germany, because this gave me a chance to visit my real dad, who at that time resided in a little town called Wengern, near Wuppertal in the Ruhr coal mining area. I also got to see my two half-brothers, Karl-Heinz and Peter, with whom I have a warm relationship to this day and the word half-brother is never used because we think of each other as full brothers.

Sergeant Hubert Marlow
From MP to Provost Marshal Investigator
to Criminal Investigator
My First Stateside Assignment
School at Aberdeen Proving Grounds,
MD and an assignment to Fort Benning, Georgia

I arrived at Aberdeen Proving Grounds (APG), Maryland, during September 1960, to attend the U.S. Army Wheel and Tracked Vehicle Mechanics School. I had re-enlisted for the school because there were no promotions to Sergeant in the MPs in those days. I finished the school and was then assigned to Ft. Benning, GA.

When I arrived at Ft. Benning and went through the Processing Detachment, the commanding officer of the Main Post MPs and the Provost Marshal Office Operations Sergeant were there, looking for some MPs because there was a shortage of MPs at Fort Benning. The commanding officer spotted my MP brass, which I was still wearing, and tried his best to talk me into coming back to the MP's. I told him if he could promote me to Sergeant, I would return to the MPs. The good lieutenant told me that the only way he could promote me to Sergeant was if I attended Ranger School and that he was willing to send me to Ranger School. I could not see myself being out in the woods eating snake meat and declined the offer. After arriving at my new unit, and having to pull guard duty and KP again, as an E4, I regretted not having taken the lieutenant up on the offer to return to the MP's.

I was assigned to the 151st Engineer Brigade, 806th Combat Engineer Battalion, Fort Benning, Georgia, and to my great dismay ended up in a Private First Class slot as an Specialist four (E4). On 05 July 1961, I managed to get out of that outfit after my neighbor introduced me to the Fort Benning Classification and Assignment Sergeant Major, who cut orders assigning me to the Fort Benning Main Post MPs.

The good news came to me while I was on KP, getting ready to do pots and pans, when the mess sergeant came to me and said "Marlow, you have been assigned to the MPs, you better get over there before they mark you AWOL." I needed no further encouragement and left immediately. The commander of the Military Police Company was Second Lieutenant John M. Turner. My initial duties were as a patrolman, next I moved up to radio operator and desk clerk, and on 16 April 62, I was promoted to Sergeant and assigned duties as desk sergeant.

What were the circumstances of me joining the CID? As a desk sergeant I had more contact with the CID warrant and enlisted agents, and in those days (before command) warrants performed duties as MPOD and duty agent and the enlisted agents performed duties as duty agent, with duties starting at 0800 hrs through 1200 hrs the next day. The MPOD slept in a room downstairs by the MP desk, and the CID duty agent slept in the CID office. The desk sergeant had to notify the MPOD and/or the duty agent of incidents pertaining to them. Ben Tuten (a desk sergeant at the time, later a CID agent, but now deceased) and I would notify the MPOD and/or Duty Agent in those instances which warranted their personal attention. If an incident occurred, that we knew they could do nothing about until duty hours, we would let them continue to sleep. Tuten and I developed a reputation as using good judgment, and so were well liked by the members of the 86th MP Detachment (CI). Shortly after the 11th Air Assault Division was formed, CID at Fort Benning, always undermanned, was in need of help, and Criminal Investigators Francis J. "Frank" George and Charles R. Alsip nominated Tuten and I to be assigned to the CID. I became aware of this one afternoon, when I was scheduled duties as the desk sergeant, and found Sergeant Hicks behind the desk. I asked Hicks "What are you doing behind the desk?" and he replied "Haven't you heard?" I said "Haven't I heard what?" He then said "You are supposed to report to Mr. Miller (Elmer C. "Al" Miller) at CID." I promptly reported to Al Miller, operations officer of the CID, and he handed me a book of regulations on arms room surveys, and said, "take them home, read them, and report back in civvies in the morning." On 12 April 1963, Tuten and I received orders stating that we were appointed to special duty with the 86th MP Detachment (CI), as provost marshal investigators (PMI), and neither of us ever returned to the MPs.

CHAPTER THREE

The CID from its Birth to the Present.

From local provost marshal (PM) control, to CID Agency, and then to CID Command

The CID investigator is reflected by two different titles in this book. While working under the control of the local PM, he was called a CID Criminal Investigator, this would be from the beginning of the CID during WWI in 1918 until 15 September 1971, when the U.S. Army Criminal Investigation Command (USACIDC) was created. USACIDC is one of seventeen major army Commands, USACIDC being the smallest Command. After the creation of USACIDC, the title changed to Special Agent and he was issued a new badge, the shield. Throughout the book the title will change from Criminal Investigator to Special Agent, depending on when the investigation was conducted.

While the CID was under the control of the local PM, often pressure was put on the PM by the respective base commander or post commanding general (CG), to drop an investigation. Naturally the PM would comply in most instances, since he was as eager to get promoted as the next guy. Of course if the investigation involved a murder or rape it was difficult to drop such a case. The Department of the Army and the Department of Defense realized this problem and it was under the reign of Defense Secretary Melvin Laird that something was finally done about this situation.

During WWI CID Investigators were drawn from the Military Police. During WWII the CID began usually with twelve man teams, one officer, normally a lieutenant and eleven or twelve non-commissioned officers (NCOs), eventually forming into Detachments.

Colonel Henry H. Tufts close ties with the CID came during November 1968 when he was assigned to the Department of the Army, Washington, DC, as the chief of the planning group for the centralization of CID activities in the army. He was directed by the Army Chief of Staff to create an organization concept and implementation plan to assure that worldwide criminal investigative resources would more readily and efficiently respond to the present day needs of the U.S. Army. In the beginning it was only Colonel Tufts and a Colonel who was a finance officer, who put their heads together and set about determining the course of action and cost of a centralized CID.

The evolution of the centralization of the CID involved several dates of significance. In 1964 the HQ, Department of Defense concluded that CID investigative services were not satisfying the army's needs. In order to improve criminal investigative capabilities, CID elements were consolidated during the period 1965 - 1969 into eight CID groups, which generally corresponded to the eight army areas worldwide. The CID elements of Vietnam and Europe were the last to be consolidated into CID Groups. Command and control of these groups was on an army area basis, which did not provide complete and positive direction to the army's worldwide CID effort. At this time however, combat divisions still had one warrant and one enlisted agent assigned to them under the control of the division PM.

Colonel Tufts did not have an easy task because there were severe time constraints to implement a command structure to centralize the CID. Drawing heavily on personal experience and observations gained through twenty-one years of military police service, Colonel Tufts reviewed and analyzed the configuration of the existing criminal investigation system. His study served to reinforce an earlier conviction that increased centralization of CID resources was the key to integrity, professionalism, and greater effectiveness in the criminal investigative program. Of course he did not do all this single-handedly, but assembled a small staff of experienced officers, to include the author's future commander, then Major M. Thomas Fairris, to accomplish the job.

The efforts of the planning group paid off, when on 5 September 1969, at the direction of the Army Chief of Staff, the US Army Criminal Investigation Agency (USACIDA), as a class II activity under the Provost Marshal General, was created. This was done after the Army Chief of Staff approved Col. Tufts' recommendations concerning the structure of USACIDA. USACIDA had no command or operational authority; its mission was to provide guidance to CID the world over. In further recognition of Colonel Tufts' integrity and talents he was appointed as the agency's first and only commander.

I am not aware of warrant officers and enlisted personnel being part of the initial planning group. However, once the CID Agency was created, most of the officers of that group became part of the agency and at this time warrant officers participated and the modern CID was created.

During this period of reorganization and restructuring of CID assets, Colonel Tufts directed the organizing of a special investigative task force to probe allegations of criminal activity within the Noncommissioned Officers Open Mess system in Vietnam, Europe and elsewhere (with the Sergeant Major Woodridge case being the best known), and to investigate allegations of war crimes, the most well-known being My Lai. Initially the My Lai investigation was in the hands of the Inspector General (IG); however, on 5 August 1969, General Westmoreland ordered that the investigation be turned over to the Office of the Provost Marshal General (OPMG), after the IG preliminary investigation indicated murder was the principal offense. At that point none other than my fellow agent, and friend, Bob Zaza, was assigned to the investigation. He later received assistance from several other CID agents, after the creation of the CID Agency on 5 September 1969, due to the immensity of the case. Both task force efforts were successful and supported the fact that further centralization of control was needed in the CID Program.

On 16 March 1971, the Department of Defense requested that a CID Agency with vertical control of all CIDs worldwide be established. The next move came in April 1970, when control of CID shifted to the Deputy Chief of Staff for Personnel at Headquarters, Department of the Army. This objective improved communication with the highest levels of government and elevated the criminal investigative effort to public view. The establishment of the U.S. Army

Criminal Investigation Command (USACIDC) became a reality, when at the direction of the secretary of defense, Melvin Laird, USACIDC was established on 15 September 1971. It evolved from a concept to reality, as a result of Colonel Tufts and his planning group's hard work, confident in its ability to accomplish its formidable mission: "To exercise centralized command, authority, direction, and control of army criminal investigative activities worldwide; provide support to all U.S. Army elements on a geographic basis and perform other CID functions assigned by Headquarters, Department of the Army."

Colonel Tufts and his team had a difficult task in the formation of the CID command. There were many things that had to be worked out to create all elements of a major command, such as the Staff Judge Advocate, Personnel and Administrations Directorate, Comptroller, Logistics Directorate, Inspector General, Investigative Directorate, and Crime Records Directorate, just to name a few, not to mention the resistance of major commanders not wanting to lose control of the CID under their jurisdiction. Of course this also meant that combat divisions no longer would have a warrant officer and an enlisted agent assigned directly to them. This also spelled the end of the Provost Marshal General's position, a two star general position.

Colonel Tufts was deservedly named as its first commander, and he commanded the USACIDC from September 1971 to August 1974. The initial table of distribution and allowance (TDA) authorized 54 officers, 53 warrant officers, 74 enlisted soldiers and 44 civilians. The CID agent strength was always 1,200 until the Vietnam era when it went up to 1,400. Today the CID agent strength, including the civilian agents, is around 800. Colonel Tufts never was promoted to general, although he should have been, largely due to the fact that in creating the USACIDC he stepped on many toes, of high ranking officers who did not want to let go of their control of CID.

A new CID badge was created, today's CID Shield, replacing the old PMG badge. New credentials with the Pentagon and the letters CID on them were also created and issued. After the terror attack on the World Trade Center in New York City and the Pentagon, CID Agents worked side by side with FBI Agents on twelve hour shifts, seven days a week. One CID Agent, Chief Warrant Officer (W2) Hogan, in a press interview on 20 September 2001 said:

"Any CID Agent can open their credentials and see the Pentagon on them. This was an attack on us. We're soldiers and we're CID agents. Our motto is 'Do What Has to be Done' and that's our motivation. And we'll continue to do the work here till we've finished." How true, and all CID Agents have always been proud of that motto.

Many changes have occurred since the creation of the USACIDC but central control of worldwide CID elements is still in effect. CID went from the old typewriter to the computer age and DNA, keeping up with new technology all the time, and the title of the investigator changed from Criminal Investigator to Special Agent.

The CID Agent's Oath

I do hereby swear (or affirm) that I shall support and uphold the Constitution and the laws of the United States: that I shall endeavor to discharge my responsibilities as a United States Army CID agent in accordance therewith; that I shall at all times seek diligently to discover the truth, deterred neither by fear nor prejudice; and that I shall strive to be worthy of the special trust reposed in me by my country, the United States Army, and the Criminal Investigation Command.

U.S. Army Criminal Investigation Command

The U.S. Army Criminal Investigation Command (USACIDC) is responsible for investigating felony crimes of army interest. This worldwide command has fewer than two thousand soldiers and civilians. CID is organized into six major subordinate organizations: 202nd Military Police Group (CID), 3rd Military Police Group (CID), 6th Military Police Group (CID), 701st Military Police Group (CID), U.S. Army Criminal Investigation Laboratory, and the U.S. Army Crime Records Center.

The acronym USACIDC retains the "D" as a historical reminder of the first Criminal Investigation Division formed in 1918 by Gen. John J. Pershing during World War I.

The CID special agents; enlisted, warrant officer and civilian, are the backbone of this command.

USACIDC has undergone many changes during the years, during the time when I was on active duty we had First, Second, Third,

Fourth, Fifth, Sixth, and Seventh Region with Subordinate Field Offices and Resident Agencies, but all that has changed, as reflected above and one has to take into consideration the reduction in numbers that the Army underwent. At the height of the Vietnam War, CID had one thousand four hundred CID agents, today there are less than eight hundred.

"USACIDC's Mission"

- Investigate all felony crimes in which the army has an interest.
- Provide worldwide criminal investigative support to all U.S. Army elements.
- Deploy on short notice in support of contingency operations worldwide.
- Conduct other sensitive or special interest investigations as required or directed.
- Conduct protective service operations for Department of Defense, Joint Chiefs of Staff, and Department of the Army.
- Provide forensic laboratory support for Department of Defense investigative Agencies.
- Maintain the repository for Army crime records.
- CID Command supports the army in peacetime and in war. Its investigators are capable of performing professional criminal investigations anywhere in the world. In addition to the basic mission, CID provides felony crime investigative support to field commanders, which includes: general crimes (against persons or property), economic crime and counter-drug operations.
- Besides its peacetime functions, its soldier agents must also possess battlefield survival skills, as CID units provide direct support to army divisions and corps. CID's contingency operations and battlefield missions include logistics security, criminal intelligence, criminal investigations-expanded to include war crimes, anti-terrorism, protective service operations and force protection operations. Force protection protects soldiers, civilian employees, family members, facilities, and equipment in garrison and deployed scenarios by providing investigative and criminal intelligence support to combat-

ing terrorism, physical and personal security, information, and law enforcement operations other than war requires the same skills the CID uses every day in its support to commanders during peace.

The USACIDC Crest

The Crest, with a white star on a background with gold grid lines, Be Done" in gold on it has the star symbolizes centralized allude to the latitude and referring to the worldwide red circle in the center on a blue and the words "Do What Has To following meaning: The central command. The grid lines longitude lines of the globe, thus activities of the organization. The grid lines also suggest a stylized web, with eight sides representing the original eight geographical regions of the command. The web, a symbol of criminal apprehension, is the result of methodical construction alluding to the scientific methods of criminal investigation. The outer points of the star further symbolize far-reaching authority. Red, white and blue, are the national colors and gold is symbolic of achievement.

The USACIDC Shoulder Sleeve Insignia

The central star and the lines of globe, together with the a compass, symbolize the basic command: to perform and authority, direction, and control activities worldwide. Red, white latitude and longitude suggesting a arrowheads marking the points of worldwide mission of the exercise centralized command of Army criminal investigation and blue are the national colors.

CID Rates as Army FBI

An Article that Appeared in the *Army Times* Approximately 1975 - 1976

While assigned to the Fort Gordon Field Office, the following article appeared in the *Army Times* (toward the end of 1975, but before my retirement in April 1976). I thought it might be worthwhile repeating the article, written by Jim Tice, Times Staff Writer.

WASHINGTON – The Criminal Investigation Command, with headquarters here, just may be one of the least known, but most misunderstood, agencies of the army.

That many soldiers associate the activities of CID agents almost exclusively with drug-related investigations is understandable. Last year more than one-third of the cases investigated by CID's world-wide network of agents and laboratory technicians involved drug-related offenses.

What many soldiers may not know is that CID also investigates:

- Violations of the Uniform Code of Military Justice, federal statutes or other regulations which result in one year or longer imprisonment upon conviction.

- Larcenies of property worth $250 or more and burglaries of sensitive items such as firearms, ammunition and narcotics. (*I might add also burglaries of quarters or vehicles*)

- Non-combat deaths due to other than natural causes.

- All sex crimes including homosexual activities.

- Procurement and conflict of interest offenses against the government.

The key to the management of CID, which officials say closely parallels the Federal Bureau of Investigation in structure, is *centralization*. As a Major Army Command, CID has been vested with the authority to conduct uninhibited investigations of felony crimes within the Army at any time and any place in the world.

Under this charter, the CID commander answers to the Chief of Staff and the Secretary of the Army for command control.

Such centralization has not always been the case. It wasn't until September 17, 1991, that CID was established as a major Army command. For some fifty years before that, the Army had been struggling with a number of different criminal investigation organizations – all seemingly plagued by problems of decentralization. Even though the Provost Marshal General (PMG) in many instances had supervision over investigations, most operations were controlled at the local level (local Provost Marshal (PM)).

Today's 2200-man command (I'm speaking of 1971) is broken down into four regions, eight field offices and three laboratories (one at Fort Gordon, Georgia, one at Frankfurt, Germany and one in

Japan. During the Vietnam War, there was a small laboratory at Long Binh. The Command makes the most of the latest crime investigation techniques, officials claim. Basic to the operation are computers, document evaluation experts, chemical laboratories, firearms and fingerprint specialists and an unencumbered communications network with local and national law enforcement agencies.

CID officials point to several examples of how centralization and major Army command status have increased the efficiency of the CID.

When the president announced an energy crisis, CID, fearing a wave of petroleum associated thefts, immediately began working with the Army Logistics Management Center at Fort Lee, Virginia, to arrange for instruction in POL management for CID agents. In less than two weeks a course had been adopted, students identified and en route for instruction. This course provided selected CID agents with the necessary expertise to investigate POL systems at any point in the logistics system.

Another example cited is the celebrated landing of a stolen Huey helicopter on the White House lawn. Within two hours of landing, CID special agents were at the White House working with the Secret Service unraveling the strange tale of the soldier pilot and his now nationally famous flight.

Within forty eight hours of the incident CID was able to provide the army staff a detailed report of criminal activities associated with army airfields over a four-year period. This information was beneficial, officials say, in directing a worldwide crime survey of army airfields in an effort to reduce the vulnerability of such facilities to criminal acts.

For increased efficiency, CID officials also point to improvements of criminal information reporting. According to one source, the 1973 report system as it pertained to drug suppression activities "surpassed all expectations," as 619 or 61 percent of all criminal reports dealt with illicit narcotics traffic.

The information gleaned from these reports helped CID agents identify the APO system in Thailand as one avenue used by smugglers to ship controlled substances to the U.S., locate marijuana and opium fields in South Korea, and identify an international cocaine ring in the Panama Canal Zone.

Who are the investigators at the heart of the CID operations? They are officers, warrant officers and enlisted personnel to begin with, but they're also a group of soldier/detectives who have passed rigid screening and training standards.

Specific requirements for EM who want to carry MOS 95D20 (special agent) are outlined in AR 195-3, though generally the soldier must be at least twenty two years old, have completed a minimum of two years service, be an E4 or above, have no convictions (either military or civilian), have completed two years of college, and be eligible for a top secret security clearance.

Applicants for warrant officer MOS 951A (criminal investigator) and the commissioned officer MOS 9150 (criminal investigative supervisor) must meet the requirements stated in AR 135-100 and AR 195-3. One stipulation for new warrant officers requires all applicants to have a baccalaureate degree in law enforcement. Officers who wish to specialize in CID under OPMS should consult AR 614 for details.

When enlisted men are first assigned to CID they serve as apprentice special agents. For one year they are in a probationary status.

Of course, as I stated this article appeared in the *Army Times* in about 1975 – 76 and things have changed in CID. Today CID Headquarters is located at Fort Belvoir, Virginia, the strength of the special agents has dropped to around eight hundred , which includes one hundred + civilian special agents, assigned to the procurement fraud units. The structure of CID also has been changed but CID remains as a major army command.

Chapter Four

CID Investigations

The following chapters will reflect investigations that were conducted by the author and by my fellow Criminal Investigators/ CID Agents, many of whom are personal friends. If the investigation was conducted overseas it will be reflected by continent or country. You will see some very good investigations and also some very funny cases. This includes cases going back to WWII.

Working at the 86th MP Detachment (CI), Fort Benning, Georgia

Going from Provost Marshal Investigator to Criminal Investigator

Provost Marshal Investigator Tuten and I were supposed to conduct arms room surveys of the arms rooms of the 11th Air Assault Division and other units and complete these surveys in a three months period. We did it in two and were then asked to stay and work in the Larceny Squad for warrant officer Carlos E. King. Next the question most frequently asked was "When are you going to put in your papers for CID?" Provost Marshal Investigator Tuten held out six months longer than I did.

On 04 October 1963, I was accepted as an Apprentice Criminal Investigator, and on 09 March 1964, I reported to the CID School, Fort Gordon, Georgia, graduating seventh among thirty three graduates. I remained at Fort Benning, Georgia until August 1964. During my time at the 86th MP Detachment (CI), the commanding officer was Lieutenant Colonel Edwin P. Gebhardt; the operations officers were Elmer C. "Al" Miller, Francis J. "Frank" George, and Arthur E. "Bud" Schuder. Agents assigned or attached from the 2nd Infantry Division, were Marvin T. Farmer, Ellie F. Rollison, Edward Z. Whitehead, Robert L. Romano, Carlos E. King, Earl J. Bodyford, Gloria W. Brophy, John W. Tilson, Fred Tinsley, Joseph O. Roque, James O. Yerby, and Mickey Payne.

I recall an interesting case during the infancy of my career as an Investigator's. This occurred after I received orders placing me on special duty with the 86th MP Detachment (CI), Fort Benning, Georgia. An accredited Criminal Investigator and a PMI Investigator had a young soldier in their office who had been accused of stealing a Red Cross canister (remember in those days CID investigated any theft over $50.00). They had this kid handcuffed, and had slapped him across the face several times (this was just around the time of Miranda) but he would not confess to them. I asked the Criminal Investigator if he would allow me to talk to him and he said "go ahead." I took him to the office I worked in, this was before I joined Carlos King in the Larceny Squad, and started to talk to him about anything, his family, baseball etc., anything except the crime. After doing this for about twenty minutes, I began to talk, in a very pleasant manner, about the theft of the money, and how it was morally wrong and that he was basically an honest kid, etc. After about fifteen more minutes, the kid pulled out his wallet and began to separate the bills into two piles. He then handed me one pile and informed me that this was the money he had stolen from the canister. I might add that I never believed in using physical force to obtain a confession, only those who don't have the intelligence to obtain a confession through investigative skills would resort to that type of tactic. It certainly is not something the CID School taught or advocated.

I asked him how he knew that was the stolen money, and he pointed out to me that he could tell by the creases in the bills, because in order to put the money into the Red Cross canister, the money had to be folded to get it through the slot. Boy, was I proud of myself, because I was just a new PMI kid and had not attended CID School as yet.

Now that I have told you of a proud moment, prior to attending CID school, let me tell you of an embarrassing moment. Due to the shortage of agents the Provost Marshal Investigator, backed by an accredited Criminal Investigator on call, worked initial cases (except really serious cases of course). One night while on duty I got a call from the desk sergeant informing me of a bad accident on the four-lane highway that ran right through Fort Benning. I was told that a lady was very seriously injured and not expected to live. I proceeded to the scene with the Speed Graphic camera in tow. When I got there, I did not know how to hook up the flash unit, however you could activate the flash unit by pressing a button on it. Being a smart and resourceful kid (so I thought) I handed the flash unit to an MP and told him "when I count to three, press the button." Of course none of the photos turned out, but the lady did me a big favor and survived so I got away with that one.

Another interesting period at Fort Benning was a time when several rapes and burglaries had occurred in one of the housing areas and CID had no leads. So the operations officer had half of the detachment on surveillance each night, this went on for about two weeks before we got positive results. We had guys on top of the commissary and at various places. I was on top of an embankment with Sergeant Cash, another Provost Marshal Investigator, when one night a black soldier came waltzing across the lawn, proceeded to a window, and made it very obvious by his actions that he was going to enter the residence. Sergeant Cash fired a round, from his caliber .38 revolver into the air and told the young man to hit the ground or be shot. He followed his instructions. We determined that he was assigned to a medical unit of the 2nd Infantry Division (at that time based at Sand Hill, Fort Benning, Georgia). A search of his wall and foot locker disclosed eight watches and some other jewelry items he had taken from victims during his nightly escapades. Needles to say he was court-martialed.

During that same period of surveillance, I was seated in a car with Criminal Investigator Mickey Payne, and we were along the main road, in front of a driveway that led into an elementary school compound on Fort Benning. While sitting there, we heard a car horn beep several times and next saw car headlights flashing and shortly thereafter the car came out of the wooded area towards the main highway, where we were located. We blocked the exit and before the driver of the car knew what was happening, his (I use the term loosely) car was surrounded by CID and Provost Marshal Investigators. It turned out the driver was an escaped prisoner from the stockade at Fort Benning. Needless to say, he was promptly returned to the stockade and received additional punishment.

Now it seems that every CID Unit has at least one jerk assigned to it at one time or another. While at the 86th MP Detachment (CI), and already assigned to the Larceny Squad, a new man came in from CID School. This individual was formerly assigned to a Military Intelligence unit (MI) and spoke good German; I will give him credit for that. He had the nerve to tell me that I spoke German with an accent. He would tell all types of wild stories about how he used to go into East Germany on MI assignments. Later I found out he had been a clerk in a MI unit. Anyway, the larceny squad had two 1957 Chevys assigned to it to be shared by all six of the investigators of the Larceny Squad, consisting of two accredited criminal investigators and four PMI investigators, of which I was one, since I had not attended CID School yet. The new man, and I don't honestly recall his name, took possession of one set of car keys, even though he was not going anywhere. I had been instructed to do something and was in need of a car, so I just took the keys from his desk and went on my merry way. Oh boy, how could I have dared to take "his" car keys?

When I returned he actually invited me to go outside to fight him because I had the gall to take "his" car keys. Chief warrant officer (W4) Bud Schuder, a fine and fair gentleman who did not put up with any type of nonsense, was the operations officer. I told the new *jerk* if he had any problems to come with me and see Mr. Schuder. Of course he did not go with me but I informed Schuder of what had occurred and he wasted no time in calling the *jerk* into his office, and then commenced to chew his ass up one side and down the other.

CID School at Ft. Gordon

I attended CID School and managed to graduate seventh out of thirty-three students. What I remember about CID School the most was the good instructors we had, all dedicated men such as our CID Agents Association Historian, Clarence Romig and Director Thomas J. McGreevy, who had made it from Enlisted to Warrant to

Commissioned Officer. McGreevy was a captain when he was my instructor, and many of my classmates will remember, and chuckle, about the day he made us close all of the windows of the classroom and told us we had to keep the information he was about to pass on to us confidential. Captain McGreevy then proceeded to tell us how to catch a queer (remember in those days CID investigated all homosexual cases). Tom said, "you walk up behind the suspect, kiss him behind the ear, and if he giggles he is queer."

Criminal Investigator Hubert Marlow
My first time in the Far East. Assigned to the 65th MP Detachment (CI), Pusan, Korea

Next came my first CID reassignment to the 65th MP Detachment (CI), Pusan Sub-Detachment, from September 1964 to October 1965, where I worked for Chief Warrant Officer (W2) Donald H. Weaver and Chief Warrant Officer (W2) Ronald A. Whitecliff.

It is funny how things will turn out, and it also seems that the real jerks never lasted in CID, with the exception of a very few. While assigned to the 65th MP Detachment (CI), Pusan, Korea, and just about the time I finished my tour of duty in Korea, I found out that Mr. *Jerk*, from Fort Benning, Georgia, had been assigned to one of the division area CID units, some time after I departed from Fort Benning. One day he took a jeep to Seoul to see his girlfriend, and was told, so I was informed, to stop taking the jeep to Seoul. The reason was that it was a well-known fact that the Korean *Slicky Boys* (Korean thieves) could dismantle a jeep in a very brief time. As the old saying went, "They can steal a radio and leave the sound behind." Well, Mr. *Jerk* did not listen and took the jeep to Seoul again one day, and he totally forgot that he had the unit's Speed Graphic camera in the jeep. When all was done, the camera had been stolen and Mr. *Jerk* was reassigned to an infantry unit walking the DMZ with a rifle. Justice was served.

It was in Pusan, where I had the pleasure of meeting and working with William J. Fitzpatrick, and Special Agents RB Stanton, Jack Teal, Jackson E. Smith, Al Moody, and several others. The thing I remember most about my tour in Korea was eating good steaks. Bill Fitzpatrick knew an army veterinarian who would now and then condemn a case of filet mignon as being spoiled. The steaks were destined for the generals in Seoul and ended up in the stomachs of the Pusan criminal investigators. German ships would stop at Pusan and I would get some good German bread and beer from the ships.

Chief Warrant Officer (W2) Weaver was a good boss, he was a fair and pleasant man to work for, and I had the pleasure of working for him for nine months. Then came Chief Warrant Officer (W2) Ronald Whitecliff, I was under his supervision for a period of three months and spent three weeks of that time in the hospital with hepatitis. Chief Whitecliff was a pretty good cook, and since we were on separate rations, he would cook at times. Later while working for the Defense Investigative Service (DIS) I would have contact with him again during the course of an investigation, he was employed by DIS at Las Vegas, Nevada. For some reason Whitecliff gave me a low evaluation of which I became aware shortly after I arrived at Fort Sheridan. Those were the days when enlisted soldiers did not get a copy of their evaluation; thank God the army has changed that policy.

Fort Sheridan, Illinois

Getting Promoted to Specialist 6 (E-6) and Warrant Officer Within Six Weeks

From Korea I was assigned to Detachment A, 5th MP Group (CI), commanded by Lieutenant Colonel Alfred R. Jefferson, one of the greatest guys to work for. 5th Army Provost Marshal was Colonel Hobart W. Sharp, and the commanding officer of Detachment A was Captain Robert K. Ressler, later of fame with the FBI as the man who got Profiling started. The operations officers, during my stay at Fort Sheridan were Stanley L. Hobson and William W. Giehran. Members of the unit were Special Agents William E. Lowry, Richard E. Proof, Daniel F. Kiburz, Donald R. Fisher, Donald Arness, Frank H. Kucera, James Durand, and George Rakas, plus a few others.

I had worked at the Fort Sheridan Office for about a month or a little more, when the operations officer, Stan Hobson, a fine man to work for, called me into his office. He said to me, "If I had received this before your arrival I would have said" 'I don't want this man, he should not even be in CID.' He was referring to my combined evaluation.

Since I had worked for him for a little while and he had observed me and gotten to know me, he and Sergeant Major James F. Coonce (Sergeant Major of 5th MP Group (CI), Fort Sheridan) tried their best to have the report thrown out and prepare a new one, but were unable to do so.

While at Fort Sheridan, I was sitting in my office writing up a case. This was in April 1966, when a lot of CID personnel were sent to Vietnam, creating a shortage of criminal investigators in our office. While writing the case, Chief Stan Hobson came to me and said, "Hubie, what are you doing?" I said, "writing up a case Chief" (he had heard my mom call me Hubie one time and from then on he called me "Hubie"). Chief Hobson then said "Stop what you are doing right now, and go to personnel and pick up this form and that form (I don't recall the form numbers anymore), you are putting in for warrant officer right now". I had about fifty four college credit hours at the time, and this was when Major General Carl Turner, The Provost Marshal General (PMG) lowered the requirements for applying for warrant to one year of college, with the provision that the person making warrant would complete the two-year college requirements later. It took only about two months, after I submitted my papers for warrant officer, until I was sworn in as a warrant officer, on 12 July 1966, by Colonel Hobart Sharp, at 5th Army HQ, Hyde Park, Illinois. This was due to the efforts by Stan Hopson and Jim Coonce, who knew a lot of people, and had my application hand-carried everywhere, and I am grateful to them forever.

A funny thing happened after I made warrant officer. I had to interview a SP-5 from personnel, who had made it a point to check my record for my rank, and when he came to the CID office he asked me what my rank was and I told him that in CID agents did not disclose their rank. His reply to me, every time I would ask him something was "Yes, Specialist Marlow" or "No, Specialist Marlow." Unfortunately he failed to check the records again, after I made warrant officer, and so one day I walked across the parking lot, near the Personnel Office, when he came bouncing across the parking lot and said, "How are you, *Specialist* Marlow?" (He always would put special emphasis on *specialist*). I pulled out my wallet, showed him my ID card, told him to come to attention, and said to him, "Is that how you address an officer?" All I heard was, "Yes, sir." I just could not let him get away with his sarcasm.

Many years later, in 2001, a funny thing happened. I have a friend in Germany, who is a *Kriminal Haupt Kommissar* (equivalent to a Major in the police), and the boss of the profilers for the Police Department of the city-state of Hamburg. He sent me a letter and asked me if I knew a Bob Ressler, I did not answer his letter immediately, since I am still in contact with Colonel Robert K. Ressler, who became famous as the head profiler for the FBI, in that he really got profiling started in the FBI. Ressler, at the time a captain, was my commanding officer when I was at Detachment A, 5th MP Group (CI), Fort Sheridan, Illinois. He was on active duty for ten years, rose to the rank of Major, and then got out and was a special agent with the FBI for twenty years.

Initially he worked as a street agent, and then got into the profiling. He retired from the FBI with twenty years of service, and he also remained in the Army Reserve, performing his duties with the CID, and retired as a colonel (O6), and has authored five books. I obtained a poster, with Colonel Ressler and Anthony Hopkins (from the movie *Silence of the Lambs*) on it, and had Colonel Ressler autograph it with a personal note to Horst Kukies. Needless to say he was quite surprised when he received it.

I was notified that my real father was very sick in Germany and for that reason requested a compassionate reassignment to Germany. This took longer than I anticipated but I did finally get an assignment to Zweibruecken, Germany. Unfortunately, my father passed away prior to my arrival in Germany.

CHAPTER FIVE

Africa

Serving in CID during WWII
Criminal Investigator Werner Loewenstein
Talk about strange ways to become a Criminal Investigator

Criminal Investigator Werner Loewenstein was in basic training during the winter of 1942 – 43, and around New Year's he was in advanced basic training in California. The first sergeant called him into his office and said: "Congratulations, Loewenstein, you have been transferred to the CID", and Werner Loewenstein replied "Well thank you, Sergeant, but what is the CID?" Loewenstein was another of the chosen few involuntarily inducted into the CID.

At the CID School in Battle Creek, Michigan, Werner Loewenstein reported to a Lieutenant Eugene Smith, saying, "Well Lieutenant, I guess I am a little late." The Lieutenant replied,"Oh, that's all right, just go to the barracks." Werner felt that Smith, who later became head of what was then known as the Air Force CID before being named the Office of Special Investigations (OSI), was one of the nicest guys he had ever met in the army. Smith later died in an airplane crash.

At the barracks his fellow soldiers asked Loewenstein, "What foreign languages do you speak?" He thought they were kidding, but it turned out the army was looking for individuals who spoke foreign languages to be assigned to a newly formed investigator group (CID).

When training ended the class transferred as a group to Governors Island, New York, and two weeks later was on a troopship headed for

Oran, French Algeria, North Africa. The army had not provided written orders or placed anyone in charge of the group, so they selected a member of the group named Encoe to be in charge.

No one in Oran knew what the unit was to do or where it was to be assigned. A sergeant at the replacement depot issued written orders sending one of the group, named Paradise, to the front in Tunisia. The entire group went to the sergeant and told him, in no uncertain terms, that he would be court-martialed and suffer dire consequences if he acted to transfer any of them. The order was revoked.

In the meantime, having learned that there was a CID office in Oran, they sent Criminal Investigator Encoe and another fellow to that office to make their presence known. From the officer in charge (OIC), Captain Dunkley, they learned that the provost marshal (PM) of the African Theater of Operations, Colonel Maglin, stationed in Algiers, had been looking for the group.

Colonel Maglin was very solicitous of the CID, and had the strange notion that CID investigators should always be in uniform showing their rank (he re-instituted this policy later when he was the Army Provost Marshal General). General Dillon, a West Point officer and lawyer soon replaced Colonel Maglin as the PM African Theater of Operations, and Colonel Maglin was reassigned to the continental U.S.

General Dillon, the father of the modern CID, before CID became a separate command, ordered U.S. insignia were to be worn on either side of the collar. No insignia of rank was to be worn, and CID investigators could wear civilian clothing if necessary to accomplish their work. A story circulating had it that General Dillon had dressed down a colonel who had refused to give a CID investigator a statement unless the agent disclosed his rank.

It was believed by many that Colonel Maglin sorely resented this change of his dress code and agent status and harbored a strong prejudice against the CID which was reflected in policies he issued when later he became the army PMG.

Prior to General Dillon's arrival Criminal Investigator Loewenstein's group had been disbanded, and investigators were sent to various offices in North Africa. Investigator Loewenstein was sent to Oran, and was cordially received by Captain Dunkley, who said, "Loewenstein, I will lend you to the OSS". The Office of Strategic Services (OSS) was a famous and somewhat secretive organization consisting half of civilians (many of them academicians) and half of military, headed by General Donovan. Investigator Loewenstein always felt that Dunkley had overstepped his authority when he did this.

Among the many intriguing tales of the OSS, Investigator Loewenstein gave great credence to the claim that Admiral Canaris, head of the German Counterintelligence, was an OSS agent. The publication, *World War II – Strange & Fascinating Facts* by Don McCombs and Fred L. Worth, portrays Wilhelm Canaris, the German Navy Admiral as head of the German secret service and clandestine warfare section of the armed forces, the *Abwehr* (Counter Intelligence), from 1935 to February 1944. He began his career in WWI on the cruiser *Dresden,* which was scuttled off Chile. He made his way back to Germany and joined the intelligence service until 1917, when he became a submarine commander credited with sinking seventeen ships in the Mediterranean sea. Admiral Canaris was a monarchist and was opposed to Hitler and the Nazis. Horrified by Nazi excesses he used his position to plot against Hitler. He helped victims of Nazi tyranny to escape, falsified reports to dissuade Hitler from invading Spain, and saved the lives of French Generals Henri Giraud and Maxim Weygand after Hitler ordered them killed. Admiral Canaris kept a card file, beginning in 1933, of all crimes by Nazi leaders. He was dismissed as commander of the *Abwehr* at the urging of Heinrich Himmler, head of the Nazi SS, who never trusted Canaris. Admiral Canaris was involved in the attempted assassination of Hitler on July 20, 1944.

He was arrested by the Gestapo after the assassination attempt on Hitler and imprisoned in Flossenburg concentration camp where he was executed on April 9, 1945, just one month before the war's end.

After the war General Donovan related the following to show the caliber of persons serving in OSS. An American OSS man, serving behind German lines in Italy, was caught and was being transported to the German headquarters in Merano. The German military men stopped for lunch and left the American in the custody of the Italian driver, who (unbeknownst to the Germans) was also an OSS agent. The driver said to the American, "Now is your chance to escape. If the Germans take you to Merano they will beat you." The American replied "It is more important that our cover will be preserved than that I escape."

When Criminal Investigator Loewenstein was lent to the OSS he was placed in civilian clothes and given a new identity and his name was changed to William Louis. He was issued ID documents under that name, retaining the initials of his real name, and was made a vice-consul in the American consulate in Oran.

The Frenchmen in Algeria, with few exceptions, both civilians and government officials, were loyal to the Vichy government of Laval-Petain in occupied France but did not openly admit this.

It was Criminal Investigator Loewenstein's job to determine the Vichy members of the Oran Harbor Administration past and present loyalties and affiliations. Werner was puzzled as to how to accomplish this but luck was on his side, and it resulted in his greatest coup in the OSS.

Criminal Investigator Loewenstein had been given quarters with a French couple who had left France to escape from the Germans and they were very much anti-Vichy. The man was employed as a courier by the Harbor Administration and Investigator Loewenstein figured he might have access to records. Investigator Loewenstein asked and to his amazement the man replied, "Oh sure, the records of all the members including their past on the Continent and under Vichy are lying all over the place."

Investigator Loewenstein obtained copies of the records and quickly and successfully identified known Vichy loyalists among the Oran Harbor Administration.

Marshall Philippe Petain, head of the Vichy government in occupied France, was sentenced to death after the war, but had his sentence commuted to life imprisonment by General Charles De Gaulle because they had served together during WWI. Pierre Laval, premier of the Vichy government under Petain was executed by firing squad on 15 October 1945.

Criminal Investigator Loewenstein did some additional work for OSS at Oujda, a Moroccan town on the Trans-North African Railroad, at the border with Algeria and then requested, and was granted a transfer back to the CID in Oran. Captain Dunkley, his old commanding officer was a changed man, no longer the friendly man Investigator Loewenstein had met when first assigned to the unit. Captain Dunkley had changed completely; was now surly and would not allow anyone to get in a conversation with him. Investigator

Loewenstein later heard that Captain Dunkley had made many anti-Semitic remarks, but he never did so in his presence.

What was known at the time was that Captain Dunkley had transferred some of Uncle Sam's funds into a bank account of his own. This was confirmed later through an investigation by CID Captain Turrou. Captain Dunkley was subsequently tried and sentenced to six months in the Disciplinary Training Center.

Criminal Investigator Loewenstein was sent to Casablanca. The Casablanca CID office, under command of Lieutenant Aubey, had become a den of thieves and was known to the French police in Casablanca as a good place to engage in black market activities.

CID Criminal Investigator Fisch, who was one of the investigators in Investigator Loewenstein's original group, was the most notorious in that respect and was later dishonorably discharged from the army (but not while in CID).

Then there was the case of a French officer, riding a bicycle, who was run over and killed by an American army truck. By the time Investigator Loewenstein got to the outfit the truck had been washed and cleansed of all blood and nobody knew anything about the accident. Investigator Loewenstein developed some French witnesses who said they could identify the Americans involved. Investigator Loewenstein had the whole outfit lined up and had the French witnesses look at them. They reneged on their promise and said they could not identify anybody.

Criminal Investigator Loewenstein, who spoke French and German, was no dummy. Since the GI's did not know what the French witnesses had told him, he told them the French witnesses had identified those involved in the accident, and if the culprits came forward and gave statements leniency would ensue. It worked, all except the driver of the vehicle gave statements and those who gave statements implicated and identified the driver. Case solved.

CHAPTER SIX

Austria

The Great Train Robberies
Criminal Investigator Virgil V. Becker

Early on Criminal Investigator Virgil V. Becker and his fellow investigators were made aware of a problem with supplies being shipped by rail to Vienna, Austria shortly after the war. As the trains passed through Linz, Austria, en route to Vienna, they were stopped at a Russian blockade and searched for contraband by the Russian soldiers. When the trains reached Vienna it was discovered that some of the boxcars had been opened and a sizable amount of the shipment had been removed.

American army guards were posted on every train. It was reported to CID investigators that the Russians were opening the cars and removing the contents. This was happening in the middle of the Russian zone, which made visual surveillance difficult.

To learn the truth and to observe firsthand, Agent Becker climbed aboard one of the Vienna-bound trains at Salzburg, Austria, dressed in the fatigue uniform of a sergeant, with a barracks bag loaded with cartons of cigarettes from the Post Exchange. Agent Becker announced to the train guards that he wanted to get to Vienna to peddle his cigarettes amongst the black market groups in town. This was acceptable to the train guards. Off he went, heading to the big city.

In the Russian zone, when the train reached the Russian blockade, Investigator Becker noticed that the Russian soldiers did not touch any of the American army boxcars. Surprisingly, it was the American army guards who opened the doors by breaking the locks. At this point the rail line passed near the adjoining American sector. The train guards proceeded to distribute the supplies to their friends who were stationed nearby in the American sector. The supplies were then trucked by the American soldiers to distributors on the black market.

When the train finally reached Vienna the American soldiers who had been guarding the shipment reported the thefts, blaming the Russian soldiers. Of course, Investigator Becker had been an eyewitness and could identify the American culprits. This black market operation came to a screeching halt when Investigator Becker and his fellow Criminal Investigators made mass arrests at the U.S. Army units involved and recovered some of the stolen merchandise. Another job well done by the CID.

Criminal Investigator Virgil V. Becker
A Slip of the Lip
Not only Enlisted Soldiers Get in Trouble, Officers Do Also

It was certainly a "cold case" in the sense that it had occurred some months previously, and was being investigated by the local Vienna, Austria police. It was brought to the attention of Investigator Becker's CID unit for the first time, when the local police reported that they were investigating the murder of an Austrian woman whose body had been discovered in the woods several months ago. She had been shot with what was believed to be a small caliber pistol. The Viennese police had recently discovered information leading them to believe that an American officer had been the last known person to have been with the decedent prior to her death.

The suspect was described by witnesses as a young man, possibly a lieutenant in the Air Force who had been driving a jeep with U.S. Army markings not specifically identified. A witness described a gas mask hose covering the stick shift lever, a common feature on army jeeps at that time (Remember at that time it was still the Army Air Corps).

With the foregoing information it was only natural that the Viennese police strongly suspected the perpetrator was an American and they were seeking CID assistance to identify the alleged American officer suspect.

After reviewing all the information the Viennese police had gathered Criminal Investigator Becker called a meeting of his CID Investigators in the 12th CID Detachment, and representatives of other agencies with experience and technical training in homicide investigations.

Some of the investigators spent time in the PX and bars looking and listening to the stories told by American military personnel, all the while being sure to consume beverages as part of their undercover assignment. Someone, somewhere knew something that the CID needed in order to identify the subject.

Forensic evidence indicated that the homicide victim had a venereal disease. It was possible that her murderer might have contracted the disease.

One of Virgil Becker's investigators overheard a discussion by hospital personnel, at one of the bars, about an officer who had contracted VD and was awaiting the arrival of his wife from stateside. This was a lead worth pursuing.

The officer was identified as a lieutenant in the military police station in Vienna. Agent Becker and his agents learned that he had set up a furnished apartment in the Inner City where he and his wife would reside upon her arrival.

Everything began falling into place. The officer had in fact contracted a venereal disease. Subsequently, the apartment was searched and a pistol was recovered. The crime lab results identified this pistol as the murder weapon. The wife arrived only a few days later to learn of her husband's arrest for murder.

CHAPTER SEVEN

France

The Paris Black Market Investigation
Criminal Investigator Anthony F. "Tony" Correri

Criminal Investigator Correri entered the Army in July 1943, and right off the bat started CID training and became a member of the 4th CID Section and would have the distinction of serving in that unit for the duration of his CID career. During that time CID units consisted of one officer, normally a Second or First Lieutenant, and nine enlisted men ranging in rank in rank from corporal to master sergeant. After additional training with the Chicago Police Department and the Michigan State Police, Investigator Correri finally found himself on the move to London, England, where he experienced some of the horrifying V2 rocket attacks. Some time after the Invasion of France Investigator Correri became involved in the famous Paris black market investigation involving the large-scale theft of American cigarettes. The frontline troops were not getting their cigarette rations, and General George Patton started the ball rolling, initiating the investigation. Investigator Correri was sent to the replacement depot at Etampes (outside Paris, France) and assigned as a "gandy dancer" tightening bolts on the railway tracks. He dressed as a Private without any insignia indicating what branch of service he belonged to. Investigator Correri had an appetite for a cold beer one night, and so he stole a pass to get out of camp (Imagine a CID criminal investigator and attorney in civilian life, committing theft).

Investigator Correri went to a bar and ordered a beer. A soldier next to him said, "You're a disgrace to the Army. Have a cognac and champagne chaser". Investigator Correri replied: "I can't buy you a drink back. How can I drink with you?"

The slightly inebriated soldier then told Investigator Correri how he got his money on the black market. He told Investigator Correri the secret of how it worked. A railway car was caused to develop a "hot box" and was stopped at a designated location where it met, by pre-arrangement, with a truck from the famous WWII "Red Ball Express." The contents of the railway car were transferred to the truck and subsequently sold on the black market.

The commanding officer of Investigator Correri's unit, a Major, upon learning of the presence of CID, assembled his men and after cautioning them said, "Ali Baba had forty thieves. I have a thousand." Correri included that remark in his report of investigation and the incident was extensively reported in the newspaper, *Stars & Stripes*.

In November 1944, Major General Milton A. Record, the Provost Marshal of European Theater of Operations (ETO), ordered all efforts of the investigating agencies of the theater to be centralized. More than one hundred agents were put on the cigarette investigation. After having made sufficient progress they made their first strike. Four hundred military police were called in to assist the criminal investigators in conducting simultaneous raids at sixteen major points from Paris to Cherbourg.

On January 12, 1945, the *Stars and Stripes* reported that the trials of five more GIs, part of the band of two officers and one hundred eighty two enlisted men (EM) accused of the theft and black market sale of cigarettes and rations were scheduled for that day. The trial judge advocate was quoted as saying that it was probable that before the court-martials ended, at least two more officers and some additional key enlisted men would be tried. He went on to report most of the men seized were from one railway operations battalion. Investigator Correri's Major was right, he did have almost a thousand thieves.

Criminal Investigator Correri was discharged from the Army on 31 October 1945, and returned to his peacetime job as an attorney, he was also one of the founding fathers of the Criminal Investigation Division Agents Association (CIDAA).

The Oil Tanker Larceny Case

Criminal Investigator Oscar Michaud
A Case He Worked before He Became a CID Agent

After his troop transport tied up at Greenock, Scotland, Investigator (by appointment) Michaud was initially assigned to the office of the Judge Advocate, HQ, Eighth Air Force. During mid-May 1944, he was reassigned to HQ, 9th Tactical Air Command, and landed in Normandy on either 11 or 16 June. Eventually he ended up in Paris, France, however prior to arriving in Paris Oscar was assigned to Headquarters, 27th Air Transport Group, located at Le Bourget Airport near Flanders Road, which bypassed the airport.

In either late November or early December of 1944 Lieutenant Colonel Wendell L. Covalt appointed Michaud as an investigator, and gave him an investigative assignment, relative to the larceny from oil tankers, because of his ability to speak French fluently. Covalt was also in charge of the Le Bourget CID criminal investigators. According to rumors, Patton's tanks and other armored vehicles were running out of gas near Strasbourg, France, a city adjacent to the South-Western border of Germany.

A young Frenchman had immigrated to the United States prior to WWII. After the onset of the war, the Frenchman, whom Investigator Michaud referred to as "Pierre," was drafted into the U.S. Armed Forces. When he arrived in Paris he was assigned to a Petrol, Oil, and Lubricants (POL) unit.

Pierre's mother and father owned an old hotel on a side street off Flanders Route, just a short distance from Le Bourget Airport. Prior to Investigator Michaud's going to the hotel, Colonel Covalt said it was a suspected headquarters in the larceny of fuel, which had been destined for use in combat operations. Colonel Covalt stressed the importance of developing hard evidence, which his office did not have.

Pierre deserted from his unit and, with some AWOL GIs, was able to build a lucrative business stealing from tankers from POL units. These oil supplies which came from the Normandy beach were being sold on the black market by the group of thieves.

Investigator Michaud proceeded to the hotel, dressed in a dirty field uniform. Sitting at the hotel bar and drinking wine sparingly, he spoke to Pierre in English. Michaud did not let on that he understood or spoke French. He kept up a conversation mostly with Pierre and avoided talking to the AWOL GIs who formed a part of Pierre's oil tanker larceny group. Pierre's mother also worked behind the bar.

After about two hours Investigator Michaud told Pierre he had better get the hell out of there before his unit found out that he was AWOL. Pierre asked him where he was assigned, and Michaud answered "With a POL unit at Le Bourget." Pierre then asked, "Can you get me some gas?" and Michaud replied, "I can get you a tanker of gas if you want one." He explained that he was anxious to get a lot of gas. Michaud told him, "I'll return to my unit and come back later with a tanker." Pierre had taken the bait and now the hook was in.

About an hour later Investigator Michaud returned with a weapons carrier and seventeen Jerry cans, each containing five gallons of gas. Before reaching the hotel, Michaud stopped at the café and had a good slug of wine. It helped him play the part that he was partly drunk. Investigator Michaud then continued on and stopped his vehicle in front of the hotel and blew the horn. Pierre came out asking,"Where's the tanker?" Michaud told him "It was too late but I'll get one tomorrow morning." He added, "There are some five gallon cans of gas here in the truck."

Pierre asked Investigator Oscar Michaud to unload the cans from the truck and put them on the sidewalk. Michaud refused, saying, "The MPs might come along, see us and arrest me." Pierre insisted that Oscar unload the cans, and Oscar said "Forget it, I know somebody else that wants a tanker of gas." He started the vehicle and Pierre shouted, "Wait! I'll get my father." He and his father climbed into the front seat and directed Michaud to a place about a block or so distant from the hotel. Pierre and the father got out of the vehicle and opened two massive doors, exposing an oil tanker parked in the center of the huge walled-in courtyard. Next to three of the walls were hundreds of U.S. Army Jerry cans, apparently filled with gas. Pierre and his father took the seventeen gas cans from Investigator Michaud's vehicle and paid him in French francs.

Michaud knew that he had to do something to prove that he had been at the courtyard. Still playing the part that he was drunk, Investigator Michaud backed into the garage door and did quite a bit of damage. That's when he learned new French swear words. The father yelled, "The %#@,!&*+ is drunk!" Michaud then backed the truck onto the road and yelled at Pierre, "I will bring the tanker in the morning." Some fifty or so feet away from the courtyard stood an old electric streetlight. Knowing that the bumper on the truck was very durable Michaud bumped into the streetlight and busted it. He wanted absolute evidence that he had been in the area.

Returning to Le Bourget with the truck, Investigator Michaud reported to Colonel Covalt, who was seated in a room twenty feet wide by thirty feet long. A couple of uniformed gendarmes, two CID agents, and a French detective or two were in the room. Colonel Covalt told Michaud to have a good meal, clean up, and get dressed in his good uniform. He and his men would raid the hotel, arrest Pierre, his mother, and father, and a few AWOL GIs and secure the oil tanker and gas found in the courtyard. Michaud had been instructed to be back to the room in one hour. When he returned, Colonel Covalt and his men had already returned from the raid.

The colonel instructed Investigator Michaud to sit in a chair at the end of the room behind a field table. He then asked, "Which one do you want to interrogate first?" Michaud was stunned. He had never interrogated anyone in his life. So he gave it his best shot and said "Call Pierre's mother." After she stepped into the room, Michaud said to her, in French of course, "Please step forward." At first she did not recognize Michaud. He was clean-shaven, and dressed in a well-pressed uniform. As she drew closer she recognized him. She spat in his face, yelling, "You are worse than the Germans." One of the gendarmes slapped her face very hard and she fell towards the wall. He said, "The gentleman asked you to step forward. You had no reason to spit on him."

At this point Investigator Michaud was relieved from conducting the interrogation. It was an easy, but very important case. Oscar could not believe what he had accomplished in a matter of a few hours (remember at that time Investigator Michaud was not a CID Criminal Investigator yet).

Colonel Cowalt, in a letter of recommendation stated, "Sergeant Michaud has handled delicate investigations of suspected pro-Nazis, black marketing, and worked with Criminal Investigation Agents interrogating prisoners (French civilians). I do not hesitate to recommend that he be given the opportunity of further training in either the Counter- Intelligence Department or the Criminal Investigation Division, as the knowledge and experience of this man in the intelligence services can be of great help to our armed forces."

Investigator Michaud was discharged from the Army on 2 October 1945, worked in a civilian job for eleven months and in September 1946, came back into the army, attending CID School with five years of investigative experience.

SHAPE HEADQUARTERS
A Funny Thing Happened (Not funny at the time)
Criminal Investigator Alfred L. "Al" Cummings

While Criminal Investigator Cummings was assigned to the 16th MP Detachment (CI), the Supreme Allied Commander Europe was Geneeral Lyman L. Lemnitzer. The 16th MP Detachment was charged with providing personal security for General Lemnitzer, his residence which was in a large compound along with the residences of other high ranking officers assigned to SHAPE Headquarters, and other classified installations. Additionally, the CID conducted criminal investigations and at times fulfilled personal requests made by the general. One such request begs revealing now that so many years and the general have passed on.

Most of the CID and other security personnel knew that a fox often walked casually through the compound, very early, most mornings. The fox did not bother anyone or anything and so was left to enjoy his early morning strolls. Al, when he was the duty agent checking the compound, often met General Lemnitzer taking his usual evening walk through the compound.

Mrs. Lemnitzer was the proud owner of some ducks and baby ducklings at a small lake within the compound. One evening the general told Criminal Investigator Cummings that the fox had killed some of the ducklings, and he wanted Cummings to kill the fox. Investigator Cummings informed the general that he did not think the fox had killed the ducklings, but the general insisted that the fox be killed, and who would argue with a four star general?

Investigator Cummings asked his fellow members of the 16th MP Detachment if they knew anything about fox hunting, and only Criminal Investigator Max Williams came forward. Cummings was a good shot and Williams had the know-how on foxhunting, so they agreed to stake out the area. They planned that when Williams positively identified the fox he would give the signal. Cummings was supposed to be the executioner.

A few hours of stakeout brought results and Williams gave the signal. Cummings aimed the shotgun and let loose one good blast. Then he observed his victim fly fifteen feet in the air and let out a very loud and forlorn cry of "MEOW." Cummings immediately knew that he was in trouble and immediately called the veterinarian, a captain, who in no uncertain terms let him know that he was not getting out of bed at 0500 hours for a cat, that is until Investigator Cummings informed him it was Mrs. Lemnitzer's pet, which she treated like a member of the family. The veterinarian arrived minutes later, extracted the cat from a drainage pipe, took it to his hospital and operated on the wound. As the general and Mrs. Lemnitzer were out of town and not due back until later in the day Cummings had some time to worry about how they would react to the shooting of their cat.

Lady Luck was with Investigator Cummings that morning. The general did not seem to be too upset when Cummings explained what had happened to the cat, although the general did tell him that Mrs. Lemnitzer was not very happy about it. The moral of this story? Take your cats out of town when Investigator Cummings visits, and never take Cummings along when you go foxhunting.

Criminal Investigator Cummings promotions in rank were almost as rapid as his uncanny ability to solve all types of crimes. In less than four years he served in all the ranks from corporal to master sergeant. As with so many other CID Investigators, what really hurt his pride was the mass conversion of so many from Master Sergeant to Master Specialist (E-7) in July 1955. The army finally saw the light and today the only Specialist rank left in the Army is that of Sp4 (E4). Cummings was appointed to warrant officer in March 1960, and retired in Jun 1966 with the rank of Chief Warrant Officer (W3).

Criminal Investigator Cummings has had his share of exciting adventures, thrills and once-in-a-lifetime experiences. But for one unusual occurrence, Cummings has to reach all the way back to when he was in the Sea Bees in the U.S. Navy. His Sea Bee Unit was selected to play a supporting role in the movie, "The Fighting Sea Bees", starring none other than John Wayne. He may have had only a fleeting part to play, but there was Cummings on the screen with the likes of Dennis O'Keefe, the lovely Susan Hayward, William Frawley, and many others. How could anyone else in the CID top that memorable experience?

CHAPTER EIGHT

Germany

Mannheim

Criminal Investigator Oscar Michaud
Perjury and Prostitution

Investigator Michaud was assigned to the 481st CID in Heidelberg, Mannheim and Karlsruhe, Germany, during the period July 1947 to Sept 1952, and had many interesting investigations. Here is another interesting case Investigator Michaud worked on.

In view of the fact that the CID was responsible for protecting the military from unseen dangers, CID had to investigate reports of prostitution. Keep in mind that Germany was still an occupied country in 1951, when this investigation was conducted. Two agents from Investigator Michaud's unit had investigated a Sergeant Harold Green and a German national, Helga Hendricks. Michaud had seen Green but once at the CID office prior to 5 October 1951. Green had a very mean and intimidating look. Two criminal investigators from Investigator Michaud's unit had conducted a thorough investigation and had done a superb job with what evidence they had. A U.S. Military Government court in Mannheim tried Green and his girlfriend, Hendricks, for running a house of prostitution. Certain German witnesses, in fear of their lives, refused to testify. Both of the accused were acquitted.

Subsequent to the trial, Judge Paul E. Madden, of the government court, was fuming about the acquittal. Judge Madden called

Investigator Michaud's office and spoke to the CID chief, Captain Milton Marcus, stating that "Green's acquittal was a travesty of justice." He demanded that Green be investigated for the possible commission of perjury when he testified in the Mannheim Military Government court regarding the acquisition of the furniture and sundry supplies used in the establishment and operation of the house of prostitution. Subsequent to that call from Judge Madden Captain Marcus assigned the case to Investigator Michaud.

When Michaud interviewed Judge Madden all he said was "I can't put my finger on it. I know damn well he lied."

Investigator Michaud reviewed the testimony of Green and Hendricks and proceeded to conduct his Investigation of perjury. His investigation did not delve into the prostitution charges because Green and Hendricks had been acquitted of those charges.

Green and Hendricks had taken ownership of a large building and supplied each room with furniture and other supplies. They testified that the purchases were normal business transactions, legitimately purchased in the course of furnishing the building. However, as Investigator Michaud's investigation progressed, it was found that most of the furnishings and supplies had come from two German manufacturing companies. In trying to verify how the merchandise had been purchased Investigator Michaud learned that Green, an American, had claimed to have been a gangster in Chicago working for the legendary Al Capone. He demanded that the German merchants supply him with the necessary furniture for all the rooms that he and Hendricks were furnishing in their house of prostitution. Only, he was not paying for the merchandise! Rather, Green and Hendricks were obtaining the merchandise through intimidation and threats of bodily harm. They had deliberately lied when they originally claimed that they had legitimately purchased the furniture and sundry items. Green's demeanor, in claiming to be a Chicago gangster, was such as to be believed not only by the Germans, but also by some of the American military. That is how much BS he threw around while at the same time giving the appearance of being a mean individual. By interviewing those involved with the threats, Investigator Michaud was able to convince the German witnesses that Green was nothing but a cheap punk and would not have the guts to shoot anyone. The statements of the Germans that Oscar interviewed, helped to convict Green and Hendricks for having committed perjury in Judge Madden's court.

Green was convicted of perjury, discharged dishonorably from the service, and was confined to Leavenworth Prison for several years.

Criminal Investigator Oscar Michaud
Before DNA there were Spectro-Secretions —
an on the spot invention

CID Criminal Investigators are also great inventors. During the summer of 1951 Investigator Michaud was assigned to the sub-detachment of the 481st CID in Karlsruhe, Germany. In late spring of 1952 he was detailed to instruct six military policemen concerning the values of the preservation of evidence and the process involved in the art of interrogation. Upon completion of the training, those qualified were assigned as Provost Marshal Investigators.

The Karlsruhe MP Headquarters was set up so that one phone call would automatically alert all the army units in the vicinity of Karlsruhe that an offense had been committed and to be on the lookout for anyone suspected in a reported crime. On a night, during the spring of 1952 when a stabbing was reported, one of the units alerted apprehended a black soldier, Private first class Larry Smith (not his real name), trying to scale a wall adjacent to his barracks. It was well past curfew, 2300 hours, when the Karlsruhe, Germany, military police were notified that a German taxi-driver had been stabbed and the suspect was believed to be a black U.S. soldier. Keep in mind that in 1952 Germany was still an occupied country under military rule.

At the scene of the stabbing military police had found a two-bladed jackknife with a white handle, in the back seat of the taxi. The largest blade was about three inches long. On the morning following the stabbing Investigator Michaud's office received a statement concerning the event and the knife recovered at the scene of the stabbing. Michaud assigned the questioning of the suspect, Larry Smith, to a student named Baumgartner. Michaud could not recall his first name or rank; however, of the six Military Police students working with CID, he was by far the most capable interrogator.

He was doing an excellent job of trying to get Smith to admit to the stabbing. It was a very hot day, hot enough to make a person sweat easily. Larry strongly maintained his innocence with the excuse that he had been drinking at a German bar, which he could not identify, and had just lost track of time. When questioned by the Karlsruhe military police, on the night of the stabbing, he said he did not want to get caught coming back late to his unit, so he had attempted to scale the wall near his barracks.

The desks in the CID office were located in such a way that Investigator Michaud could observe the students interrogating a suspect. Having listened to Baumgartner question Smith for nearly an hour, and watching the sweat drip from his forehead, Michaud offered to help Baumgartner, who of course was relieved after trying so hard to get Smith to confess.

Investigator Michaud picked up the knife from Baumgartner's desk and proceeded to the large hallway adjacent to his office. About midway down the hall he stopped at one of the windows. Michaud did not have the slightest idea how he was going to get a confession from Private first class Smith. Baumgartner had progressed so well with his questioning of him, but just could not find the key to obtain a confession.

While standing at the window with Smith, Michaud noticed that his hands were very sweaty. A light in his head went on so brightly he could not believe what he was thinking. Looking at Smith, Michaud explained to him that their bodies, made by God, had an emotional system that was so intricate it was only recently that the FBI laboratory was able to differentiate between secretions of the body, like sweat, that are necessary in keeping us healthy, and spectro-secretions that calcify and are present only when a person commits a crime. "You can't destroy spectro-secretions, except with a special acid that is known only to the FBI" he told Smith.

Investigator Michaud picked up the knife from the windowsill and rubbed his hands all over the knife. Then he said to Larry. "I know that five or ten years ago, if I had rubbed my hands on this knife, I would no doubt have been thrown out of the army for fear I would have destroyed fingerprint evidence. Today, it is not necessary to worry about holding the knife in my hands because the FBI has developed a secret system to separate sweat from spectro-secretions." Michaud explained that it was very easy to know if he, Smith, was the one who held that knife and stabbed the German taxi-driver. He then said to him, "When you held this knife and struck the German taxi-driver with it your sweat immediately became spectro-secretions. Spectro-secretions calcify. Calcified secretions only occur when a person is involved in the commission of a crime. Your spectro-secretions cannot be removed from this knife because they are calcified."

Investigator Michaud then told Private first class Larry Smith that he could send the knife to the laboratory in Frankfurt or if he continued denying he was involved he would have to send it on to the FBI in Washington. The sad part about sending the knife to the FBI in Washington would mean he might have to be detained for three months or more while waiting for the FBI report showing that his spectro-secretions were on the knife. His cooperation could be noted by the military court and might have some impact on their deliberations.   .

Smith indicated that he was now ready to tell the truth in regards to the stabbing. Baumgartner resumed the interrogation and took his statement, confessing that he had stabbed the German taxi-driver. The taxi-driver did not have life-threatening injuries. He was the only witness to the assault. So you see make-believe, or do we call it CID inventions, can bring out the truth.

Investigator Michaud missed the boat. He could have been world famous had he registered the Spectro-Secretions System with the US Patent Office.

Heidelberg

Criminal Investigator Oscar Michaud
The Chief of Chaplains was a Thief

It was 1948 and prior to the money reform of a defeated Germany, when Criminal Investigator Oscar Michaud was assigned to the 481st CID, at Heidelberg, Germany. Things had not improved too much in Germany and food was still a scarce item with most Germans just getting by on what rations were doled out. There was one program that was of tremendous help to many Germans, and that was the distribution of CARE packages which had started out as part of the Marshall Plan, named after the famous WWII General George C. Marshall who later would become the secretary of state. These CARE packages contained all kinds of goodies, mostly canned goods such as meat products, vegetables, lard, milk powder etc. These CARE packages were destined for delivery to orphanages, hospitals, and various other qualifying agencies responsible for delivery of the CARE packages to the legal recipients. CARE packages could also be purchased by relatives or friends of German nationals in the United States, which was the case with the parents of Special Agent Hubert Marlow (author of this book), who had an aunt, who resided in the suburbs of Chicago. This aunt would send a CARE package once a month, which to the delight of Marlow's parents would contain a can of coffee. Naturally CARE packages were a sought-after item and sold well on the black market which was thriving at that time. Germany was still governed by the military and for that reason someone in the military had to be responsible to oversee the distribution of CARE packages. This is where our good Chief of Chaplains came into the picture.

Now as any good CID Investigator, Oscar Michaud had his snitches (informants) that he at times relied on for information. Oscar had one snitch, a Hungarian by the name of Janus Szluka, who in the past had given him some information in cases of a minor nature, which Oscar had always been able to verify. However it was during early 1948 that Janus provided Oscar with information regarding the sale of CARE packages on the black market. It would prove to be correct and valuable, and spelled the doom of one colonel. Colonel Maddox, the Protestant Chief of Chaplains, was the responsible officer, charged with seeing to it that the packages were properly distributed.

Janus had informed Michaud during a prior meeting, that Colonel Maddox was selling CARE packages on the black market. Oscar asked Janus if he could set up a meeting with Colonel Maddox, posing as a buyer of CARE packages, and see if he could get a truck load for the Chief of Chaplains apparent rate of two thousand dollars. No sooner said than done, and Janus had made a deal with the thieving chaplain to receive a truckload of the packages in a very narrow alleyway in Heidelberg. The good colonel of course thought the narrow alley was chosen for both his and Janus's protection from being discovered. Little did he know that during this late summer night, his downfall was about to occur. Hidden in two doorways were two CID investigators that would assist in the arrest of Colonel Maddox, as soon as he had accepted an envelope containing the payoff, which he of course assumed to be two thousand dollars. In actuality Oscar had taken some cut paper and placed a one dollar bill on top, to give it the appropriate color. Oscar did not want to take a chance and lose a bunch of money. The colonel took possession of the envelope and was promptly arrested by the two investigators, who then escorted him to the CID office in Heidelberg.

After arriving at the CID office, Oscar asked Colonel Maddox to take a seat in the coffee room, while he went to brief his chief, Major Booth. In the meantime the vehicle and CARE packages had been properly secured as evidence. Major Booth walked to the coffee room with Oscar, greeted the colonel and escorted him to his office, with Oscar following them. A funny thing happened when they arrived at the major's office. He turned around, looked at Oscar, and said, "You can't come in, this is private, and besides what you did is entrapment." Of course it was not entrapment but good police work, and Oscar did not hesitate for one moment to let the major know. He said to the major "You have no authority to take me off this case. Besides, you know the regulations. You will have to put it in writing as to why you are taking me off this case." Of course Major Booth declined to do so because it would have been evidence of his real intention to let the colonel off the hook. It did not take Oscar very long to know the reason for Major Booth's actions. He spotted masonic rings on the fingers of both Booth and Maddox. No further conversation took place between Booth and Investigator Michaud at this time.

Michaud walked to his office and wrote a detailed account of the incident. The next morning he gave the written report to one of his investigators, Investigator Heidom, who was on his way to CID Headquarters in Washington, D.C. He would make sure headquarters would be made aware of the investigation.

More than two weeks went by, and Investigator Oscar Michaud heard nothing, and was starting to wonder if the good colonel had indeed gotten divine intervention for his thievery. But then one fine morning a CID investigator from Washington, D.C., popped into his office and informed him that he and several other investigators were there to investigate Colonel Maddox and that he could not assist them. Oscar was a little upset, to say the least, and told the investigator that he had initiated the investigation and saw no reason why he could not participate. The other investigator had a good reason for not wanting to permit Oscar to be further involved in the investigation. He said to Oscar "You are Catholic and Colonel Maddox is Protestant. We don't want any claim of bias by the Colonel's defense."

Besides selling CARE packages on the black market, Colonel Maddox, as the investigators from Washington, D.C., had discovered, had also shipped twenty six baby grand pianos to a warehouse in Texas. Colonel Maddox had been in charge of the CARE package distribution throughout the U.S. Zone of Occupation. He would ask various Protestant Chaplains under his command for some of their weight allowances. In this manner he had been able to ship the twenty six pianos to Texas.

On completion of the investigation, Colonel Maddox appeared before General Huebner and was given the choice of resigning or facing a court-martial. Wisely he resigned, and of course lost all pay and retirement benefits. He got a second jolt some time after leaving the Army, when he was required to pay heavy customs duties on the pianos. It couldn't have happened to a nicer guy. You might say God took care of him.

Kaiserslautern

Special Agent Courtland D. Bradbury
A Reported Rape

Special Agent Bradbury was assigned to the CID at Kaiserslautern, Germany, referred to by most soldiers as K-Town. He received a call during the middle of the night that most CID agents hate: A sergeant had reported his wife had been raped.

Agent Bradbury arrived at the sergeant on post government quarters, one of the two story type quarters with stairs going up to the kitchen. The MP met Bradbury at the door and gave him a quick briefing, informing him that the rape allegedly had occurred weeks before, but the wife had not told anyone. Bradbury walked upstairs and there was the husband, a sergeant who was a member of a unit involved in highly secret matters. He was about six foot three inches tall, and consisted entirely of muscles, it seemed. He was drinking a beer and it was apparent that he had already consumed a few. He was pacing back and forth and it was quite clear to Agent Bradbury that he was one upset individual. The wife was about five foot ten inches tall, very good looking, but had let herself go somewhat and was about fifty pounds overweight. Here she was, sitting at the kitchen table with nothing on but a nightgown that was quite revealing, showing lots of flesh. It was all Bradbury could do not to look at this woman and run the danger of having her big muscleman, who was slightly pickled, get angry and do a number on him. Here only diplomacy would work.

The lady told Agent Bradbury that about a week prior, when she returned from doing her laundry, and while exiting her car in the parking lot, a male, whom she believed to have been a black male, grabbed her from behind and held a knife to her throat. At first, according to her, he said nothing, just held her, pulled down her clothing, and raped her. She did not see him and he did not say anything! Bradbury at this point started asking some questions, like how she knew he was black if she didn't see him and he did not say anything! This is when her story started to change. She said "Oh, I saw his black penis and he might have said something. He was wearing a watch cap pulled down over his face!" The parking lot was illuminated and the incident would have been visible to anyone in the area. According to her the dirty deed was done right there in the parking lot and it lasted some time.

Agent Bradbury smelled a rat, but due to the intoxicated condition of the hunk of a husband she had, he was not about to call his wife a liar in front of him, so he just took her statement in as much detail as was possible and exited the domicile. Bradbury informed the lady that he would have to see her at the CID office in the morning at 10:00 A.M. to sign the statement and maybe have her look at some pictures. After leaving the quarters, Bradbury went back to the CID office and contacted the MP duty officer (MPOD), informing him that this no doubt was a false complaint and that he would take care of the paperwork. The MPOD was ready to put out APBs (All Point Bulletins), submit a Serious Incident Report (SIR) and notify the German Police.

After writing up his initial report, Agent Bradbury caught a few winks, and then contacted the commander of the husband's unit, requesting that he bring the husband to the CID office. It was arranged so that the wife would arrive first, and not be aware of her husband's presence. Bradbury now conducted an in-depth interview of the wife, and this time in his environment, more conducive to success. He let her know in no uncertain terms that it was physically impossible for the rape to have occurred as reported. That he did not believe one word of her story, and that she better start telling the truth. She started crying and admitted that she was not raped. She stated her husband was going to the gym nightly and working out, and she was just staying at home getting fat. She was jealous of him, and thought he was playing around. She said, that she had made up the story of the rape to make him mad and jealous, not thinking he'd go off the deep end and report the incident. Once he had reported the alleged rape, she was afraid to change her story.

Agent Bradbury turned the entire matter over to the husbands commanding officer for disposition, and wrote a CID report, reflecting in the offense block "Rape Unfounded." Case closed.

Criminal Investigator Robert L. Cherry
Nothing Unusual Happened During My CID Career,
I Just Worked Normal Cases.

When the author first met Criminal Investigator Cherry at Fort Benning, Georgia, he was new to CID and the author had just been attached to the 86th MP Detachment (CI). Investigator Cherry was reassigned shortly thereafter. The author wrote up Cherry in the CIDAA newsletter in the featured article "Someone You Should Know." Agent Cherry told the Author "Nothing unusual happened during my CID career, I just worked normal cases." He was wrong, as you will see.

Even Generals Can Get Into Trouble

While at the 6th MP Detachment (CI), Heidelberg, Germany, Criminal Investigator Cherry had an interesting investigation assigned to him by the operations officer, Chief Warrant Officer (W4) Jimmy Johnson, as a result of an article in the *Overseas Weekly*. The article reported "There is a brigadier general in Heidelberg who is not too careful about the company he keeps." The commander in chief United States Army Europe (CINCUSAREUR) wanted to know the identity of this brigadier general. Cherry, through a confidential source, identified the individual as the staff judge advocate, USAREUR.

This brigadier general had been involved in an affair with Ms. Sweden and had been involved in compromising situations with known prostitutes. The general's sexual liaisons were of sufficient importance to be a discredit to him and the military service. The CINCUSAREUR relieved him of his command and he returned to Washington DC, and was told by the army chief of staff to get a haircut and resign from the U.S. Army with the rank of colonel or be courtmartialed. It was an offer the general couldn't refuse. He retired as a colonel.

A Good CID Agent Proves a Suspect Guilty and Also Innocent of a Crime
Remember the Old Saying "All that Glistens is not Gold"

Things are not always what they seem to be; sometimes the evidence seems to indicate without a doubt that a suspect is guilty of the crime being investigated. A good investigator has to be constantly on guard not to get a one-track mind. I have always stated that I would rather see ten guilty persons go free than one innocent person convicted of a crime he or she did not commit.

A polygraph examiner can be of great help in many cases, but agents are always reminded that a polygraph exam is an aid to an Investigator, not a crutch to make life easier for an agent. Good investigative work will always be a must. As you will see both, good investigative work and work of a good polygraph examiner will have good results.

Special Agent Henry H. G. Mungle, a good polygrapher
The Apparent Guilty Were Innocent

Special Agent Henry H. G. Mungle worked as an agent for many years and then became a polygraph examiner. It seems his most important cases occurred during the period as a polygraph examiner. Agent Mungle received a lead from Germany that Staff Sergeant (E6) John Smith (not his real name) was about to be tried for the murder of his girlfriend's son, a two year-old. The agent working the case thought it might be a good idea to polygraph the live-in baby-sitter, a friend of the family, who had since returned to the USA. The case agent just wanted to tie up loose ends and thought the baby-sitter would pass the test with no problems and this would eliminate a possible defense tactic for Staff Sergeant Smith. Smith maintained he did not beat the child to death or cause his death in any way.

Agent Mungle traveled from Washington, DC, to Michigan and conducted the test at the local police station. It was a difficult test because the woman was emotional about the issue. Mungle tested her and she showed deception about causing the injuries to the child. As a result of Mungle's interrogation of the baby-sitter, she admitted to causing the death of the child as a result of injuries that were discovered during the autopsy. She was a rather large person and had deliberately stepped on the child's stomach (much of the injury was in the stomach area) causing internal bleeding and then slammed a door on the child's head. There were some old injuries also that a subsequent forensic autopsy disclosed, that occurred before Smith came into the picture. This indicated to Agent Mungle that she, and not Smith, was responsible for the child's injuries and death. Smith was released from the Mannheim Stockade (Prison), and I'm sure he will always think highly of CID Agents.

Nuremberg - Erlangen

Criminal Investigators Henry Kuhn and Frank McHargue Hot Fingers Stole the Messhall Safe

It was around 1965, and Criminal Investigator Henry Kuhn, a member of the Nuremberg Field Office, 13th MP Detachment (CI) was the unlucky guy on duty. He was notified by the MP desk sergeant around 06:00 A.M. that a housebreaking and theft had occurred at the messhall of the 84th Engineer Battalion near Erlangen, which was not very far from Nuremberg. The initial report indicated that a field safe and contents had been stolen and that the safe had contained about three hundred dollars in U.S. currency. First things first, so Investigator Kuhn called his partner, Criminal Investigator Frank McHargue, and chased him out of bed.

Investigators Kuhn and McHargue hopped into their CID sedan and proceeded to the scene of the crime. All they knew at that time was that the mess sergeant had discovered the crime when he opened the mess hall and that there had been no forced entry, so it almost sounded like an inside job. When they arrived at the mess hall the mess sergeant pointed out a single bulb light fixture on the wall and over the safe and told the two investigators that whoever the crook was, he had unscrewed the bulb a couple of turns to turn it off. Now there was good reason for him to do so, because the light bulb was directly over the safe and that way the MP's could see the safe through the window. The two investigators, also determined through questioning the mess sergeant, that someone had apparently failed to properly lock the messhall and for that reason no force was necessary to enter the building.

The 84th Engineer Battalion had its own little compound and the total number of military personnel assigned to that particular location was only approximately one hundred and fifty. This of course favored the two investigators, providing the crime had been committed by a member of the 84th Engineer Battalion and not by an outsider.

Investigators Kuhn and McHargue started by questioning the mess sergeant to get a little more information. The good sergeant told them that the safe was a small field safe with a combination lock and had been on a wooden stand in his office. He also told them that one person could easily carry the safe, which had not been chained to a permanent fixture. Next the two investigators conducted the usual crime scene search for physical and other evidence, but it appeared there was no other evidence. The two investigators had already examined the light bulb and to their amazement it had one nice fingerprint "fried" on it. Now if that print belonged to the crook, it showed that he was not too smart because there was a good chance it would lead to his identification and of course apprehension. On the other hand the two investigators would have to come up with a suspect with whom they could compare the fingerprint.

Now the next question the two investigators really wanted answered was "where is the safe?" but they would have to wait a while for that answer. Investigators Kuhn and McHargue determined there were no other witnesses to this crime and for that reason returned to the office in Nuremberg to properly pack the only evidence they had, namely the light bulb, and forward it to the CID crime laboratory in Frankfurt. One interesting fact was that the fingerprint had been literally etched into the glass of the bulb, which indicated that the crook had burnt his fingers. Kuhn and McHargue were told by some of their fellow investigators that they were wasting their time with the light bulb. Some said that even if the crime laboratory lifted the print they would probably not be clear enough and they would never find the crook. Not too long after submitting the evidence to the crime lab, Kuhn had the last laugh, when he was informed by the crime lab that they had been able to process the print on the light bulb, which they said was a thumbprint and fully identifiable.

Investigators Kuhn and McHargue figured the first step would be to fingerprint the one hundred fifty or so members of the 84th Engineer Battalion assigned to the compound. That is exactly what they did and then forwarded the fingerprint cards to the crime lab for comparison with the thumbprint on the light bulb. It did not take long and the answer came back from the crime lab that the thumbprint on the bulb was identical to a thumbprint found on the fingerprint card of Specialist four (E4) Jerry Hale (not his real name), Kuhn and McHargue had their man. The two investigators drove to the 84th Engineer Battalion. compound and informed the commanding officer of the laboratory findings and that they were there to apprehend Specialist four (E4) Hale, the criminal who had committed the dastardly deed. The First sergeant had Hale brought to the orderly room where he was promptly advised that he was under apprehension. The two agents transported Hale to the CID office and when confronted with the evidence Hale readily confessed to the crime and a sworn statement concerning the facts was obtained. Hale was then taken back to his unit and showed the two Investigators where he had disposed of the stolen and forced-open safe. It was in a wooded area not too distant from the messhall. The safe, of course, was empty because Hale had taken all the cash, approximately three hundred dollars, out of it. When asked why he committed the crime he said "I needed money." Hale was court-martialed, found guilty of housebreaking and theft of U.S. government property. He was reduced in rank and confined at the U.S. Army Stockade, Mannheim, Germany for several months. This case would subsequently serve as a learning tool at the basic course of the CID School, teaching the future criminal investigators of the value of fingerprint evidence when properly secured and submitted to the U.S. Army Crime Laboratory.

Nuremberg

Criminal Investigator Henry Kuhn
One Nut

It was around 1970, and Criminal Investigator Henry Kuhn had once again been assigned to the Nuremberg Field Office, Detachment C, 9th MP Group (CI), and it was his lucky day to be the duty investigator. Kuhn received a report from MP desk sergeant around 5:00 A.M. that the medics at the Nuremberg Army Hospital were treating a soldier for some very serious injuries. This solder, Specialist four (E4) John Nutless (not his real name), came to the medics, some time between 3:00 a. m. and 4:00 a. m. He told the medics that he had been assaulted by a group of black soldiers resulting in serious injury to his genitalia, as a matter of fact the removal of one of his "nuts."

Investigator Kuhn wasted no time, and proceeded to the hospital to get first hand information from the victim, Specialist four (E4) Nutless. Nutless gave Kuhn a little more detailed information concerning the alleged assault. He told Kuhn that while walking towards his barracks on William O. Darby Caserne, he was approached by several Black soldiers who threw a shelter half over his head, grabbed him, and dragged him to a small building. Once they had him in this building, one of the soldiers took a knife from his pocket, opened it and then proceeded to cut open his scrotum and cut out one of his testicles. The other soldiers held him down and held his mouth shut so he could not scream. After that all of the assailants fled the scene leaving him in this small building in excruciating pain and bleeding profusely. Examination of Nutless by the duty doctor and medical personnel disclosed that one of his testicles indeed had been removed and that he was in serious need of medical attention.

Now Investigator Kuhn wondered why anyone would want to do such a thing, what could possibly be the reason for the alleged attack? Nutless informed Kuhn that he believed the attack took place as an act of revenge by friends of a soldier whom he had recently testified against at a court-martial. Now this seemed plausible to Kuhn but first things first, there was still the crime scene, that small building Nutless had referred to needed to be processed. A search of the caserne disclosed that there was indeed a small two-story building at the far edge of the motor pool area. The door of this building, according to the motor sergeant, was always locked with a small padlock, which now was missing. He was unable to tell Kuhn the last time the building had been checked and found to be secured. A check of the area around the door failed to disclose the padlock. Kuhn checked the building, which he determined had been out of use for an extended period, so everything was now covered with a heavy layer of dust. A thorough check of the ground floor disclosed nothing unusual. It disclosed neither evidence of a struggle nor physical evidence. Investigator Kuhn for that reason moved his crime scene search to the second floor and as he walked up a flight of stairs he discovered a small room which contained nothing more than a desk. Kuhn did observe footprints in the dust on the floor leading to that desk. Now things started to get a little more interesting, because the next thing Kuhn observed in the dust on top of the desk, was a distinct imprint of outlines of someone's rear end, in other words the outlines of a derriere (buttocks). From the outlines position it appeared as if someone had sat on the desk with the legs hanging over the edge. On the floor, against a nearby wall, Kuhn observed a blob of flesh and thought to himself *what on earth is this?* He would soon learn that it was a testicle and apparently the one that had been removed from Nutless and it appeared that the testicle had been thrown there. Investigator Kuhn now gave the immediate surrounding area a good check and discovered a blood smeared razor blade on the nearby outside window ledge. Kuhn secured the razor blade as evidence and gave it a thorough check, which disclosed that it contained a distinct bloody fingerprint. Kuhn completed his crime scene check but found no additional evidence. Kuhn had summoned a medic to the crime scene and the medic picked up the blob of flesh and placed it in a container. A doctor subsequently confirmed that the blob of flesh was indeed a human testicle. The first thing that came to Investigator Kuhn's mind was Nutless' claim that he had been dragged to the building and that one of the Black soldiers had removed his testicle with a knife, and a razor blade certainly did not look like a knife. Kuhn smelled a rat and thought about the finger-print on a light bulb in a messhall, also in the Nuremberg area, that had nailed a crook who had stolen a safe from the messhall.

Investigator Kuhn returned to the CID office and packed the razor blade for submission to the CID Crime Laboratory in Frankfurt. He did not have to wait too long when he was informed that the blood on the razor blade, as well as the latent fingerprint, matched that of none other than our poor "victim" Specialist four (E4) John Nutless. Case solved. Now the only thing that remained was to interrogate Nutless and find out why he had made a false report and lied about the fact that he himself had cut out the testicle and the reason for his actions. Nutless was still hurting from the self-inflicted wound but well enough to be interrogated. He was appre-hended and taken to the CID office and interrogated by Investigator Kuhn. When confronted with the CID Laboratory findings he admit-ted that the reported assault was a fabrication and that he had cut out his testicle while under the influence of mescaline (a mind-altering drug). Nutless declared he had no recollection of the incident. However he admitted that he had used mescaline and thus was "out of it." When he finally became aware of his injuries, while walking back to the barracks, he went to the hospital and told the medical personnel that he had been attacked. Nutless told Kuhn that he had returned from a trip to Amsterdam, which of course was notorious for the availability of all types of drugs, and he admitted that he had purchased the mescaline while there. He was charged with "Making a False Report" and "Malingering" and court-martialed. He was reduced in rank and sent to prison for a while.

Criminal Investigator Henry Kuhn
Sugar Sweetens but can also be Destructive

It was sometime during 1971, and Criminal Investigator Henry Kuhn was still assigned to the Nuremberg CID office and once again it was his turn as the duty investigator. He was informed by the military police that someone had dumped sugar in the gasoline tanks of vehicles parked in a unit motor pool. Putting sugar in a gas tank can be very destructive if unknown to the vehicle operator, because if he starts the engine, it can freeze up the engine and cause massive damage. The crime was discovered at approximately 05:30 A.M. that morning when an alert was called. As part of the alert the artillery unit was supposed to proceed to a pre-designated area. The artillery unit was part of the 2nd Armored Cavalry Regiment, located on what was commonly referred to as the "SS Caserne," because it was near the Nuremberg stadium of Nazi rally fame. As the members of the artillery unit reported to the motor pool and their assigned vehicles, they discovered that sugar had been poured into the gas tanks of their vehicles. The bad part about all this was that some of the vehicles involved were mobile weapons carriers, vehicles that carried and were capable of firing nuclear projectiles. This was a serious matter that could take away a good bit of firepower in the event of an attack by Soviet bloc military units.

Investigator Kuhn wasted no time and immediately proceeded to the crime scene, in this case the motor pool of the artillery unit and started his crime scene search. While canvassing the motor pool area he found two empty "Domino" sugar cartons, which had been haphazardly discarded–thrown under some vehicles and obviously out of place. Kuhn retrieved the two sugar cartons, keeping in mind that he had been able to obtain fingerprints on much stranger items before. Kuhn continued his crime scene search and found obvious traces of sugar on the gas tanks, near the filler tubes of about fifty vehicles. The perpetrator made no effort to conceal the fact that he had poured sugar into the gas tanks. The gas caps had been left off and what appeared to be sugar could be seen in and around the gas filling tubes, this of course was what had saved the day because none of the vehicles were started by their drivers and thus permanent engine damage was avoided. From interviewing drivers of the assigned vehicles, Kuhn determined that the sugar had apparently been dumped into the gas tanks of the affected vehicles sometime the night before. After finishing his crime scene search and on the spot interviews, which disclosed that the motor pool was not guarded at night, Investigator Kuhn returned to his office and processed the two "Domino" sugar cartons for shipment to the CID Crime Laboratory in Frankfurt. He was able to identify the sugar cartons as the type that could be purchased in the post exchange facilities.

Investigator Kuhn had great faith in the CID Crime Lab, and once again would not be disappointed. It did not take very long and he was notified that the two "Domino" sugar cartons had been examined and processed for fingerprints, and that they had identifiable fingerprints. Fingerprints are fine to catch a crook, but of course one has to have a suspect with whom the fingerprints from the crime scene could be compared. One thing that went through Kuhn's mind from the onset of his investigation was the question *is this an act of sabotage or revenge?* If it was an act of sabotage, it might be much more difficult to identify the culprit. Kuhn therefore notified the local Military Intelligence Office and one of their agents worked closely with him on this crime. The artillery unit had approximately three hundred soldiers assigned to it at the "SS Caserne," so that would be a good start. The MI agents present soon were of the opinion that it was not sabotage but an act of mischief. The MI Agents did agree to assist in fingerprinting all members of the artillery unit based in the "SS Caserne." No sooner said than done, they proceeded to fingerprint the approximately three hundred personnel of the unit, and of course hoped to identify the criminal. Investigator Kuhn would be disappointed because the reply from the CID Crime Lab came back negative, no match was found. This was a puzzle to Kuhn until through further checks and interviews, he determined that one member of the unit, Private first class Wieser, had been confined to the Nuremberg Stockade on the morning when the incident was discovered and reported to the military police. It was also determined that Private first class Wieser had been dispatched to the stockade in connection with an unrelated offense. *Now who would be a better suspect than a jailbird?* thought Kuhn, and promptly proceeded to the stockade, fingerprinted Private first class Wieser, and advised him of his rights. Wieser chose to seal his lips and would not utter one single word to Investigator Kuhn. This would be the first and only case Kuhn handled, where an interviewee would remain completely and adamantly silent. The hopes of solving the case now rested with the CID Lab, and Kuhn wasted no time in submitting the fingerprint card to the laboratory so a comparison with the fingerprints found on the two "Domino" sugar cartons could be made with Private first class Wieser's. It did not take too long and Kuhn had a smile on his face, when informed that the fingerprints on the fingerprint card of Private first class Wieser matched those found on the "Domino" sugar cartons.

Investigator Kuhn had also interviewed the unit commander, who described Private first class Wieser as a malcontent, and it is believed that this was the motive for his destructive action of pouring sugar into the gas tanks of the unit's tactical vehicles. A court-martial was scheduled, however Kuhn returned to the United States and was never called to testify, apparently the physical evidence alone was sufficient to convict Wieser. Once again Criminal Investigator Kuhn proved the value of collecting certain types of evidence first, asked questions later, and let the CID Crime Lab do its job.

Criminal Investigator William C. Ward
Tangling With Famous Lawyers

There are times when you can, and times when you can not fool a lawyer. While still at Fort Carson, Colorado, Criminal Investigator Ward had to appear in court on one of the cases he had worked. The defense counsel asked Ward "Don't you investigators have a sense of rivalry as to who can solve the most cases?" the inference being doing almost everything, legal or otherwise in order to solve a case. Ward replied "No Sir, we do our best to solve any case but always within legal parameters. The defense counsel came back with "Oh come, Mr. Ward, surely you have a sense of rivalry in solving cases, one way or another, we lawyers do!" To which Bill Ward replied "Yes Sir, I noticed that." Big mistake, the defense counsel really raked Investigator Ward over the coals from then on. The moral of this story, never try to up one on a lawyer while you're on the stand testifying.

Outsmarting a Lawyer before Being on the Stand Testifying

While stationed in Giessen, Germany, during 1969, Criminal Investigator Ward worked a kidnapping and assault case, and the civilian defense lawyer was well known for his dislike of CID. To the best of Investigator Ward's recollection it was none other than F. Lee Bailey who was a known "Bible Thumper," as Ward would say. Investigator Ward was called before the Article 32 Board (like a jury in civilian life), and was told "Look out for this guy, he is sharp and hates CID." Ward had a good case, but felt that it was never wrong to take precautions and so he did by bringing a Bible. Now Ward sat in such a manner that no one could enter the room without him having to move his legs, which he had resting on a chair almost blocking the entrance. With his Bible open and on his lap, Ward waited for Mr. Bailey to show up, and when he did, he stopped and said, "excuse me." Ward looked up and said "Oh, I'm sorry, I was reading and didn't see you." Ward then moved, so that Mr. Bailey could enter, and as he did he looked down and saw the Bible. He then asked Investigator Ward "Do you always read the Bible while waiting to appear before an Article 32 board?" Ward answered "I read the Bible whenever I have the chance or time." Bailey grunted and entered the room. At that time Bailey had no idea who Ward was, in other words he did not know he was a CID investigator.

Finally the moment of truth arrived and Ward had to testify. He was called into the room, sworn in, and as he said "everyone had a shot at me." Finally it came to the moment when Mr. Bailey had his chance to put another CID agent through the wringer, and everyone of course was waiting for the ax to fall. A surprising thing happened; Mr. Balley said "I observed Mr. Ward in the waiting room reading the Bible, Any man who reads the Bible regularly would not tell a lie under these circumstances, therefore I have no questions for Mr. Ward." Yes, Agent Ward outsmarted a lawyer, but let me add that since that day Bill has become an ordained minister and does read the Bible.

Criminal Investigator Shel F. Miller
The Brutal Rape of an Eleven Year Old German Girl

Investigator's Miller, Pella and Lefler, members of the 11th MP Detachment (CI), Berlin, Germany, were assigned a brutal rape case, during late 1952 (Germany was still an occupied country at that time). The perpetrator was thought to be an American soldier. Miller was a newly minted, school-trained CID criminal investigator (what we would today call an apprentice CID agent) with about four or five months experience. Of course he was not the lead investigator, Criminal Investigator John Lefler was. Miller had been teamed up with Investigator Mike Pella for training in the field, and it turned out to be a fantastic learning experience for him early in his CID career.

Investigators Pella and Miller worked the case for about two weeks and were going absolutely nowhere, and we all know that feeling.

Virtually all leads were exhausted. Drinking coffee one morning, and trying to think of what else they could do to solve this case and have justice prevail, Investigator John Lefler came up with the idea of checking the detachment's newly started MO (Modus Operandi) file for possible leads. Investigators Pella and Miller, although spoofing Investigator Lefler's idea as being a waste of time, and having the feeling that they were clutching at straws, went for the file. There was a grand total of about fifteen cards (remember it was a new file) with ID photos in the box, seven of them pertaining to various types of sex offenders.

In for a penny, in for a pound, Investigator Miller thought–as they took all of the cards, even the barracks thieves to the hospital in Berlin, where the victim was being treated, for a photo line-up with the eleven-year-old victim. As Miller put it "Damned if she didn't immediately, without the slightest hesitation, pick out the photo of a soldier named Gordon Brake," (Not his real name). Investigators Miller and Pella waited for a while re-shuffled the cards and spread them out again. Again the child immediately picked out Brake. Miller and Pella went to Brake's unit and apprehended him. After putting together all the forensic evidence, including scrapings from under the girl's fingernails, the lab report came back reflecting they matched with Brake's. Brake was court-martialed, found guilty of rape, and sentenced to life imprisonment at the Leavenworth U.S. Military prison.

Investigator Miller learned a valuable lesson, early in his career, that there is no such thing as any lead being a waste of time, no matter how remote or insignificant it might appear. Sometimes it's the little things that make a difference.

Criminal Investigator Hubert Marlow (The Author)
My Third Tour in Germany

Nine Months at Headquarters and then as Special Agent in Charge of the Bad Kreuznach Resident Agency

From Vietnam I was assigned to HQ, 9th MP Group (CI), Kaiserslautern, Germany, as the standards officer (case review) from February 1971 to September 1971. Initially the commanding officer was Colonel Edward G. Luce, a nice gentleman, followed by Colonel

Edward Brakenridge. Brakenridge apparently did not have much use for Warrant Officers, because when an Specialist four (E4) was promoted to Specialist five (E5), the good colonel had the army photographer take a picture while he pinned the new Specialist five (E5) stripes on the lucky guy. A few weeks later I and two other warrant officer agents received our promotion to Chief Warrant Officer (W3) and one to Chief Warrant Officer (W4) and the good Colonel said nothing and did nothing. 9th MP Group (CI) changed to 2nd Region, USACIDC (upon the creation of USACIDC), and moved to Heidelberg, Germany, and was at that time commanded by Colonel Robert C. Yowell. At 9th MP Groupp (CI) were Chief Warrant Officer (W4) Alan T. Kokinda, Special Agents Robert W. Moody, Almondo A. Vallone and Norman E. Bilger.

My job at 9th MP Group (CI) was Standards Officer, in other words case review, it was kind of funny to have a foreign-born kid review the work of native Americans. Another job at 9th Group was to conduct inspections of the subordinate offices. One day I went on such a trip with Agent Moody, who was driving. As we went down the autobahn (Freeway), I looked over at Moody, and to my amazement he had his eyes closed and was asleep, I awakened him in a hurry and told him to pull over and let me drive. I had noticed in the office that he would hold a newspaper perfectly in his hands and if you looked behind the paper you would find him sound asleep. Later it was found out that he suffered from some type of illness, was prescribed medicine, and was alright after that.

In September 71, I was reassigned to take over the Bad Kreuznach Resident Agency when the Special Agent in Charge (SAC) Marvin Besson was reassigned to Korea. I was at Bad Kreuznach from Sep 71 to January 74, as Special Agent in Charge and Investigator. This office initially came under Detachment G, 9th MP Group (CI) which upon the creation of USACIDC became the Kaiserslautern Field Office, Commanded by Captain William E. Flanigan, Jr. with Operations Officers Gene C. Griffin, followed by Mr. Kokinda.

This was during the summer of 1973, when Major General Davis, the first black general to command a combat division, had taken over the 8th Infantry Division. During this period we had seven or eight robberies and aggravated assaults occur in Bad Kreuznach, with the offenders being a group of black individuals. Neither we (CID) nor the German Kripo had any leads. General Davis was asking the Division Provost Marshal, Lieutenant Colonel Carl Allen, "What is CID doing about these cases?"

As luck would have it I had gotten Specialist four (EE) Lewis (a black soldier) off the hook when he was accused of rape and drug use. All because I remembered the so-called victim, a German lady, from an incident six months prior and after checking a few things proved her to be untruthful.

The building the CID office was in had an archway leading to the parking lot, and on the left side (downstairs) was the CID office and on the right side the MP station and station commander's office. The entire upstairs was the education center and Lewis was taking some college courses and would always stop by my office and say hello (he was grateful I had gotten him off the hook). So when he came into my office I said to him "Lewis, I need your help." To make a long story short, about two weeks later he came and gave me a list of about seven black soldiers who he said were a gang and troublemakers and could have committed the robberies and aggravated assaults.

Now we had something to work with, and I of course briefed Lieutenant Colonel Allen. I, or one of my warrant officers, would brief Lieutenant Colonel Allen on the status of cases every week. I requested that he not say anything to General Davis until we had worked on the cases some more and developed more information. Obviously he must have said something, because two days later Colonel Thomas, Commander 8th Infantry Division Support Troops, whose brother Major Thomas was the commanding officer of the Alaska Field Office (CID), came into my office and said "Mr. Marlow, the general wants to break up this group (referring to our suspects) and split them up all over Germany. I want you to hold a line-up this afternoon." Of course no criminal investigator in his right mind would have done that because you want all suspects to remain in the area, so they can be interrogated if need be. I replied "Colonel, I will hold the line-up when I think it will benefit me as an investigator the most, not to get the general off your ass." Colonel Thomas did not like my answer, and I took some heat and back-stabbing for it. Our patience paid off because a couple of weeks later we solved seven of eight of the cases as a result of Lewis providing the suspects names.

Special Agent Martin W. Quattlebaum
The Supreme Sacrifice: Dying in the Line of Duty

During the summer of 1992, Special Agent Martin W. Quattlebaum attended a ceremony at Headquarters, U.S. Army Europe (USAREUR). Mrs. Charlotte Walliser was presented an International Narcotics Enforcement Officers Association (INEOA) Medal of Valor in memory of her late husband Volker Walliser.

This case clearly reflects the close ties that exist between all law enforcement officers, and how they work together. Unfortunately, this work may result in the deaths of officers/agents while pursuing their duty to suppress the illegal drug trade.

German Police Officer Volker Walliser was one of those officers. Known to a number of former Level I Drug Team agents by his covert name "Ritchie," he was murdered by a drug dealer, in December 1991, during negotiations for a controlled delivery of twenty five kilos (a little over fifty pounds) of heroin. Luckily the killer was arrested before he had the chance to murder Officer Walliser's undercover partner, U.S. Army CID Special Agent Jim Bean.

Special Agent Jim Bean was a warrant officer assigned to the Second Region Level I Drug Team, which consisted of seven agents who worked with the state police "covert" drug teams throughout Germany. They were targeted against major drug traffickers involved in smuggling large quantities of illicit drugs.

The CID agents handled incidents involving major military traffickers involved with organized civilian drug dealers. Being non-German, the CID agents were not suspected of being police by the civilian traffickers. The system worked very well for both the CID and the German police. When the concept was first implemented in the early 1970's, the Germans did not have much experience working drug investigations. Many of the supervisors of the teams today learned their trade from CID agents who worked with them.

Around May or April 1991, while Agent Bean was working with a Baden-Wuerttemberg source that had connections with an international arms dealer who wanted to meet a buyer. Bean met the arms dealer after the informant traveled to Switzerland and described Bean as an American who was involved in different business ventures and might be interested in the weapons for sale. When Bean met Maurice they eventually began discussing ways to ship heroin back to the United States, where lots of money could be made in the Northeast. Maurice was interested in Agent Bean's cover story that he shipped exotic european vehicles back to the states for resale. Maurice told agent Bean he was connected to a heroin lab and they could do some big business.

Maurice was very cautious for a good reason. Once the CID/German Police ran his name through Interpol and the NADDIS system, they learned just who it was they were dealing with. Maurice had served time for his involvement in the heroin investigations in the United States on which the movie, "The French Connection" was based. Maurice now owned a hotel and bar in Switzerland and was still wanted for crimes in France, but he seemed to be well connected. He told Agent Bean not to worry if he was with the police because they had not committed a crime by just discussing business. Maurice also warned that he had friends in the police and he was not going to jail because he was too old, (fifty five years at the time). CID/German police later learned that Bean's cover story and his cover identification was indeed checked by someone in the Munich police early on in the case.

Agent Bean was invited to come to Switzerland and visit Maurice. However the Drug Enforcement Agency (DEA) in Switzerland attempted to insert the German Federal Police into the case and refused to give country clearance for Bean to come to Switzerland. Bean ultimately told Maurice he did not want to come to Switzerland. Maurice agreed to come back to Germany.

It was at this point that officer Walliser and a second informant were introduced to Maurice. Officer Walliser played the role of a French citizen interested in some business and the other informant was a Turk who was extremely experienced in complex major heroin cases. This would enable the first informant to be worked out of the scene because Maurice knew where he lived and worked. Maurice accepted the new players immediately. It helped that they drove an expensive automobile and played the part of high-level businessmen. Maurice agreed to deliver twenty five kilograms of heroin but wanted to see some money before showing any amount of heroin. Maurice was shown three million Deutschmarks (Two million dollars) flash money near Stuttgart. The deal continued to evolve over the next couple of months and eventually Maurice was shown the money again.

The Turkish informant, who was an addict, showed up early for a meet with Maurice one night and was high on heroin. Maurice had been doing background checks on the new people brought into the scenario and he accused the Turk of being involved with the police. As it turned out, the Turk had also been involved on the fringes of the original "French Connection" case and had worked with the French police later in exchange for getting out of jail early. Maurice accused the Turk openly and the deal seemed finished.

More time went by and the Turk stayed in contact with Maurice. Maurice eventually visited the Turk at his home near Karlsruhe and continued to show an interest in doing a deal and started an operation with Agent Bean to transport heroin to the U.S. All the parties agreed to do the deal and agreed to Maurice's suggestion to deliver in Mannheim, but only after much bickering to do the deal in Freiburg near the Swiss border. Here is where, in the opinion of CID Special Agent Martin W. Quattlebaum (the provider of this information) some major errors were made. Of course it is easy to sit back after the fact and second-guess decisions. Maurice wanted to see the money again. The case agents wanted to show him one more time since there was some distrust. The head of the Baden Wuerttemberg State Police drug program did not want to show the money again. He did, however, allow the case agents to convince him it was the right thing to do. Everyone wanted to get Maurice in jail and get a good seizure of drugs. It was agreed that they would meet in a hotel in Mannheim.

Agent Bean, Officer Walliser, Wolfgang Megele (state police undercover officer), the Turkish informant, and Maurice and his partner met in a ritzy hotel in Mannheim. Everyone disrobed to prove that no one was wearing a wire or was armed. Then the group sat down and set up the delivery. The money was shown again by Officer Walliser and remained in the room. The Turk, Maurice's partner, and Wolfgang departed together with the understanding that Maurice's partner would go with them to get the twenty five kilos of heroin.

They drove to Karlsruhe and stopped at an autobahn (Freeway) rest stop identified by the accomplice. They drove to that location in a

German police car. Officer Megele and the Turkish informant waited at the rest stop restaurant while the accomplice went to get the heroin.

In Mannheim Agent Bean, Officer Walliser, and Maurice settled down in the hotel to wait for several hours. There were several phone conversations between the players, often spoken in French. Officer Walliser spoke German, English and French, as did Maurice. Agent Bean was fluent in German but did not understand French. Maurice recommended that Bean accompany him to his hotel and wait in his room in the event Maurice's wife or some other partner called looking for Maurice. Agent Bean refused to leave Officer Walliser alone, but Officer Walliser persuaded him that it was a good idea for someone to wait in Maurice's room by the phone.

Maurice walked the short distance with agent Bean to Maurice's room. Maurice changed a one thousand Deutschmark note at a local bank, probably to verify its authenticity. He and Agent Bean conspicuously entered Maurice's hotel through the downstairs elevator. No hotel workers saw them enter the building.

A surveillance team followed them in the transition from one hotel to another, while another team was set up in the adjacent room beside Officer Walliser's location. German police specialists had the entire scene covered inside and outside the hotel. Surveillance cameras installed within the television set continued to monitor events in Officer Walliser's room. Protection was as tight as possible without the teams being detected. No one knew whether or not the ever-cautious Maurice had his own counter-surveillance. All the players remained tense and ready to react instantly to any perceived trouble. Maurice left Agent Bean at his hotel room, telling him to make himself comfortable and offering him whatever he wanted from the room refrigerator/bar. Maurice used the latrine in his room before departing and then went back to the room where Officer Walliser was waiting. Maurice and Officer Walliser talked with Bean on the phone several times in the ensuing few hours of waiting. Bean talked with Officer Walliser and Walliser said, "It'll be over soon." The surveillance team watched Walliser and Maurice talking and then saw the two pour some Sekt (champagne) to celebrate the deal.

Maurice then calmly reached into his jacket, draped over a chair behind him, withdrew a .32 caliber automatic pistol, and shot Officer

Walliser six times. Walliser was still holding his glass as he fell dead to the floor.

Maurice picked up the suitcase of money and started for the door as the arrest team burst into the room. Maurice was immediately arrested while the team watching Agent Bean was alerted. Bean was immediately covered and removed from the area under tight security. Officer Megele and the Turkish informant remained at the rest stop waiting for Maurice's partner to return to them with the heroin. When they were alerted to the murder they discovered that the keys to their vehicle were missing. Shortly afterward, Maurice's accomplice was arrested traveling toward the German-Swiss border.

Agent Bean was in all likelihood another intended target of Maurice. Maurice was likely enroute back to his hotel to obtain his personal belongings and his car. He did not have other ammunition in his possession, but why would he leave a witness behind in the person of Agent Bean. As far as Maurice knew, Bean was the last person to see him with Officer Walliser.

The gun used to kill Officer Walliser? Maurice likely had hidden it in his hotel latrine. He was watched going and coming but the surveillance team was only loosely trailing him. What about Officer Megele and the Turkish informant? It can only be speculated what plans there were for them. It is possible that Maurice's accomplice was supposed to kill those two but became too scared to go through with it. The keys for their car were never found, nor was it determined how they had disappeared.

CID Special Agent Martin W. Quattlebaum, will never forget that night. After waiting all day to hear that "the deal had gone down", he got the call from Agent Bean informing him there had been trouble. He said "Chief, Walliser has been shot." Agent, Quattlebaum, supervisor of Agent Bean, thought he was joking, and then he detected a different tone in Agent Bean's voice. Agent Quattlebaum still finds it difficult to believe that such a careful and confident police officer as Officer Walliser, was killed.

Those who knew Officer Walliser could not believe the sad news of his death. He was the first German undercover agent ever killed in the line of duty. But all drug investigators can learn from his sacrifice. There were mistakes made that need not be made again.

Perhaps his death can save the life of some other agent who works in this dangerous profession. Maurice and his partner are serving life sentences in prison. CID Special Agent Jim Bean retired from the U.S. Army CID and now resides in the United States. As long as Maurice is alive there has to be concern about the threats he made against Agent Bean.

Criminal Investigator Alvin P. Fackerell
Unusual Assignment CID Special Agents Sometimes Get
Interviewing German Luftwaffe Field Marshal Albert Kesselring

Criminal investigations usually deal with the more sordid and unpleasant facets of life and people. The incident related here, although its cause and background are certainly sordid, is a more pleasant interesting, and somewhat unusual investigation.

Searching for a German Gestapo General

During 1955 Criminal Investigator Alvin P. Fackerell was assigned as the chief criminal investigator and provost marshal (PM) at the Flint Caserne Barracks, Bad Toelz, Germany. The resident troops were the 10th Special Forces (ABN). The caserne was located at the foot of the Bavarian Alps and south of Munich. This was a perfect location for the jump and ski training of these troops. About twenty Kilometers (twelve Miles) from Bad Toelz there is a small town named Tegernsee. It is named after the lake upon whose shores it is located

A German national, Herbert Heuer was assigned to Criminal Investigator Fackerell's office as an interpreter, and he is part of the story. Interpreter Heuer served in the German Army as a lieutenant, and was wounded on the Eastern Front, then sent to a hospital in Bad Toelz. He was taken a Prisoner of War (POW) by General George Patton's forces, checked out, and subsequently released at the end of the war. Although a native Berliner he chose to remain in Bad Toelz, and who could blame him since Berlin was surrounded by the Russians. Interpreter Heuer was fluent in English, obviously, or he would not have been hired by the U.S. Forces as an interpreter.

One day a courier from headquarters, Southern Area Command (SACOM), Munich, arrived at Investigator Fackerell's office with a letter classified "Secret." The letter contained information to the effect that a continuing search was underway in an effort to locate a former German Gestapo (*Geheime Staats Polizei*-Secret State Police) general named Wolff. Wolff had been in charge of Gestapo activities in Italy during 1943-1945. He was wanted for war crimes committed by the Gestapo during his period of command.

The letter further stated that during this period all German forces in Italy were under the overall command of former Luftwaffe (Air Force) Field Marshal Albert Kesselring. Field Marshal Kesselring was now residing in the Tegernsee area. Field Marshall Kesselring was to be interviewed to obtain any knowledge he had concerning General Wolff and his present whereabouts.

Investigator Fackerell had Interpreter Heuer telephone the office of the local *Landespolizei* (State Police) at Tegernsee. They confirmed, through the use of the very efficient citizen registration files maintained by the *Einwohner Meldeamt* (Citizen Resident Registration Office), that Kesselring resided in Tegersee. It should be mentioned that all residents of Germany were (even before WWII, and still to this date) required to report their resident address each time they moved, to the *Einwohner Meldeamt*.

An interview was arranged between Investigator Fackerell and Field Marshal Kesselring for the following day. The German military officer caste system began making its presence felt. Interpreter Heuer said to Fackerell, in a mixture of fear and awe, "So, we are really going to talk to a field marshal."

At the post library Investigator Fackerell found an autobiography of Field Marshal Kesselring which had been written shortly after the end of WWII. Kesselring had served in WWI as an artilleryman. In 1933, after twenty-nine years in the artillery, he was transferred to the famous Luftwaffe (which was not his personal preference at the time). Even at his advanced age he took flight training, and made steady promotional progress. In the early years of WWII he commanded various Luftwaffe elements engaged in the "Battle of Britain," on the Western Front. In spite of the fact that he never joined the Nazi Party, and never became a member of the German officer clique known as "Hitler's Gang", his command posts became higher, and his influence greater, as the war progressed. In 1941 he was sent to Italy as Commander-in-Chief, South, where he attained the rank of field marshal. By the fall of the following year he was in command of all German and Italian forces in the entire Mediterranean area. He was the only Luftwaffe field marshal to command ground and naval forces in addition to air forces.

After the Italian surrender in September 1943, Field Marshal Kesselring continued to command the German retreat through Italy. His command provided some of the stiffest opposition encountered by Allied troops during WWII. Upon the capitulation of Germany in 1945, Field Marshal Kesselring was imprisoned by the British forces. After a hasty court-martial he was sentenced to death. Later, a full investigation of Field Marshal Kesselring's command activities resulted in the death sentence being vacated. He was released and allowed to return to Germany. After his capture the field marshal had been stripped of his baton, and all his orders and decorations, by souvenir-hunting British officers. (Note by the Author-Field Marshal Kesselring was responsible for saving many Italian art treasures and historical buildings)

Upon arrival at Tegernsee for the interview Investigator Fackerell and Interpreter Heuer were directed to a small house, looking much like an American vacation cabin, located on the south shore of Lake Tegernsee. Field Marshal Kesselring, a widower, lived alone, except for the presence of an elderly woman housekeeper. Fackerell's first impression of the Field Marshal was of a well-built man who wore a big smile. There was a patch on his trousers.

Upon entering the small living room Fackerell and Interpreter Heuer were greeted by Field Marshal Kesselring. Heuer came to ram-rod-attention, bowed from the waist, and clicked his heels, sounding like a rifle shot. The Field Marshal merely nodded at him and walked over to shake hands with Investigator Fackerell.

The interview began, carried out in English, between Heuer and Fackerell, and then entirely in German between Heuer and Field Marshal Kesselring. In a very short time Field Marshal Kesselring stated that he had no useful knowledge concerning General Wolff. He said "I was a fighting general. General Wolff was a Gestapo man. I never met him or saw him on the front line". After ascertaining that the interview was not going to produce any information about General Wolff the conversation became more general and enjoyable.

The housekeeper served coffee as Investigator Fackerell, and Field Marshal Kesselring talked, interpreted by Heuer, about WWII and its aftermath. The Field Marshal seemed quite interested in Fackerell's war service in the Pacific Theatre where he had served in the U.S. Navy. He also talked to Interpreter Heuer about the Russian Front. At one time Fackerell asked him if he had ever had his baton and medals returned to him. He sadly shook his head, and said, "No." Time slipped by, and Fackerell realized they had talked for more than two hours, it was time to go. As Fackerell and Heuer were leaving, Field Marshal Kesselring said in perfectly accented British English, "Thank you for coming to see me. I have enjoyed the visit I wish you both all good luck". The only reason Investigator Fackerell could suggest for Field Marshal Kesselring carrying on the interview in German, through Interpreter Heuer, is that he might have felt more in control and more comfortable that way.

Since the day of the interview, Investigator Fackerell has read many books about WWII, written by people on both sides of the war. Fackerell never read a derogatory word about Field Marshal Kesselring. Fackerell later learned he was known as "Smiling Albert" by his intimate friends, such as Field Marshal Erwin Rommel. Historically he is known as a leader of men, a brilliant general, and above all, a "good soldier". Field Marshal Kesselring died a few years after the interview. Agent Fackerell stated "To this day I have not learned any more about a Gestapo General Wolff. During a visit to Germany several years later Fackerell found Heuer still living in Bad Toelz. He was in a very responsible position with American intelligence.

Information concerning Kesselring and Wolff

Field Marshal Albert Kesselring (1887-1960) was promoted to Field Marshal on 14 July 1940, transferred from the Eastern Front to Italy about Nov 1941. The book *World War II Strange & Fascinating Facts* by Don McCombs and Fred L. Worth reflects the following concerning Albert Kesselring "Luftwaffe general who commanded all Axis forces in Italy. He was a very versatile commander who was in charge of Luftwaffe units in the Battles of Britain and North Africa and later conducted an excellent defense of Italy. Kesselring was tried and convicted by the British for his part in the massacre of 335 Italians at Ardeatine Caves in Rome on May 23, 1944. He was sentenced to death, but this was commuted to twenty years imprisonment. He only served five years, having been released in 1952 on medical grounds."

The book *Leaders and Personalities of the Third Reich* (1984) by Charles Hamilton reflects the following: "Karl Wolff (1900-). Head of Himmler's personal staff; military governor of Northern Italy. Born in Darmstadt on 13 May 1900, Karl Wolff served in WWI, winning both classes of the Iron Cross. After the war he became a member of the Hessian Freikorps. In 1931 he joined the NSDAP (National Socialist German Workers Party) and the SS. Wolf rose quickly in the SS, serving briefly in 1933 as Ritter Von Eppl's personal adjutant. He came to Himmler's attention while in this post, and the *Reichsfuehrer* SS soon took the young officer as his own adjutant. Until 1943 Wolff served also as head of Himmler's personal staff and liaison officer for the *Reichsfuehrer* with Hitler. In 1942 he was promoted to lieutenant general in the SS (SS-*Obergruppenfuehrer*). Wolff was dismissed as Himmler's personal adjutant in 1943 because he insisted on divorcing his wife, which was against Himmler's wishes.

Wolff was sent to Italy in 1943 as military governor of Northern Italy. He was also Plenipotentiary General of the Wehrmacht in Italy. In effect Wolff controlled German-occupied Italy for the last two years of the war. By February 1945 he was convinced that the war was lost, and he opened negotiations with the Allies in Switzerland which resulted in an early surrender in Italy. This step, which could have cost him his life, would serve him well in the postwar years.

Because of his record in Italy, Wolff was hardly bothered by the Allies after the war. Sentenced by a de-Nazification court to four years, he served one week of his sentence before being released. He later became a successful advertising executive.

In the aftermath of the Eichmann case, however, he was arrested and charged with complicity in the "Final Solution" by the West German government. In 1964 he was sentenced to a prison term of fifteen years and was not released until 1971."

Hanau

Criminal Investigator Robert A. Cappuccio and Robert Babbin
The Burglar was wearing the Evidence

It was during the spring of 1968, and Criminal Investigator Bob Cappuccio was assigned to the Hanau Field Office of the 52nd MP Detachment (CI). Bob was the duty agent when the MP desk sergeant informed him that someone had broken into the dry cleaning store on base and that the thief had made off with items of clothing and money from the cash register. Bob and his partner Robert Babbin went to the crime scene and did the usual, dusting for fingerprints and taking photographs, showing the damage the thief had caused by his forced entry.

What now? There were no other leads at that very moment, however we all know that criminal investigation depends on a lot of skill and some luck. It was Bob's lucky day, because about a day later Investigator Cappuccio got a tip from one of his informants that he had seen a young soldier, Private fist class John Smith, a member of Headquarters Company, parading around wearing a suit that had been stolen from the dry cleaning store. Now the mere fact that this Private first class Smith was wearing one of the stolen suits did not necessarily mean that he was the culprit who had forced his way into the store and stolen the merchandise and money, but it was a good start. If nothing else Smith would have some explaining to do and certainly should be able to provide information as to how he obtained the suit he was wearing. So the next move was to arrest this Private first class Smith and interrogate him. No sooner said and done. Investigators Cappuccio and Babbin went to Private first class Smith's unit and arrested him and took him to the CID office. Once at the CID office Cappuccio advised him of his rights, informed him that he was suspected of the offense of burglary, and asked him if he wanted a lawyer to be present during the interview. Of course Cappuccio said interview and not interrogation, no need in helping him shut up. Private first class Smith indicated that he was willing to talk to Investigator Cappuccio without a lawyer being present. So the first thing he told Cappuccio was that his girl friend was pregnant and that he was in dire need of money and clothes, and that was the reason he had broken into the dry cleaning store. In other words he confessed. In essence he told Cappuccio that he had some fun, got his girlfriend pregnant, and now had to pay for it. There was one little problem however, and that was the fact that this young soldier was not willing to make a written sworn statement. Since he had indicated this to Investigator Bob Cappuccio at the beginning of the interview, Bob had a way of dealing with this situation, as any smart CID agent would. He simply started to write everything down verbatim and when the interview was finished he asked Private first class Smith if it was alright for him (Bob) to type this statement and if he would then sign it. Once again the young soldier informed Investigator Cappuccio that he would not sign a formal statement. What to do now? Cappuccio simply asked Smith, very politely, if he would be so kind as to read his notes to make sure everything was accurate and truthful. To this he readily agreed. Once he had reviewed the notes Cappuccio asked him, "Would you mind signing my notes?" and to his surprise he did. Now this in itself would most likely not have been enough to convict or even have the soldier tried by court-martial. Private first class Smith had forgotten one thing, that Special Investigator Babbin had been present during the entire interview and recording of the notes by Investigator Cappuccio. So case solved, Babbin signed the notes as a witness and when the court-martial was in session Private first class John Smith's lawyer had him enter a plea of guilty. He was convicted, sentenced to be reduced to Private (E1), ordered to be confined for two years at the Leavenworth prison and received a dishonorable discharge from the army.

Zweibruecken

Criminal Investigator Hubert Marlow (The Author)
My First Assignment to Germany in CID
Working as a CID Agent and MP Station Commander

Next came an assignment to the 52nd MP Detachment (CI), Mannheim, Germany, with duty station Zweibruecken, Germany, from Oct 67 to Dec 69. The commanding officers were Lieutenant Colonel David T. Stewart and Major Robert G. Spann, Operations Officers George Bonville, William E. Joyce and Tim L. Mayfield. My duties at the Zweibruecken CID Office started off with a bang, when Lieutenant Colonel Robert Goggans, area provost marshal, informed me that I would also be the station commander (local PM). This meant I had operational control over twenty nine MP's, one of whom was none other than our associate member of the CID Agents Association, John K. Groves, at that time an Specialist four (E4), to retire as a Lieutenant Colonel.

A sad day occurred, involving Specialist four (E4) John Groves, on 19 November 1969. John had worked a double shift, as the desk sergeant and then had filled in for the road supervisor. John, a newlywed, had picked up his wife to take her to the doctor that morning, after finishing work. John had just left his off-post residence with his wife and eight-months-old son, driving his VW Beetle on the cobblestone street in Zweibruecken, when a big Mercedes came barreling down the street, which had big sturdy trees lining one side of the road that had a big drop, and struck John's VW, pushing it into one of the trees. The German driver of the Mercedes was drunk. John's wife died a couple hours later at the hospital in Landstuhl, Germany, his eight-months-old son was in a cast for six months, and John suffered extensive injuries to his mouth. I assisted John, who, along with his infant son, was medically evacuated to the United States, as best as I could and then heard nothing further from him until the Fall of 1996.

I came home from work and had a message on my telephone answering machine and the caller said "Mr. Marlow, this is Lieutenant Colonel John Groves, you probably won't remember me. I was one of your MPs at Zweibruecken, and always wanted to thank you for what you did for me after my wife was killed in the car accident." I immediately knew who Lieutenant Colonel Groves was and called his office at Fort Bliss, Texas, where he was the provost marshal. Additionally he had the job of battalion commander of an MP unit, which covered Panama and other locations. He was on a trip to Panama. I called one more time a week later and he still was not in. One day while at the Defense Investigative Service (DIS) office, in Chicago, Illinois, where I was assigned as a special agent, a call came in and it was John Groves. The funny thing is that we would only go to the office once every two weeks at most. I said, "Well, I suppose I will have to call you sir now" but he declined and we have been good friends ever since. I determined that, after returning to the states, he had been a deputy sheriff and a detective for a local police department for seven years. He had attended Missouri Southern State University and Webster University. He had been in ROTC, gotten a reserve commission, went on active duty and two years later got a Regular Army Commission. He had also worked for 6th Region CID and I even got him to join the CIDAA. This only shows you how small this world is. John found me while talking to several individuals from the El Paso Law Enforcement Group Association. One of the members was retired CID agent Al Yost who worked for the U.S. Marshal's Service and when John mentioned my name, he said he knew where I was and gave him my phone number. John's commanding officer, before transferring from the 564th MP Company, Massweiler, Germany, to a platoon of the 533rd MP Company, Zweibruecken, was none other than First Lieutenant Daniel A. Doherty, who would become the commanding general of the CID.

A Case of Rape

It was at Zweibruecken that I worked a case I would not consider the most important, but it certainly enhanced liaison with the German police in the state of Saarland, and the state of Rheinland Pfalz. On 04 Feb 68, a fifteen-year-old German girl reported she had been raped by an American soldier. She described the soldier as being dressed in fatigues and that he drove an American Army sedan with a big antenna on the back. The girl reported that the soldier picked her up while she was hitchhiking, in Zweibrueken, Rheinland Pfalz, and then drove into the state of Saarland where he raped her. Those were my leads. Since the subject was alleged to be a U.S. soldier, I started the investigation. Due to the victim reporting the car was an army car with a big antenna on the back, I made checks with various motor pools, inquiring who had checked out a staff car with a big whip antenna on the back. When I talked to the dispatcher in Kaiserslautern, Germany, he apparently was intimidated by being questioned by a CID criminal investigator, since I detected nervousness in his voice. After questioning him for a few minutes, he informed me that one member of the Labor Service Unit had checked out a staff car and told him not to tell anyone that he had checked it out. A little more work, and I was able to notify the Kripo

Zweibruecken and Saarbruecken, that I had a suspect, and asked them if they were ready for a line-up.

We all drove to the MP Station/PMO, Kaiserslautern, and the victim picked the subject out of a line-up without hesitation. The subject, a German national and member of the Labor Service, was married, and had two children. He appeared in court and was sentenced to fifteen years imprisonment. The Labor Service initially consisted of displaced persons, but later primarily employed Germans. It was a semi-military organization in that initially the members wore a uniform, which displayed an insignia of rank. This was later dropped. The duties consisted of guarding depots, gates of casernes, and driving trucks hauling supplies. As a result of solving this case, I was given a letter of commendation, by the chief, State Criminal Police Office (Landeskriminalamt), State of Saarland, with the normal endorsements Brigadier General Harley Moore, PM U.S. Army Europe,

Colonel William T. McClary, Commander 15th MP Brigade, and Chief Warrant Officer (W4) William E. Joyce, operations officer, 52nd MP Detetachment (CI)). In addition I was given a letter, with my photo attached, signed by the president, State Criminal Office, Saarland, instructing all policemen in the state of Saarland, to assist me in any matters within my jurisdiction. I never used my CID credentials again in the state of Saarland thereafter, and boy did they give me the royal treatment when I asked for assistance.

Powers of a Little Chief Warrant Officer

Besides Specialist four/Lieutenant Colonel John Groves, mentioned previously, I had a Sergeant Weicker who was the nephew of the senator from Connecticut. Weicker was one of my desk sergeants, and a very good one at that. One evening he called me, sounding somewhat alarmed. He informed me that the Community Leader, a Lieutenant Colonel, was in the station somewhat intoxicated raising hell with him and trying to pull his rank. I proceeded to the MP Station and in my position as station commander politely informed the good colonel that if he did not depart and go to his quarters immediately, I would place his ass in the cellblock. Furthermore, that he and I would then have a, conversation with Brigadier General Donley in the morning, which might be rather unpleasant for him. I had an open door policy to General Donley, a very nice gentleman, who subsequently was promoted to Major General and became the commanding general of Red Stone Arsenal, Alabama. I saw the Lieutenant Colonel several times thereafter and I have to say he never carried a grudge, but appeared to be grateful that I had him taken to his quarters.

Goeppingen and Schwaebisch Gmuend

Special Agents Martin Quattlebaum and Timothy R. Lane
The Army had some Stupid Criminals

Agents Quattlebaum Lane and Edward Rall worked in support of the 1st Infantry Division and the 56th Flield Artillery Brigade, Goeppingen, Germany, during the period Jun 81 to Jun 86. Agent Quattlebaum was in charge of the Goeppingen Resident Agency (RA) and the Schwaebisch Gmuend Branch Office (BO). Rall was at the BO, and Quattlebaum and Lane at the RA. Lane was assigned all drug cases, with Quattlebaum working all other cases, and Agent Rall taking care of cases at the BO. This of course did not mean they did not work as a team, regardless of the location or offense at hand. One case involved an Specialist four (E4) John Smith (not his real name), assigned to the Support Battalion of the 1st Infantry Division, who apparently considered himself a "self employed businessman" because he was dealing in hashish and other drugs.

One night Agents Quattlebaum and Lane were coming back on the train from Saarbruecken to Goeppingen. They decided to give a soldier, also a passenger on the train, some business by purchasing some hashish from him. They did, and then put the long arm of the law on him and convinced him that it would be a good idea if he became their confidential informant (CI), he did. The informant set up suppliers and sellers making about ten to fifteen cases for Agents Quattlebaum and Lane.

One night Agents Quattlebaum and Lane were out pretty late. Their CI had set up a buy from Smith, and just as Agent Lane was breaking down the door, Smith tried to throw some of his hashish out of the window and one of the two agents caught the tell-tale merchandise. After a long night, Lane obtained a confession from Smith.

The next morning, when Agent Quattlebaum got to his office, his German interpreter/investigator informed him that Smith was waiting for him in his office. Now Smith was not a puny little guy but a husky six foot six inches specimen of a soldier, and as Agent Quattlebaum entered his office he got a shocker. There was Smith, seated in an easy chair, with an M-16 rifle, magazine in place, across his lap. Agent Quattlebaum jumped back and drew his .38 revolver faster than the Lone Ranger ever could have, and he then instructed Smith to put the M-16 on the floor and walk towards him. Agent Quattlebaum does not remember who was more startled, he or Smith, but he definitely got Smith's attention and he promptly complied with his instructions, at the same time he yelled, "I'm here to see Mr. Lane!"

Agent Quattlebaum kept Smith's M-16 and instructed him to go sit in the waiting area outside his office until Agent Lane arrived. Lane arrived shortly thereafter and took Smith upstairs to his office and asked him what he wanted. Smith, on the other hand, acted as if Lane was his best buddy and pulled out a cloth bag, which contained about fifteen pieces of hashish, each with a street value of about fifty Deutschmarks (Approximately twenty five dollars each). Smith then said to Lane (his buddy, you bet) "You guys missed this last night when you searched my room. This was hidden behind the picture hanging on the wall." Agent Lane took the hashish from Smith and had him sign a receipt releasing it. Later during that week Smith set up his supplier and Agent Lane and a local criminal police detective (*Kriminal Polizei*) busted the supplier and confiscated another half kilo of hashish (a little over one pound).

Smith had his trial, and proved just how stupid he was. When the judge asked him if he had made very much money selling drugs, Smith replied, "Yes I did, your Honor." Smith then informed the judge that he had been dealing in drugs, mostly hashish, for the past two years and had earned about thirty to thirty five thousand dollars (tax-free money) during that period. Smith just about fainted when the judge sentenced him to fifteen years confinement and a fine of, you guessed it, thirty five thousand dollars. Smith told the Judge he could handle the jail time, but how did he expect him to pay the thirty five thousand dollars. He then added, "I guess I will have to sell my stereo equipment and some other stuff I bought."

Schwaebisch Gmuend

Special Agents Quaddlebaum, Lane and Rall
A Rape and a Not So Smart Subject

Agent Lane, single at the time, resided in the Bachelor Officer's Quarters (BOQ) at Goeppingen, Germany, and to make it real convenient for his boss, Agent Quaddlebaum, the BOQ was located across from his house and next door to the Officers' Club. Agent Quaddlebaum was full of mischief and unfortunately for Agent Lane he was the victim of these mischievous acts. Agent Quaddlebaum would go across the street, knock on Lane's door and say "Get up. We've got to go to Schwaebisch Gmuend, there has been a rape. Lane would rush and get dressed, complaining all along, then open the door only to hear Quaddlebaum say, "I was just joking." Well you know the old saying about crying "Wolf" too often, and that is what Quaddlebaum had done.

One fine Saturday morning, when normal people look forward to being able to sleep in, Agent Quaddlebaum received a call from Special Agent Edward Rall, informing him there had been a nasty rape at Schwaebisch Gmuend, and that he (Rall) was on his way to the hospital with the victim. Rall requested that Quaddlebaum and Lane proceed to Schwaebisch Gmuend, about twenty five Kilometers (approximately fifteen miles) miles from Goeppingen, and process the crime scene until he (Rall) was able to return. Quaddlebaum thought "No sooner said, no sooner done," but had forgotten about the pranks he had pulled on Lane. Determined to get started he went to Lane's room, knocked on the door and announced to Lane that there had been a bad rape at Schwaebisch Gmuend, and that they (he and Lane) had to go there and process the crime scene. Now Lane might not have the memory of an elephant but neither did he suffer from Alzheimer's. So when Quaddlebaum knocked on the door he simply refused to open it. It took Quaddlebaum about fifteen minutes to convince Lane that he was serious, and when he finally did open the door he was still not fully awake. Agent Quaddlebaum told Agent Lane that the victim, a female soldier, had been injured in the rape attack.

Agents Quaddlebaum and Lane drove to Schwaebisch Gmuend, and were briefed by the military police (MPs). The unfortunate victim had been raped only four months prior by a foreign national (non-German and non-American) and that offense for that reason came under the primary jurisdiction of, and was investigated by the German Criminal Police.

Agents Quaddlebaum and Lane learned that the victim had jogged out of the main gate at 0400 hours (4:00 A.M.) and was running on the track in the housing area, when someone suddenly grabbed her from behind, dragged her to a sand pit, struck her numerous times on the head and then raped her. Her assailant then left her, apparently thinking he had killed her.

Quaddlebaum and Lane located the crime scene that included both sides of a quarter-mile running track and a long jump pit on the other side of the track. Agents Quaddlebaum and Lane located some boot prints at several locations, including a spot behind some bleachers that the Subject had hidden behind waiting for the unsuspecting victim to jog past. They also located some bootprints in the long-jump pit. Agents Quaddlebaum and Lane took photographs of the prints and general crime scene. Unfortunately for them, it started to rain and the best boot impressions began to fill with water, making it difficult to obtain casts of the prints, this of course does not mean the two agents did not attempt to obtain casts. The local 56th Field Artillery Brigade Trial Counsel (district attorney) even showed up and Quaddlebaum and Lane politely told him to stay out of the crime scene until they were finished with it, since they had no desire to have someone contaminate the crime scene.

Next Agents Quaddlebaum and Lane started to interview possible witnesses. They started by interviewing the German gate guard, on duty at the main gate. The interview of the gate guard disclosed that an American soldier had been at the main gate at 0400 hrs (4:00 A.M.) and then left to "go to the bathroom" just after the female (victim) ran past the gate. A little later this same soldier came back to the main gate and told the gate guard that he had to go home and change his uniform, because he had soiled it when he went to the bathroom. Agent Lane's first remarks were "Quaddlebaum, that's our boy." Quaddlebaum and Lane picked up this soldier and started to question him concerning his whereabouts after he had departed from the main gate shack, and as Lane expressed it "we razzle-dazzled that ol boy." They told him that they knew exactly what kind of a watch he wore, this was because they had recovered the watch at the long-jump pit, and before long the subject confessed to the rape. He then took Agents Quaddlebaum and Lane to his off-post quarters, to retrieve the trousers he had worn before and during the rape, which were extremely wet and muddy. Subject's wife confirmed that subject owned a watch of the type the two agents had recovered at the crime scene. The wife asked if she could ride back to the caserne with her husband and both agents agreed, and she sat next to her husband who by now wore two connected bracelets, better known as "handcuffs." Agent Quaddlebaum will never forget what occurred as they proceeded to the caserne and drove by the track (crime scene). The subject gestured with his head toward the track and whispered loud enough for Agents Quaddlebaum and Lane to hear him say to his wife "That's where it happened honey!" I'm sure his wife really appreciated him saying, "honey" to her.

Subject was court-martialed and entered a guilty plea; he was sentenced to forty five years confinement. Unfortunately the victim, as you might say, "got life" because two rapes in four months were more than she could emotionally handle. She was medically evacuated and received a medical discharge from the army.

Agent Quaddlebaum remarked "It was a good thing subject entered a guilty plea, because the victim would not have been able to testify." Another successful investigation due to a good job done by CID agents.

Talk about funny things happening, after the case was adjudicated, Agent Rall was presented an impact Meritorious Service Medal by the commanding general, 56th Field Artillery Brigade. Quaddlebaum and Lane, who had gotten the confession from the subject and gathered the evidence, were spectators in the audience during the presentation of the medal. But neither of them begrudged Rall getting the medal. Unfortunately Rall only lived two more years and died of a brain tumor. CID lost a good agent.

Heidelberg

Special Agents Steven C. Volk, Samuel J. Owens and James R. Herndon CID's Heidelberg Drug Team

The Junkies went from the Sweet Smell of Victory to Utter Defeat

Herndon was an apprentice CID agent. Working on a drug team is very hard and dangerous work and at times involves long hours on the job and agents on drug teams have to possess acting talents for the protection of their life, the lives of fellow agents, and of course to have a successful drug bust.

In January 1974, it was a cold wintry day in Heidelberg. A drug bust was to go down, based on information obtained from a junkie. Special Agent Steve Volk was the man in charge of the drug team and on this day worked the case with Special Agents Samuel J. Owens and James R. Herndon. Special Agent Herndon, doing his undercover work, had met a certain young German male, who went by the name of "Dave", at Untere Strasse, Heidelberg a few days before the drug bust went down. Dave was a heroin addict and claimed to have a connection for large quantities of heroin. Agent Herndon promised to give Dave five grams of heroin if he would introduce him and his buddy, agent Owens, to his drug connection. Herndon introduced Owens to Dave as the moneyman. Herndon and Owens met Dave at the Heidelberg *Bahnhof* (Train Station) on the day that would culminate in the arrest of Dave. They showed Dave a large amount of Deutschmarks (German currency) they had received from *Kriminal Hauptkommissar* (KHK), the equivalent of a captain of detectives, Hans Astor, the boss of the narcotics section of the detectives division, Heidelberg police. The money was in one of those rental lockers and as they departed the train station Owens slipped the key to the rental box to one of the drug team members, without Dave observing this. They told Dave that they would return for the money once they had seen the heroin.

After Owens and Herndon, both real workhorses, had shown Dave the money it developed into a productive fast-paced police operation, which had a certain comical side to it that left eight unsuspecting civilian drug dealers and users in a German jail. It also resulted in the confiscation of a considerable amount of heroin and other illicit narcotics, as well as an illegally owned high-powered rifle that could have caused the death of law enforcement officers. The matter fell under German jurisdiction and would have to go before a German court for justice to be dispensed.

It was planned that Dave, who was a German national, would be arrested by German detectives after the sale of the drugs to the two undercover CID agents, Owens and Herndon, but we all know that plans and reality are two different things.

Everything seemed to move along well and Agent Volk thought to himself, *Pretty soon we'll nail these bums and their drugs,* but then plans are made to be changed and in this case Dave threw a monkey wrench in the wheels. He informed Agents Owens and Herndon that they would have to drive to Darmstadt, about a forty-five-minute drive from Heidelberg, where they would meet Dave's friend who had the heroin. The change of location did not present a problem to Owens and Herndon, but it did create a problem for the German police involved because it resulted in a change of jurisdiction. If the police from Heidelberg suddenly conducted moving surveillance of drug dealers in Darmstadt it could well compromise ongoing police drug suppression operations in Darmstadt. So quick action to coordinate between the two jurisdictions was a must. A number of alternate plans were discussed between the German police and CID and it resulted in agreement that the German "Mobile Reaction Team" (MRT) called in German the "*Mobileseinsatzkommando,*" a specialized team for long-term surveillance operations and unconventional tactics against organized crime, would have to participate. With the help *of Kriminal Haupt Kommissar* (Police Major) Hans Astor, the assistance of the MRT was quickly gained. The on-duty eight men, GMRT unit responded within the hour with four specially equipped unmarked and unconventional undercover vehicles. The team was led by *Kriminalkommissar* (Police Lieutenant) Bertram Bauer, who had been the boss of the Heidelberg police narcotics unit prior to his transfer to the MRT, and also included two German customs officers, Karl Singer and Walter Fleischhauer.

Special Agents Owens and Herndon and Dave piled into Owens' old bright yellow VW beetle, which in its heyday was lucky to top out at seventy five miles per hour and headed down the *Autobahn* (freeway), which had very little traffic, followed by the high powered MRT vehicles. Normally Dave might have gotten suspicious seeing the high-powered cars in back of the beetle not flying by at one hundred plus miles per hour, but this was during the oil crisis and the German government had restricted the speed to one hundred Kilometers per hour on the *Autobahn* and therefore Dave had no reason to be suspicious in that regard.

Special Agent Steve Volk, the boss of the CID drug team, had agreed that once it was known that the drugs were in possession of either Dave or one of his cohorts, either Owens or Herndon, would signal this information by tying their shoelaces and the German police teams would spring into action to make the arrests and conduct searches. Volk had provided the signal to the participating German police. However, first there was the forty five or so minutes drive from Heidelberg to Darmstadt, to a park commonly known to the police and drug dealers as "shit" (denoting drugs) park. Agents Owens and Herndon arrived at the park, discreetly followed by Steve Volk and his German police colleagues. Owens and Herndon straddled Dave and purposely entered the park with him in search of his cohorts. Owens stalled Dave to allow the surveillance team time to park and exit their vehicles. Herndon spotted several of the surveillance team members as they entered the park, recalling one was carrying a violin case, which he was sure contained a machine pistol. Shortly after entering the park, Dave approached a couple of fellow junkies and exchanged a few words with them. Owens and Herndon, it should be said, fit right in with the crowd if you judged them by their appearance. You might say they looked rather shabby and sleazy, a trait desirable for undercover agents. Dave and his two cohorts agreed to take Owens and Herndon to the drug dealer as they headed back to the old VW bug. Upon entering the car, Owens acted as though the car wouldn't start and Herndon knew he was stalling again to give the surveillance team a chance to get back in their cars. Owens went to the rear of the vehicle to look into the engine compartment and then gave the circling finger up sign (the mount-up sign in the U.S.). This is when things went wrong and did not go according to plan.

Volk and two of his German officers, Astor and Bauer, waited on the outside of the park not too far from Agent Owens' ugly VW beetle, where it was planned to make the arrests if the deal went down. Astor and Bauer joined other German detectives and members of the MRT units. Agent Volk, ever cognizant of the danger Owens and Herndon were always exposed to on a mission like this, kept his eyes keenly focused on the entrance/exit of the park awaiting the return of Owens and Herndon with whatever drug scum accompanied them. It seemed like an eternity to Agent Volk, but in reality it was not that long, when both Agents Owens and Herndon, along with Dave and his two cohorts came walking out of the park and returned to the VW. Volk said to himself, *soon the signal will be given*, and for that reason kept his eyes fixed on the two agents, one of whom he expected shortly to bend down and tie his shoe-laces, thereby giving the signal for action. Volk lost momentary eyeball contact with the two agents, as he was walking on a sidewalk opposite from where the VW was parked. This was due to a van being parked along the sidewalk, which momentarily blocked his view and it was at precisely this point that Volk failed to see the circling finger sign Owens had given. As he emerged from behind the van he observed Agent Owens bent over at the rear of his VW with his foot resting on the bumper and the hood of the rear-mounted engine open. Agent Herndon, Dave, and his two buddies were in the process of getting into the VW. Agent Volk had a big problem at this point, had Owens given the signal and was he just completing it as Volk emerged from behind the van? Or why was he bent over? What to do now? A quick radio check failed to alleviate the doubt because no one had been in a clear position to observe Owens and all had depended on Agent Volk to maintain eyeball contact with Owens.

Agent Volk had to make a quick decision to make the arrest now, or to allow the group to leave and follow them in an inconspicuous manner. Volk opted for the arrest. Events unfolded very quickly. Known for their unequalled efficiency, German police quickly moved in for the arrest. The suspects, including Owens and Herndon, were taken from the VW and ordered to the ground. Volk made sure that he positioned Owens a short distance from the others. A quick exchange of quietly spoken words as Agent Volk "wrestled" Owens to the ground brought light to the situation. Volk learned that the drugs had not been turned over to any of the individuals just arrested. Owens had not given the signal; he had merely attempted to stall for time by "checking" his engine to give the surveillance team time to get into position. Agent Herndon's heart sank when he saw Volk and the German cops run towards the VW. One of the officers pulled a syringe, a couple of hits of heroin, and a hash pipe from Dave's pocket.

Agent Volk quickly asked agent Owens if he thought the mission could be salvaged and he replied "I think so." At this point Volk made good use of his native tongue. He spoke very loudly in German, addressing the German policemen and loud enough so Dave and his two junkies could hear him. Volk said "*Haben Sie den Sprengstoff gefunden?*" (Meaning, "Did you find the explosives?"). At first the German policemen were confused by the question, but very quickly one of the officers picked up on the decoy and replied "No explosives have been found yet," in German of course. Agent Volk then suggested that the door panels be removed from Sam's (Owens) pride and joy, his beloved old VW. The German officers immediately went to work tearing away the panels, while Agent Owens watched in disbelief as his beetle was being dismantled. Volk, in the meanwhile, walked up to Dave, whose head was raised and who obviously followed the action with intense interest. Volk bent down to Dave and made it clear to him that he knew he was involved with the two Americans who were suspected of cooperating with German terrorists and transporting explosives. Volk told Dave if he wished to help himself, now was a good time to do so and come clean and tell him what he knew about these two American terrorists. Dave's tense facial expression relaxed. He had a sly smile on his face as he said in German: "You mean you're not with the narcotics police?" Agent Volk assumed an air of surprise at this question then said to Dave "No, we have no interest in narcotics, our only interest and mission is catching terrorists." This obviously saved the day for Dave and his fellow junkies, or so he thought at that time.

Now why did Dave and his two fellow junkies fall for the terrorist story Agent Volk told Dave? It was a matter of the times. During the period when this drug action took place the German Red Army Faction (Commonly called the "RAF") a terrorist group, were involved in at a least three major bombing attacks against U.S. Forces, killings of German politicians, and bank robberies. The author was involved in one of the investigations, during 1972, when a U.S. Army captain and two enlisted men had been killed at Heidelberg as a result of a bomb the Bader Meinhof gang, the criminals who would later call themselves "*Rote Armee Fraktion*" (Red Army Faction), had set off on the grounds of USAREUR (U.S. Army Europe) headquarters. It was at that time also that the author met Agent Volk. Most of the members of the Bader Meinhof gang were eventually caught and tried and some committed suicide while in jail.

At this point agent Volk and the German police officer huddled for a brief moment and decided to "release" the three junkies, along with the two undercover agents, and then to continue to keep them under surveillance. It was agreed that the arrest signal would remain the same. The three Germans could not believe their luck that day. All smiled, as did the two undercover agents, when they were told to pack up and get out of the area by a good acting "angry-looking" German cop who had failed to bag his terrorists. Dave was so over-joyed at his luck, and Singer, the German customs officer, even gave him his syringe, the two hits of heroin, and the hash pipe back. Dave became outright polite, wishing all a good day. As the VW bug moved from the area their smiling faces could be seen, in the rear window of the car, looking backward where the "Political Police" were standing. After they all had entered the VW, Owens and Herndon told the three junkies things were way too hot and that perhaps they should return at a later date. But this is where the three junkies were thinking about only one thing, the five grams of heroin they had been promised, and so insisted that they continue and go through with the deal.

The moving surveillance continued, but now with extreme caution. The undercover cars trailing the suspects rotated frequently with the officers in the cars continually changing disguises, even switching vehicles. Several kilometers (One Kilometer = five eighth of a mile) outside of Darmstadt the drug dealers in the VW had become so self assured that they had fooled the cops, that they no longer glanced backwards to see who was following them. Dave directed Agents Owens and Herndon to a high-rise apartment building in Darmstadt. Owens had to park his VW across the street from the-high rise apartment, and they then had to walk across the street at a traffic light. While waiting for the traffic light to change to green several of the surveillance cars drove through the intersection. To Herndon's utter disbelief, neither Dave nor his two buddies noticed this. Two police officers continued the surveillance on foot but lost sight of everyone after they entered the elevator. On the way up the elevator made two stops, and for that reason the undercover policemen had no idea at which stop the drug dealers and two agents had got off the elevator. Now all depended on a signal from one of the two agents.

After Herndon and Owens entered the apartment, Agent Owens went to another room with the dealer and checked the merchandise. After that they both, Owens and Herndon, were in a room of the apartment with the drug scum, and both were concerned that Agent Volk and the German police would not know which apartment they had entered. Owens thought about it and decided that Herndon should go down to the car and retrieve the money. Dave was not too sharp, because had he thought about this he would have realized that the money had been left in the security box at the train station. Herndon immediately left the apartment, not wanting Dave to realize the money was not in the car. When he got to the first floor elevator he met Agent Volk and some of the surveillance team members, who after a very tense wait of approximately thirty minutes, which seemed like an eternity, were very happy to see Agent Herndon. Herndon told him the apartment number and number of persons present, which was a total of eight persons. Herndon also told Volk that some of the persons in the apartment were high on drugs and that he had observed a rifle in the apartment. Volk felt much relieved after this. *Kriminal Haupt Kommissar* Astor determined that there was not enough time to obtain a search warrant, taking into account the current circumstances and consideration for the safety of the two undercover CID agents. Astor therefore ordered an immediate raid on the apartment. Agent Herndon, after passing the valuable information on to Agent Volk, timed his arrival at the apartment in such a manner that Volk and the German officers were right on his heels. Herndon rang the doorbell, someone in the apartment looked through the peephole, and seeing his newly-made American "friend" and "drug dealer", unhesitatingly unlocked the door. Herndon slipped to the side of the door and the police officers quickly entered the apartment and quickly brought the situation under control. Two or three of the people in the apartment were so strung out on drugs, that they had no clue as to what was happening. Others were in shock, in particular Dave, who spotted Agent Volk and then, addressing no one in particular, said in German, "I thought you said you were not with the narcotics police but with the political police?" To which Agent Volk replied "I lied!"

One thing not known to Agent Volk and the German police was that when Agents Owens and Herndon entered the apartment, and realized that Volk and the German police did not know which apartment they had entered, Agent Owens had marked the trail for them by dropping his black U.S. government ball-point pen just outside the apartment door. Smart thinking on the part of Agent Owens. Another successful drug raid, resulting in justice being dealt to the scum of the world, drug users and dealers.

Special Agent Steven C. Volk
A Drug Bust, Attempted Murder and Justified Homicide

Once again the "CID Drug Team" (CID DT), led by Agent Volk, and supported by Military Police Investigators (MPI) of the 17th MP Detachment, Heidelberg, consisting of Staff Sergeant Arthur Spell and Sergeant Willie Walker, and the always-important members of the German Criminal Police Narcotics Division, headed by *Kriminal Haupt Kommissar* Hans J. Astor and his colleague Kriminal Kommissar (KK) Klaus Rostock. Again this operation was assisted by the members of the German "Mobile Reaction Team" (MRT), under the leadership of *Kriminal Kommissar* Bertram Bauer, who were an important part of this mission.

It was some time during October 1975, and the CID DT had obtained information from an informant that a certain black American Army staff sergeant (SSG) was selling heroin. The information from the informant was subsequently verified through another source. The plan of action was coordinated with all involved. The initial action contemplated was to introduce, through a confidential source, one of the CID DT members, Military Police Investigator Walker, to the seller and then do the usual thing, set up a buy and arrest the dealer and his cohorts and bring all to justice, so they would get what they deserved for spreading misery.

On 30 October 1975, things seemed to be clicking. The black staff sergeant had been in contact with a CID informant and a member of the CID DT who was posing as the interested buyer of the heroin.

With the deception in progress, the black staff sergeant was to meet the informant and the undercover CID DT member (Walker) in a parking lot of a cemetery, on the outskirts of Kirchheim, a good out-of-the way location only a few kilometers from Heidelberg. The arrangement was for the staff sergeant to sell fifty grams of heroin to the CID undercover man during the early evening hours on Friday, 31 October. The plan was for the members of the CID DT and the German MRT to make the arrest of the staff sergeant immediately after the sale of the heroin, and the CID undercover man would either "escape" or be "arrested" with the others involved.

The first step in the plan was for the police to clear away anyone in the parking lot, to keep innocent people from getting hurt, and to find suitable vantage points for the arrest team members to conceal themselves from the staff sergeant and his cohorts. Normally visitors to the cemetery would use the parking lot, but on this cold and wet fall day there were no cemetery visitors present, only one apparently deeply in love couple was in the parking lot necking and having a good time, oblivious to their surroundings. German police quickly sent them on their way. Having done this, all hoped that the good staff sergeant would cooperate and go through with the deal.

The informant and Military Police Investigator Walker (CID undercover man) arrived, as planned, and waited. After a short wait the black staff sergeant also arrived and a discussion ensued. It would have been nice if Walker could have worn a wire, enabling the surveillance team to listen in, but in those days CID did not possess such badly needed equipment. The only means to let the surveillance/arrest team know that the heroin was in possession of the staff sergeant or the sale had been made was to wait for a prearranged signal given by Military Police Investigator Walker. On this dreary night that was to be a difficult task because nature played a nasty trick in the form of a quickly arriving heavy blanket of fog. After what seemed to be an hour, but actually was not much more than fifteen minutes, a set of headlights suddenly appeared in the fog and a car slowly entered the parking lot, circling the area obviously looking for any unusual activity. The car backed into a parking space where the three men waited. The driver did not shut off the engine or turn off the headlights. Then things moved quickly, Military Police Investigator Walker gave the signal, barely visible in the fog, indicating he had seen the heroin. Radios began crackling, ordering hidden police officers to close in for the arrest. As this occurred, the driver of the car apparently spotted one of the approaching police officers, put the car in gear, gunned the engine and came flying out of the parking spot. While fleeing the area, the driver clearly aimed his car at one of the approaching German officers. Sensing the imminent danger, the German detective escaped the oncoming car by throwing himself backwards, and while doing so, fired one round from his pistol at the passing car. Another German MRT officer, who saw what was happening, aimed his submachine gun at the fleeing car and fired several rounds at the car as it disappeared and was enveloped by the dense fog.

Unmarked police cars, which had been strategically placed in the area, took up the chase of the fleeing car. Unfortunately they lost sight of the car in the thick fog just after entering the outskirts of Kirchheim at a five-corner intersection, where one of the pursuing police cars collided with another car, which was going through the intersection. Fortunately no one was killed in the accident.

Back at the parking lot the staff sergeant, informant, and Military Police Investigator Walker were quickly arrested and the heroin was confiscated and marked as evidence by German police officers. The black staff sergeant, the informant and Military Police Investigator Walker were shocked by the unfolding events. The staff sergeant obviously had no idea he was dealing with police, because he flatly refused to identify the black American driver of the fleeing car. The car was identified by the detective whom the driver had tried to run down, as a Ford Capri with U.S. Army Europe (USAREUR) license plates, and a "For Sale" sign displayed in the left rear car window. Due to the heavy fog the license plate number could not be identified.

Now that the narcotics-dealing staff sergeant had been placed in cuffs, it was time to track down the guy who came close to being a cop killer, namely the driver of the Ford Capri. There was no time to waste, so for the remainder of the night the locating of the Ford Capri became a priority. Members of the CID DT got in contact with their informants but none were able to provide any leads, so the informants were sent on a mission to various clubs and see if they could pick up any information from their friends. While the informants were busy keeping their eyes and ears open, members of the CID DT and German detectives were checking criminal intelligence reports, hoping that somewhere in one of the reports the Ford Capri would pop up and identify its owner. At the same time members of the German MRT reconnoitered the areas in Heidelberg and surrounding towns looking for the Ford Capri.

Everyone was getting pretty tired, after having been up all night, but as dawn broke luck was on the side of the cops. An informant reported he had overheard people talking about a Ford Capri that was offered for sale by its owner. The big break came from the CID and German police intelligence files, which contained a record of the Ford Capri. As a matter of fact, German police at one time had impounded this car, when it was suspected it was being used to smuggle drugs from the Netherlands to Germany. At the time they had to release the Ford Capri to its owner, a U.S. Army soldier, due to lack of sufficient evidence that the vehicle had in fact been used for drug smuggling. But now the files provided the name of the owner, which then led them to his address in a town near Heidelberg. An unmarked police car was dispatched to the residence, and found the Ford Capri with the "For Sale" sign in the window and what appeared to be a bullet hole in the left rear of the car in an underground garage.

German police wasted no time in getting an arrest warrant for attempted murder for this soldier, an Specialist four (E4), and also a search warrant to search his off-post apartment. Shortly before noon, 1 November 1975, German police and members of the CID drug team–who were invited by German police to accompany them–were on their way to the suspect's residence.

Attempts to gain access to the apartment with a ruse failed, so German police identified themselves as police officers and ordered that the door to the apartment be opened immediately. Those inside the apartment ignored the order and the police officers could hear a commotion in the apartment and the sound of toilets being flushed repeatedly as well as the opening and closing of doors. There was no time to waste, fearing the destruction of evidence German police forcibly opened the apartment door, entered the apartment, and took up defensive positions. No one was observed in the hallway or the living room, which was to the right of the hallway. It could be heard as doors to other rooms in the apartment were being closed, and then there was utter silence.

All law enforcement officers involved knew this was a potentially dangerous situation. *Kriminal Kommissar* Rostock, *Kriminal Ober Meister* (Detective Sergeant) Klaus Paehler and CID DT member Military Police Investigator Spell checked the first two rooms to the left of the hallway and the living room, but found no one. Detective Rostock was out of sight in the kitchen, Military Police Investigator Spell was concealed behind a cabinet in the hallway and Detective Paehler was standing in the living room, slowly turning as he was checking the room. It was then that a black American man came silently out of the bedroom, at the end of the hallway with a revolver in his hand. He stealthily approached the unsuspecting Paehler, who had his back turned towards him. Both Rostock and Spell saw the subject raise his revolver to point at the back of the unsuspecting Paehler and both fired their weapons simultaneously, fatally injuring the black man, who was subsequently identified as Specialist four (E4) C.M. O'Neal Jr., the owner and driver of the Ford Capri. What the law enforcement officers in the apartment did not know was that the revolver brandished by the black man was only a starting pistol, which looked like any normal revolver.

Taken into police custody for questioning were several senior U.S. Army Non-commissioned officers, who were apparently frequent and routine guests of the heroin- dealing Specialist four (E4) O'Neal playing all-night poker games. During the previous evening they had played poker while O'Neal made his heroin delivery. He sat out for a few hands and returned to the game after he had intentionally almost killed a German detective in the cemetery parking lot by attempting to run him over with his car. Now he had unnecessarily paid for it with his own life. Investigation also revealed that the Specialist four (E4) and his poker-playing friends had believed that the police entering the apartment were actually criminals out to rob them, as a carry-over from the previous night's incident. The death of the Specialist four (E4) was investigated by German police from higher headquarters in Karlsruhe, and after a thorough review by the district attorney it was determined to have been a justifiable homicide.

Bad Kreuznach

Special Agent Hubert "Herb" Marlow (The Author)
and MPI Jim Sims
A Senseless Murder

It was just before Christmas when the desk sergeant of the military police, Bad Kreuznach notified Special Agent Marlow, the special agent in charge (SAC) of the Bad Kreuznach resident agency, and the duty agent that day, that a murder had taken place on Rose Kaserne. Rose Kaserne was the Headquarters of the 8th Infantry Division.

Agent Marlow proceeded to Rose Kaserne and processed the crime scene, with the assistance of Military Police Investigator James Sims, who was attached to the CID office and would in many instances assist Marlow. The room was in the process of being re-painted and somewhat in disarray and the walls clearly reflected that a crime had occurred, because there was blood all over the wall and on a mattress.

Initial investigation revealed that Specialist four (E4) Ituralde had stabbed Private first class (E3) Peiffer after an argument about Peiffer not doing his part in helping with the painting of the room. The argument got heated to the point that Ituralde pulled a knife and stabbed Peiffer in the heart. Peiffer ran down the hallway, towards the Orderly Room, but collapsed before getting there with blood spraying from his heart.

Ituralde was apprehended and taken to the CID office, where Agent Marlow, with Military Police Investigator Sims present, interrogated him. After about an hour Ituralde admitted stabbing Peiffer, and in a written sworn statement related that they had been instructed to paint and spruce up the room for an upcoming inspection, and that Peiffer was lazy and did not help. Ituralde said he got so angry that he stabbed Peiffer.

A general court-martial was convened and Ituralde was found guilty of murder and sentenced to reduction to the lowest rank and fifteen years confinement in the penitentiary, Fort Leavenworth, Kansas. Ituralde's sentence was appealed to the Military Court of Appeals on the grounds that the trial judge, a colonel, had not permitted the defense counsel to present information about the victim's juvenile record to the court.

Prior to coming on active duty in the Army, Private first class (E3) Peiffer had had a little juvenile run-in with the law, which had occurred before he became a member of the United States Army and for that reason the trial judge had not permitted it to be presented to the court. The Court of Military Appeals sided with the defense counsel and ordered a re-trial of Ituralde.

By now Agent Marlow had been reassigned as the operations officer of the Fort Gordon Field Office, Fort Gordon, Georgia, and it was just a few weeks before his scheduled retirement after twenty years of active duty. Marlow was notified that a re-trial of Ituralde was scheduled at Fort Leavenworth and that he would have to appear as a witness. Military Police Investigator Sims and Special Agent Terry Rhodes were also summoned to appear.

Agent Marlow was happy to see his old co-workers Sims and Rhodes, and unfortunately learned that Rhodes was in bad physical condition and given only two more years of life by his doctors due to an incurable illness.

Things really got a little comical now. Marlow was outside the courtroom prior to the beginning of the trial and so was Ituralde with his mother and defense attorneys. Ituralde had been released from Leavenworth prison after spending five years in confinement, and had received all back pay as an Specialist four (E4) for the five years he had spent in confinement. Ituralde had money now and had hired his old defense attorney Captain Davis, now out of the army and a civilian attorney in North Carolina, to defend him. He also had an assigned military defense lawyer. Ituralde walked up to Special Agent Marlow, acting as if they were old buddies, and in a very friendly tone said "Hi, Mr. Marlow, how are you? I would like you to meet my mom." With that he introduced Agent Marlow to his mother, who had flown in from Puerto Rico to appear as a character reference for her son. Ituralde had been a model prisoner, and had learned the upholstery trade while in prison. The Staff Judge Advocate's office at Rose Barracks, Bad Kreuznach had lost the murder weapon (the knife) Ituralde had used to kill Peiffer with. Ituralde had claimed self defense and this time around it worked for him and he was found not guilty of murder and became a free man. From conversations with Ituralde during the period of the court-martial, Agents Marlow and Rhodes and Military Police Investigator Sims, all came away with the impression that Ituralde indeed had become a changed man, changed for the better. Ituralde told Agent Marlow that he was going to return to Puerto Rico and get a job as an upholsterer. Special Agent Rhodes sadly passed away less than two years later. The assignment to Bad Kreuznach, although not without problems, was a good one for Special Agent Marlow. He had good agents and Militry Police Investigators working for him and the best secretary/interpreter he could ask for in Frau Renate Maahs. Frau Maahs advanced to the position of Interpreter/Investigator not long after Agent Marlow left Bad Kreuznach. Actually she did a lot of investigative work while Marlow was the boss of the Bad Kreuznach resident agency and to this date Agent Marlow has maintained contact with her. She retired a few years ago and Bad Kreuznach no longer has U. S. Forces stationed there.

CHAPTER NINE

Italy

Vicenza

Special Agent Daniel E. "Danno" White
Peddling a Bike and Peddling Drugs

Special Agent White was the chief of the Drug Section, at the CID office, Fort Huachuca, Arizona. It was during the summer of 1981, and White was in a relaxed mode, when the secretary informed him he had a call from CID Headquarters. Any time CID Headquarters is mentioned you wonder "what now?" Agent White took the call and found out it was the drug coordinator at headquarters, CID Command, who informed him that the United States and Italy had finally reached an agreement to allow the forming of a Joint Drug Suppression Team (JDST). The team would consist of CID agents, military policemen, and Italian police officers (carabinieri) assigned to the Southern European Task Force (SETAF). Now at first White thought, *Why is he telling me about things in Italy?* but then the man from Headquarters offered Agent White a change of scenery with a little more pleasant climate, to be reassigned to Italy and start up the JDST. White felt a change of scenery might not be such a bad idea and since he was a newly-wed, and he and his new bride, who was an MP, had not been on their honeymoon yet, Italy sounded like a pretty romantic place to do that. Before long White and his wife were in Vicenza, Italy. White was in for another surprise, when he found out that the special agent in charge (SAC) of the Vicenza CID office was none other than his old friend, John Henderson, with whom he had served, during the mid 1970s, at the CID resident agency (RA), Mannheim, Germany.

Special Agents White and Henderson enjoyed several lunches and evenings together and Henderson explained the strange ins and outs of working in Italy to White. It was the first time White had been assigned to Italy, but Henderson had been stationed in Italy before as an MP, was married to Chris, a wonderful Italian lady, and had learned much during his first stay in Italy. Agent Henderson knew the "politics" and "problems" with which CID agents would be confronted and just as in the United States, Italy also has a variety of law enforcement and investigative agencies. There were two types of carabinieri (police) in Italy; the "real" and "powerful" Italian police were the carabinieri who take care of the Italians, in other words outside the Military Bases. The second type of carabinieri were those assigned to military bases that were known as the "SETAF carbs", they were more like military police. Agent White, if he wanted to succeed and get the greatest possible cooperation, had to learn the workings of the Italian police. He then had to train his JDST how to work with that variety of police and at the same time please all of them and establish the best possible liaison with all of them.

It did not take long before Agent White became well acquainted with Paolo Corradi, the interpreter/criminal investigator, with whom White shared an office. They would become good friends and to this day still maintain contact. Corradi, an Italian national, would become Agent White's right-hand man. Through him White would wine and dine (officially called liaison) the chiefs of the Italian narcotics units in the Veneto region of Northern Italy.

There were two main chiefs; one was Federico Peri, in charge of all drug activities and investigations in the Vicenza, Italy area and a Mr. Scala, in charge of all drug activities and investigations in the Verona, Italy area. To get things rolling, Corradi, with the assistance of Federico Peri, arranged a luncheon to be attended by Agent White, Interpreter Investigator Paolo Corradi, Chief Frederico and the chief prosecutor for drugs, who would turn out to be very important in the operation of the JDST. Now the Italian lunch was a new experience for Agent White, because you have to have plenty of time and be relaxed to enjoy one of those laid-back Italian lunches.

The purpose of the luncheon was to come to an understanding of the "terms of engagement" and make it clear to the Italian authorities that Agent White's sole purpose was to stop the flow of drugs to U.S. Army soldiers. White succeeded in explaining the importance of the use of informants for the purpose of making controlled purchases of drugs, and the use of informants to "introduce" White and his team members, in an undercover scenario, to drug dealers as "interested" buyers, with the purchased narcotics becoming evidence. White received the green light and started working drug suppression activities. In Italy it is not only against the law to sell drugs, but it is also against the law to purchase drugs. The peculiar thing about all this is the fact that Italian law makes no provision that would exclude law enforcement officers from being considered as breaking the law when making "controlled buys" to be used as evidence. For that reason it was a major victory for White when the chief prosecutor agreed to permit various test cases to be brought before him as a result of JDST members making controlled buys.

No drug team can operate successfully without having some good informants and sometimes you can get informants by holding out a carrot or a stick to them. Agent White had meetings with the major army commanders for two reasons: to introduce himself and explain the mission of the JDST, and to solicit their assistance in "secretly" identifying a few soldiers, involved with drugs, whom they thought worthy of giving another chance and thus saving their army career. These soldiers would be identified through positive urine drug tests; they would get another chance providing they cooperated with law enforcement agents. It was a simple matter, Agent White would "make them an offer" to work for him by identifying their sources of drugs and arrange for a covert purchase of drugs from their sources. If they cooperated, their commanders would not have the soldier discharged from the army because of their positive urine drug test, but would give them one more chance. The arrangement worked out quite well for both the new informants and White.

Special Agent White wasted no time; he had been in Italy only about two weeks, got himself an informant, and wasted no time in putting him to work. The informant set up a deal with his Italian drug dealer for the purchase of some hashish. The dealer was to meet him in a park by a residential area where he had always met him in the past and made his purchases. This was at the edge of the park at a park bench and the plan was for White and his informant to walk to the bench, sit down and wait for the drug dealer to arrive. Once he arrived and they made contact with him, a plan had been worked out to affect the arrest of all but White who would escape with the drugs (evidence).

Interpreter/Investigator Corradi had made contact with Frederico Peri, who in turn strategically positioned his covert team of police officers on the streets disguised as telephone company employees. He had managed to borrow a telephone company repair truck from the telephone company and had the area covered pretty well. Additionally two of Agent White's military police investigators (MPI), members of his JDST, were jogging around the park with other civilians also jogging. White had designed a system of signals so that all members of the JDST would know when to spring into action. The plan was for White to obtain the hashish, turn over the payment money to the dealer, then pull out a pack of cigarettes and offer the drug dealer a cigarette (first signal). He would then drop the pack of cigarettes (second signal) and his informant would bend down and pick up the pack of cigarettes (third signal). Of course this entire sequence of events would occur in a matter of seconds and would be the signal that a drug deal had been made and for the covert officers and investigators to move in and attempt to arrest all involved with the exception of Agent White who would be allowed to escape with the evidence.

Everything went as planned. The deal was set. The surveillance team was in place. Agent White and his informant were seated on the park bench and the two MPI men were jogging and all were in the "wait" mode for the drug dealer to show up. In typical Italian laid back fashion the drug dealer was late and the poor Military Police Investigator guys were breathing heavily from the prolonged jogging, now at a somewhat slower pace, and as they passed White on the park bench they would mumble a few unkind words in his direction.

Agent White's informant finally spotted his drug dealer approaching on a bicycle. He rode the bike all around the park, checking out the area and White and his informant noticed that he had a plastic shopping bag attached to the handlebars. After circling the area, riding right past White and his informant, he finally stopped. The informant introduced White to the drug dealer. White told the drug dealer that because of his tardiness he was now in a hurry and was late getting back to work. The Italian drug dealer, who spoke broken but understandable English, apologized for being late. Now started what you might call the "show and tell" phase of the deal. The Italian showed White the hashish in the grocery bag without removing the bag from the handlebars and told him he wanted to see the money. White reached into his pants and pulled out a wad of money, and of course did not yet give it to the dealer, but spread out the money in his hand like a Las Vegas card dealer, then put it back in his pants. To reduce the chance of the dealer escaping on his bike, White told him that he felt uncomfortable with him sitting on his bike, and for him to join them on the park bench. The drug dealer hesitated and indicated that he wanted to complete the deal right then. White initiated a delaying action and told the drug dealer that he had seen the hashish plates, but that he wanted to touch and smell them to confirm it was really hashish. White then made a motion that he wanted to look in the bag again, and the dealer allowed him to do so. White broke the seal on the wrapping and scratched the hashish plates with his fingernail, then examined and smelled his fingernail and said "it's hashish." He then randomly did the same to another hashish plate and again said "it's hashish." Then followed a little price haggling and the dealer confirmed the asking price but did not get off his bike. White then told the dealer that he wanted to break a small piece of hashish off one of the plates and smoke it with him (the dealer); to test it and he readily agreed. He then removed a plate of hashish from the bag and Agent White reached over and took it. White then broke off a small piece of hashish (now here comes the Hollywood actor) but then dramatically pulled out his pack of cigarettes, removed a cigarette and then removed some of the tobacco to make room for the hashish. He then very conveniently offered the Italian drug dealer and his informant a cigarette, which he and the informant accepted, at the same time accidentally dropping the pack of cigarettes (signal two). The informant picked up the pack of cigarettes (as planned–signal three). Now the drug dealer was distracted watching White, with his plate of hashish under his arm, but White like a true gentleman, lit the cigarette for him to distract him a little more. While this was going on White could see the movement of the surveillance team, heading in their direction to make the arrests. As soon as one of the team members yelled "Police" in Italian, Agent White bolted like a jackrabbit and took off running, plate of hashish in hand. He ran his heart out and turned corners to get away, finally stopping to catch his breath, and to look around.

Now Agent White had really planned this drug action well, except for one little fact, he did not have the telephone number to the CID office with him; had been in Italy; a foreign country, for about two weeks, did not speak Italian, and now had no idea where he was, in which direction the army base was, or where the park from which he had escaped was. He had no Italian coins suitable for making a phone call and even if he had the coins he had no number to call. On top of all this he was holding a hundred-gram plate of hashish in his hand, was totally lost, and could have been subjected to the embarrassment of being arrested by JDST non participating Italian police.

After about twenty minutes had passed Agent White spotted the Italian police surveillance vehicle (telephone repair truck) driving around, obviously looking for him, and of course they found him and all had a good laugh. The Italian police were tickled pink with the success of the joint operation. They had bagged the dealer in possession of the remaining hashish plates and thus could charge him with "Attempted Sale of Hashish" and they also took the plate of hashish Agent White had in his hand, as evidence. All participants returned to the Italian police narcotics office where the Italian police team members took Agent White and his drug team and Interpreter/Investigator Corradi to the police coffee espresso bar to celebrate their joint success. The beginning of a pleasant and successful four-year drug operation for White, the participating Italian police officers of the JDST, and last but not least Interpreter/Criminal Investigator Paolo Corradi, who to this date maintains contact with his friend Special Agent White. Both White and Corradi have since retired from CID. Corradi also keeps White informed of the status of Federico Peri, the narcotics unit chief, who has risen in rank within the Italian police and sends his greetings to White through Corradi. This proves how through good liaison, trust, and cooperation a friendship of a lasting nature can be developed.

Military Police Investigator Donald E. "Don" Riffe
Detours to becoming a CID Special Agent

It was during 1982-83, and Don was a military policeman at Fort Polk, Louisiana, when he was dreaming of becoming a CID Special Agent and he knew that by just sitting on his rear end he would not make it. Don thought, *maybe if I volunteer for the Drug Suppression Team (DST), I will get my foot in the door.* No sooner the thought then action followed. Don went to see Special Agent Ismar Rubio, the DST boss at Fort Polk, and informed him that his valuable talents were available to become a member of his team. All seemed to being going well when disappointment struck, in the form of orders, assigning Don to the MPs in Vicenza, Italy.

After his arrival in Vicenza, Don worked as an MP for a while, and then managed to land a position as a military police investigator (MPI). He was lucky, because the CID office was located directly across the hall from the MPI office. As a member of the MPI team, Don had daily interaction with the members of the CID and of course during these contacts he kept his eyes open to see if a spot on the DST was available.

Working with the CID to prevent a Tragedy

MPI Riffe while assigned to Vicenza attended college classes at night in an effort to complete his Associates Degree, because he knew how important education was to get promoted and also to be accepted by USACIDC and become a CID agent. His primary college instructor was none other than Danno White, the drug team chief.

One night, Don was at the MP station, and had just completed working on an incident when the desk sergeant received a call from Sergeant Jimmy Gray (not his real name), the armorer of one of the local units. It seemed that Gray was having some domestic problems and was extremely depressed and despondent over the situation. Gray had consumed several beers to kill the pain and help him decide what course of action to take.

He had gone to his place of employment, the unit arms room, and locked the door so none could get in. Gray called and informed the desk sergeant that he was going to kill himself and end it all, and that he would shoot anyone who came near him in an attempt to stop him. Now luckily for Gray, Don happened to be one of his college classmates and a student of Danno White, and thereby both had established some rapport with him. The desk sergeant handed the phone to Don who talked to Gray in an effort to calm him down and reason with him. In the meantime the desk sergeant contacted Jeff Holder, the CID duty agent, since attempted suicide and possibly murder (if Gray shot someone else as he had indicated he might do) was a matter for CID jurisdiction.

While Special Agent Holder was on his way to the MP station, Don managed to calm Gray down a bit and convince him that he was his friend and that he should give him some time to try and help him. Since Danno White was also Gray's instructor, Don made use of this fact and mentioned to Gray that maybe he would like to talk to Mr. White, to which he readily agreed. There was one slight problem, it was late at night and Special Agent White was not the duty agent and might not be at home. As luck would have it he was at home and without hesitation agreed to come to the MP station and assist in this matter, after all a life might be saved.

Special Agents Holder and White, Military Police Investigator Riffe, and several MPs established a perimeter around the building containing Gray. Agent White then used Gray's commanding officer's office to establish phone contact with the depressed, intoxicated and dangerous Gray. Military Police Investigator Don Riffe was privileged to listen in as Danno White used all of his investigative skills while talking to Gray. He talked calmly to Gray about every imaginable thing except the incident, making him feel he was his friend, which had an obvious calming effect on Gray. Over the next hour or so Agent White slowly eased Gray into the subject of why he had barricaded himself in the arms room. This procedure allowed Gray to blow off some steam in a somewhat controlled environment and at the same time he was beginning to sober up. Eventually this led to Gray agreeing to come out of the arms room and talk face to face with his "new friends" Agents White and MPI Riffe. Since White and Riffe knew Gray from school, they were the ones that would meet him at the door of the unit building. This would permit Holder and some of the MPs to enter from the rear of the building and secure the arms room, preventing Gray from returning to the arms room and gaining access to firearms. The waiting was a tense moment. Danno White had gotten a promise from Gray, over the phone, that he would not bring any firearms with him. The exemplary manner in which Agent White had talked to Gray, which convinced him of the sincere concern for his well-being, not only had a calming effect on Gray, but also on Military Police Investigator Don Riffe. It just shows what experience can do. Don had already locked and loaded his weapon but Danno White made sure he understood that the use of the weapon would only be a last resort. At the same time it was important that Don took this precaution because Agent White had not brought his own weapon nor had he had time to pick up a protective vest. Gray walked out of the company building holding a large knife. Fortunately, he stopped several feet from where Agent White and Don were standing. Again the skills of Danno White came to bear as he managed to calmly talk Gray into dropping the knife so they could talk. Gray sat down on the steps of his unit building and started to cry. Danno White sat next to him and placed his arm around him and calmly told Gray that everything would be alright. The threat of the loss of life, Gray's or that of someone else, was eliminated and normal police procedure required that Gray would be handcuffed. He was taken to the CID office and an army psychiatrist, who had been alerted, met them at the CID office and they talked to Gray for a couple more hours. He was then taken to the local army hospital for additional medical care.

The professional demeanor and skill displayed by Special Agent Dan White, with the end result of possibly having saved a life, had a profound effect on Military Police Investigator Don Riffe. Don had already gotten to know and respect Danno White, but that night's experience increased the already strong desire to be a CID special agent; he wanted to be an agent just like Danno.

Shortly after this incident Danno White rotated back to the United States and the first part of Military Police Investigator Don Riffe's wish was fulfilled when he moved to the CID office and became a member of the DST. Not long thereafter he submitted his application to be accepted into the CID program. After a favorable background investigation was completed Riffe was approved to attend CID school, successfully completed the course and became an apprentice CID special agent. He returned to Vicenza, now as a proud member of the army CID.

Special Agent Don Riffe
The Importance of Little Things

Shortly after returning to Vicenza as a proud apprentice CID special agent, Don was the duty agent when the Italian police came on post and made their intentions known, that they were looking for a soldier. They informed the CID and Military Police that they suspected this soldier of having been the driver of a vehicle involved in a fatal hit-and-run traffic accident, and they wanted to question him.

They informed Don that a couple of days earlier a young child had been walking down the street in the Vicenza area, when the child was struck and killed by a hit-and-run driver. Witnesses had described the driver, who fled the scene after striking the child, as a white male with short hair driving a specific model and color Fiat. Investigation by the Italian police, determined that there were only four Fiats fitting the description provided by witnesses in Vicenza. One of the four Fiats was owned by an American soldier they now considered their prime suspect. The suspected soldier was in the field and not available and the Italian police were eager to impound the soldier's Fiat. Agent Riffe located the soldier's Fiat parked near his unit, and it was a typical young GI's car in that it was not in the best condition. There were some dents on the front portion of the vehicle that could have been consistent with the hit-and-run scenario, but on the other hand it could have been caused by other means. Since the possibility existed that the soldier had been involved in a fatal traffic accident Special Agent Riffe thought it prudent to do a little more investigating and not just accept the Italian police's views on the matter. He and the traffic NCOIC (non commissioned officer in charge) proceeded to the scene of the fatality to get a firsthand look and do their own crime scene investigation. Riffe and the sergeant spent a couple of hours at the scene and went through it with a fine toothcomb. It paid off for Riffe, because a few feet from the point of impact, Don noticed a small piece of plastic lying in the grass that just looked out of place. Don examined the piece closely and came to the conclusion that it was most likely a part of the trim on an automobile and so it became evidence as far as he was concerned.

While at the scene of the fatal traffic accident the father of the dead child walked up to Agent Riffe and the traffic sergeant and indicated that he wanted to talk to them. This was a challenge, since neither Riffe nor the traffic sergeant spoke Italian. Even though there was a language barrier, the father of the dead child made it clear that he wanted the person who had killed his son caught and brought to justice. Riffe made it clear to the gentleman that they would do everything possible to help make that happen. Being the father of a small boy himself, at that time, it struck close to Riffe's heart.

Agent Riffe and the traffic sergeant returned to the CID office and called the Italian police, requesting a meeting so they could discuss the case. After they arrived Riffe showed them the small piece of plastic he had recovered from the scene of the traffic fatality and they acted as if it was no big deal. Thanks to the dedication and insistence of Paolo Coradi, the Italian interpreter/investigator employed by the CID office; they took that piece of plastic for further investigation. Riffe's hunch paid off, because that small piece of evidence turned out to be the key to the solving of the crime. The Italian police had been convinced the U.S. soldier was the guilty party. As it turned out, further investigation by the Italian police determined that the small piece of plastic Riffe had recovered from the crime scene matched the front end of a Fiat. It was one of the four in Vicenza, and it was owned by an Italian man who also fit the physical description provided by witnesses. Good investigative work by a young and new CID special agent solved this crime and helped ease the pain of a grieving father. Not only that, it also cleared an innocent soldier whom Italian police were convinced had been the culprit. Agent Riffe paid attention at CID school and remembered the instructor's statements "Pay attention to detail" and "don't overlook the small stuff," lessons well learned and applied.

Criminal Investigators Tony Schneider and Pete Dedijer Hint, Hint, Guess Where the Hashish is hidden

Assistant Criminal Investigators Tony Schneider and Pete Dedijer were both assigned to the 25th MP Detachment (CI), at the Caserna Carlo Ederle, in Vicenza and both were happy with that assignment. What more could they want than sunny Italy? Investigator Schneider had a good informant or "snitch," as the investigators would call him as long as he was out of earshot. This informant was pretty good and had given Schneider information before. This time he told him that a certain soldier, Specialist four (E4) Richard Blyth, who resided off base and shared an apartment with Specialist four (E4) Frank Mayfield, had some hashish he was hiding in his refrigerator.

There was only one small problem, since the hashish was located in an off-base apartment; the matter would have to be handled by the Italian authorities. This would present no big problem since the CID had their two trusty SETAF carabineri (Italian federal police–quasi-military) Appuntatos (a rank equivalent to a corporal) Cocchi and Delfino, with whom Schneider had worked several cases before. Investigator Pete Dedijer, being the new kid on the block, was ready to spring into action and have the soldiers pay their dues for possessing illegal drugs. Talk about going in style, Investigators Schneider and Dedijer and Appuntatos Cocchi and Delfino piled into a nice four door, blue, Alfa Romeo sedan and headed downtown to the "druggies" off-base apartment. Since it was under Italian jurisdiction Schneider and Dedijer could accompany the two Italian investigators as observers, but could not actively participate in searching the crime scene. It would be up to the two Italian investigators to obtain a search warrant and then go through the soldier's apartment in an attempt to locate the hashish. Since the "snitch" was a pretty good one and had already told Schneider that the hashish was in the refrigerator, this information had to be conveyed to Cocchi and Delfino.

Investigators Schneider, Dedijer, Cocchi, and Delfino arrived at the suspects apartment, a two-bedroom apartment, and Cocchi and Delfino thought it might be a good idea to save a little time and get this case resolved. In their smooth Italian fashion they managed to talk the soldier's landlord into opening the apartment for them so they could look around, while the soldier occupants were at work. Investigators Schneider and Dedijer hinted to the two Italian investigators that it might be a good idea to check the refrigerator and they did. When one of them located two slabs of hashish wrapped in aluminum foil, he apparently thought it contained ham or "mortadella" because who in the world would keep hash in the refrigerator? Just not "Italian style." The investigator was about ready to return the aluminum foil packet to the refrigerator when Investigators Schneider and Dedijer, who were only "observers," started to stomp their feet on the floor and Investigators Cocchi and Delfino got the message. All four investigators left the apartment and headed to the Italian court house, to obtain a search warrant, so that they could go to the apartment of the suspects and with the full authority and compliance of the law "search it for the hashish" that was there according to the informant. Investigators Schneider and Dedijer stood in the back of the courtroom, while the two experienced Italian investigators gave their pitch to the judge, in an attempt to have a search warrant approved. After a lengthy conversation the two detectives huddled up at the judges bench and a little while later walked up to the two CID investigators with big grins on their faces. They told Investigators Schneider and Dedijer that they had obtained a search and an arrest warrant for the suspects, Specialist four (E4) Richard Blyth and Specialist four (E4) Frank Mayfield that had been named by the informant.

Investigator Pete Dedijer, who had just shortly before finished CID School, and clearly remembered what the instructors had said about the principals of search and seizure, was somewhat perplexed as to how easily the two Italian investigators had obtained a search warrant from the judge. So he asked Investigator Delfino what he had told the judge while they were huddled at the Judge's bench. Delfino gave Dedijer a big smile, reached into his jacket pocket and retrieved one of the tinfoil-packed slabs of hashish that he had removed from the refrigerator in the apartment. Delfino said, in anything but perfect English, "I show judge the probable cause, and now we go and arrest the criminals." They did and both Specialist four (E4) Blyth and Specialist four (E4) Mayfield became the guests of an Italian jail for several months and more than likely ended their army career. Investigator Dedijer learned much while in Italy and thinks back on that tour with fond memories.

SP4 Marlow – Military Police – 1958

CW2 Hubert Marlow – CID – Oct. 67

Living on the farm during WWII with foster parents. L to R: Foster father, my aunt, mother Elsie Marlow, twin brother Carlo, daughter of foster parents, my grandmother Maria Mueller and foster mother, at Zeckendorf, Bavaria (approximately 12 miles from Bamberg), Germany, 1943

L to R: Twin brother Carlo, sister Delores and Hubert (author) destined to be in the military?

L to R: *Wilhelm Gusloff* and *Cap Arcona* – "The Queen of the Atlantic" two ships that would suffer a tragedy much greater than that of the *Titanic*. This photo was taken in Hamburg, Germany, during August 1939, after the 91st and last peacetime trip of the Cap Arcona.

The *"Deutschland"* on the Elbe River, Germany.

A SPECIAL VIEW OF AN UNUSUAL AIR ENGAGEMENT DURING THE EURO-
PEAN AIR OFFENSIVE OF WORLD WAR II
"THE ULTIMATE HONOR"
Artist: R. Harper
A SALUTE BY GERMAN FIGHTER ACE IN BF-109 TO B-17 CREW, AFTER THEIR
AIRCRAFT SURVIVED EXTENSIVE DAMAGE DUE TO FLAK AND ATTACKS BY 15
LUFTWAFFE FIGHTER PILOTS.
December 20, 1943, Northern Germany
U.S. B-17 Pilot/Acft. Cdr.: Charles L. Brown, Weston, W. Va.
527 Sq., 379th BG, 1st Div., VIII Bomber Command
German Bf-109 Pilot: Franz Stigler, 6./JG 27
Source: "THE 13 MINUTE GAP"

On December 20, 1943, the 8th Bomber Command attacked targets in the Bremen, Germany,
complex. B-17-F aircraft No. 42-3167, of the 379th Bomb Group (H), marked with a large
triangle K, was severely damaged by flak on the bomb run. Shortly thereafter the B-17 was
attacked by 15 Luftwaffe fighters, with the engagement lasting between 13 and 22 minutes.
Somewhat later a single Bf-109 made a non-firing approach to the badly damaged B-17 and
ended up flying formation on the right wing. The German pilot visually inspected the damaged B-17, nodded to the American crew, and after about two minutes, saluted, rolled over and
departed. Although the B-17 had suffered severe flak and fighter inflicted damage and four
crew casualties, it successfully returned to England.

The B-17 pilot and crew feel that the untold story of this unique act of chivalry/camaraderie
during combat in World War II, should be recognized and reported. "THE ULTIMATE
HONOR" was painted by Robert L. Harper, at the time an air intelligence officer in England,
who helped remove casualties from the B-17. The complete details of the mission and post mission activities are covered in the narratives "THE 13 MINUTE GAP" and "THE 13 MINUTE
GAP – REVISITED" by Charles L. Brown, the B-17 pilot.

DETACHMENT "C" 1957 142ND MP COMPANY

CRAILSHEIM
GERMANY

SFC CAREY
OPERATIONS SGT

Sgt OWENS
DETACHMENT SGT

SP-3 WILLIAMS
DESK SGT

SP-3 SINDORF
DESK SGT

SP-3 OXENDINE
DESK SGT

SP-3 LAIK
DESK SGT

Pfc GABE
DESK CLERK

SP-3 MOKRZYCKI
TAPS

SP-3 DERMINIO
PATROL MAN

SP-3 DURKIN
PATROL MAN

SP-3 STROUT
PATROL MAN

SP-3 THOMAS
PATROL MAN

Pfc CORBIN
PATROL MAN

Pfc MARLOW
PATROL MAN

Pfc HALE
PATROL MAN

Pfc LEACH
PATROL MAN

Pfc MOORE
PATROL MAN

HQ Det., 142nd MP Co (Svc), Garmisch-Partenkirchen, Germany, 1958, with the Zugspitze, Germany's highest mountain in the background. Captain George M. Schneider, Commander, on the left side and First Sergeant Joe G. Quintana on the right. SP3 Marlow (author) is in the middle row, 2nd to the right of the guidon.

Sp3 Marlow and Pfc Leach in front of the Crailscheim, Germany, MP Station

Pfc Juan R. Torres, Sp3 Hubert Marlow and Pfc Jerry A. Hale, in Heidelberg, Germany, on a Command Post Exercise (CPX) 1958

Members of the HQ Det., 142nd MP Co (Svc), Garmisch-Partenkirchen, Germany, 1958, at the Casa Carioca Ice Show, performing duties with Capt. George M. Schneider. The Casa Carioca was destroyed by a fire a few years later.

Inspection of Sp3 Marlow by Capt. George M. Schneider. Schneider placed this photo under the dust cover of Marlow's bed, and wrote on the back "Ein guter Soldat" (a good soldier) "I wish I had a company of men like you" "Sincerely, George M. Schneider, Capt. MPC"

1LT James D. Smith, Commander, 142nd MP Co (Svc) gives away the bride "Monika" at the chapel, Sheridan Kaserne, Gamisch-Partenkirchen, Germany, on 8 Nov. 1958

A Military Police wedding – Hubert and Monika Marlow

USACIDC
Commanders

COL Henry H. Tufts
Commanding Officer
Sep 1971 - Aug 1974

MG Albert R. Escola
Commanding General
Aug 1974 - Sep 1975

MG Paul M. Timmerberg
Commanding General
Sep 1975 - Sep 1983

MG Eugene R. Cromartie
Commanding General
Sep 1983 - Apr 1990

MG Peter T. Berry
Commanding General
Jul 1990 - Jun 1995

BG Daniel A. Doherty
Commanding General
Jul 1995 - Sep 1998

BG David W. Foley
Commanding General
Sep 1998 - Jun 2001

U.S. ARMY
CRIMINAL INVESTIGATION
COMMAND

Major General Donald J. Ryder – Commanding General USACIDC and Provost Marshal General – from Jun 2001 to present.

Current CID badge used as of September 1971.

PMG CID badge used until September 1971.

One of the WWII CID badges used until the late 1940s-early 1950s.

Provost Marshal General Position Announced

Concept to Provide Better Efficiencies, Effectiveness for Law Enforcement

The U.S. Army announced on Jan. 30, the creation of the Provost Marshal General (PMG) position for the Army. The announcement is just one more step in the Army's transformation plan designed to restructure its major subordinate commands and functions while realizing the Army's vision of enhancing effectiveness and providing better efficiencies throughout the service.

"This law enforcement enhancement will provide the Army's most senior leadership with a comprehensive, single source responsibility for law enforcement, security, corrections, and criminal investigative-type requirements," said Ryder.

"This is for the betterment of the Army and the Military Police Corps as a whole, and will certainly increase synchronization within these functions."

The transformation calls for the PMG to be a part of the Army Staff reporting directly to the Army Chief of Staff, and changes the CID command from a major Army command to a Direct Reporting Unit (DRU) -- still reporting to the Army Chief of Staff -- and thereby retaining its investigative autonomy, free from the perception of outside undue command influence.

According to Army planners, a single officer will be "dual-hatted" as the PMG and the commander of

CID. Planners say the move will enhance effectiveness and synchronize efforts – ultimately streamlining critical input to senior Army leadership.

The new PMG is expected to establish policy and provide management and technical oversight of Law Enforcement, Counter-Drug Support, Corrections, Criminal Investigations, Physical Security, Antiterrorism and the Weapons of Mass Destruction Installation Preparedness Programs for the Department of the Army.

Additionally, he will act as the Department of Defense Executive Agent for the Enemy Prisoner of War/Detainee and Corrections Program; monitor and report worldwide Anti-Terrorism/Force Protection and criminal information; and provide domestic threat information to senior Army leaders and major commands.

"The new position will provide an invaluable "footprint" within the Pentagon for all law-enforcement and security issues," said Ryder. "The PMG will also be responsible

Maj. Gen. Donald J. Ryder

for obtaining and allocating resources, (including budget development and execution); and directing and organizing the PMG and CID to accomplish their respective missions and functions at the Departmental level [Army] and in support of Army operations."

Ryder stresses that "yes, there will be a new organization in town," but institutional functions will remain the same. "Most of the move will be a seamless transition to the military policeman or the CID special agent providing selfless service wherever the Army finds itself."

"I think it's critical for everyone to understand that there will be no change in CID's charter as an independent investigative agency, or in the functions performed by the Security, Force Protection and Law Enforcement Division (DAMO ODL G-3)," explained Ryder. "For the vast majority of Military Police and special agents affected by this announcement, it will be business as usual."

> "I think it's critical for everyone to understand that there is no change in CID's charter as an independent investigative agency... For the vast majority of MPs and special agents affected by this announcement, it will be business as usual."

The last credentials of Special Agent Hubert Marlow – also the current credentials used by CID.

Theater Provost Marshal credentials of Criminal Investigator Robert B. Howard – used by CID during WWII in the China-Burma-India Theater of War.

Members of the Pusan Detachment, 65th MP Det (CI), Hialeah Compound, Pusan, Korea and Korean investigative personnel. Front row, left to right: Miss P.S. Pyon, Criminal Investigator Jack Teall, J. Prisco, Al P. Moody, CW2 Donald Weaver the Officer in Charge, Criminal Investigator Jackson E. Smith, Provost Marshal Investigator Tommy D. Williams and Criminal Investigator Hubert Marlow.

Second row: K.H. Kong, T.U. Yi, C.T. Kim, T.C. Pak, K.Y. Shim, H.Y. Choe, S.A. Son, C.K. Pak, and W.Y. Pak.

Back row: F.H. Kim, S.T. Son, M.K. Kim, C.H. Kim, and C.Y. Yi

Provost Marshal and CID office, Hialeah Compound, Pusan, South Korea. (1965)

Fatal traffic accident, just outside the back gate of Fort Sheridan, IL, investigated by Criminal Investigator Hubert Marlow (author). Unfortunately, it involved two off-duty MP's.

Commanding Officer, Det. A, 5th MP Gp (CI), Ft. Sheridan, IL, CPT Robert K. Ressler, later of FBI fame as a profiler and author. Across from him (in the middle) the Operations Officer CW3 William Giehran.

Hubert Marlow (author) being sworn in as a warrant officer by Col. Hobert Sharp, Commanding Officer, 5th MP Gp (CI), Hq 5th US Army, Chicago, IL, with wife Monika and mother Elsie Marlow attending the ceremony.

John K. Groves, after recovering from his traffic accident injuries in Zweibruecken, Germany, became a police officer with the Police Department, Joplin, MO. This shows officer Groves as a traffic officer during 1969.

John K. Groves went from SP4 Military Police to Lieutenant Colonel, Military Police Corps, a great accomplishment. From L to R: CW5 Willie Rowell, BG Daniel C. Doherty and LTC John K. Groves. (1997)

LTC John K. Groves, Provost Marshal, Ft. Bliss, Texas (1997)

Staff of HQ, 6th Region, USACIDC, Presidio of San Francisco, CA, with the Golden Gate Bridge in the background. L to R, front row: CPT Townsend, CPT Susan Wood, MAJ John K. Groves, SGM Savedra, COL Linda Norman (Commanding Officer 6th Region), LTC Robert Reed, Executive Officer. Back row: unknown, unknown, unknown, unknown, CW4 William Middleton. (1993)

L to R: Col. William T. McClary, outgoing Commander, 15th MP Brigade, Kaiserslautern, Germany, CW2 Hubert Marlow, Investigator in Charge and Station Commander, Zweibruecken CID/MP Station, LTC Robert Goggans, Provost Marshal, Palatinate District, Kaiserslautern, Germany. (1968)

MP Honor Guard for Col. McClary, upon his departure, with CW2 Hubert Marlow following Col. McClary. SSG Earl J. Castle, Operations Sergeant, is stepping out of the Zweibruecken MP Station. (1968)

L to R: CW2 Carl D. Coleman, CID Pirmasens, CPT Ronald Carnevale, USAF Security Police, Zweibruecken, LTC David T. Steward, CO, 52nd MP Det (CI), Mannheim, SSG Earl J. Castle, Opns Sgt, Zweibruecken MP Station, LTC Stanley Lobodinski, CO, 94th MP Bn, Kaiserslautern, Col. Herbert Michau, incoming commander, 15th MP Brigade, Kaiserslautern, LTC Sarsfield, Community Leader, Zweibruecken and CW2 Hubert Marlow, CID and Station Commander, Zweibruecken MP Station, Germany. (1968)

CW2 Hubert Marlow, presenting SSG Earl J. Castle with a plaque upon his departure from Germany. (1969)

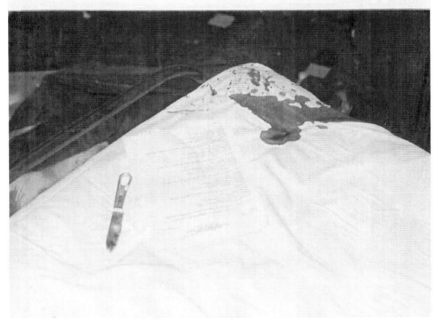

Murder scene, Rose Barracks, Bad Kreuznach, Germany. The victim was stabbed in the heart and blood immediately spurted against the wall. The murder weapon on the blood stained bed.

Sexualverbrecher wurde gefaßt
Gute Zusammenarbeit zwischen amerikanischer und deutscher Kripo

Anfang Mai wurde von der Mutter einer 13jährigen Schülerin Anzeige erstattet, weil ein US-Angehöriger versucht hatte, das Mädchen in den Radium-Stollen beim „Quellenhof" zu ziehen und dort zu vergewaltigen. Bei der Vernehmung des Mädchens stellte sich heraus, daß der amerikanische Soldat versucht hatte, das Kind durch Schläge gefügig zu machen. Durch die Hilfe eines hinzugekommenen weiteren Angehörigen der US-Streitkräfte konnte das Mädchen entkommen.

Unmittelbar nach Bekanntwerden dieses Vorfalls wurde die amerikanische Kriminalpolizei (CID) eingeschaltet. Da sich zuerst keinerlei Hinweise auf den Täter ergaben, schien zunächst eine Klärung des Falles ausgeschlossen. Erst nach mehreren Tagen gelang es den Angehörigen des CID, eine Spur aufzugreifen, die dann — dank des unermüdlichen Einsatzes der amerikanischen Kriminalpolizei — doch zum Ziele führte. Der Täter konnte ermittelt und identifiziert werden. Ebenso konnten durch die CID Tatzeugen — ebenfalls Angehörige der amerikanischen Armee — festgestellt werden, die bei der Gegenüberstellung den Täter einwandfrei wiedererkannten. Der Täter ist jedoch nicht geständig. Wenn auch gelegentlich Stimmen laut werden, daß die Zusammenarbeit zwischen der deutschen Polizei und der CID zu wünschen übrig lasse, dann muß hier einmal klar herausgestellt werden, daß sich die amerikanische Gesetzgebung und Prozeßverfahrensweise von der der deutschen in einigen Punkten stark unterscheidet. So sind z. B. für das amerikanische Strafverfahren verschiedene Fakten von größter Wichtigkeit, die im deutschen Strafverfahren nur eine nebensächliche Rolle spielen und umgekehrt. Dies verlangt großes Verständnis von beiden Seiten, und gerade dieses gegenseitige Verständnis brachte in der Vergangenheit immer wieder Erfolge.

Speziell auf dem Gebiet der Sittendelikte, bei denen Angehörige der US-Streitkräfte als Täter in Erscheinung traten, konnten im vergangenen Jahr alle Straftaten geklärt und die Täter ermittelt werden. Diese Erfolge sind nicht zuletzt auf die gute Zusammenarbeit zwischen deutscher und amerikanischer Kriminalpolizei zurückzuführen. Diese Zusammenarbeit wird vor allem wesentlich dadurch erleichtert, daß einige in Bad Kreuznach tätige Angehörige der CID die deutsche Sprache beherrschen und so der immer etwas umständlichere Weg der Verständigung über einen Dolmetscher vermieden werden kann.

Translation: EXTRACT from the Newspaper "General News"
"Excellent cooperation with US Criminal Police"

All cases involving sex crimes cleared. At the beginning of May, this year, the mother of a 13-year-old girl filed a complaint alleging that a member of the U.S. forces had attempted to rape her daughter at the Radoncave adjacent to the "Quellenhof." During the ensuing investigation it was determined that the U.S. Subject had assaulted the girl to break her resistance. The daughter was able to escape when another member of the U.S. forces arrived at the scene and came to her assistance.

Immediately after the incident was reported, the US CID was informed. In view of the fact that no leads, regarding the identity of the Subject, were developed at the beginning of the investigation a conclusion could not be drawn. After several days however, and thanks to the untiring efforts on the part of the CID, the Subject was identified and located. The CID further developed witnesses who positively identified the Subject during a line-up. The Subject, however, did not confess.

Due to comments made, that the cooperation between the American CID and the German Police was lacking and left something to be desired, the German Police feels obligated to point out the fact that compared to the German penal code, the American penal code, as well as the law enforcement procedures are entirely different. For instance facts considered very important to the German court proceedings might not be important to the American system and vice versa. This, however, requires a great deal of understanding on both sides; and this understanding was the reason for successes in the past. Especially in the case of sex crimes, involving members of the US forces as subjects, all cases resulted in identifying the subjects and bringing the investigation to a successful conclusion. Such success is the result of good cooperation between the German and American Criminal Police, additionally some of the members of the Bad Kreuznach CID are fluent in German, alleviating the need of an interpreter.

Fort Gordon Field Office, L to R, front row: S/A Craig Young, secretaries Lois Davidson, Joanne Peak and Evelyn Thompson. Special Agent Maynard Midthun and SP5 James Bignon (Admin). Second row: Special Agents John Morgan, Thom Whitrock, Eddie Jackson, Harry Nelson and Chuck West. Third row: Special Agents Stan Brown and Gene Miller. Top row: Major Tom Fairris, Commanding Officer, CW3 Hubert Marlow, Operations Officer, Special Agents Carolyn Hauser, Bob Kelly and Roy Barker. (1975)

Major James W. Macolly, Commanding Officer, Fort Gordon Field Office, Third Region, USACIDC, promotes CW2 Harry W. Kinsella to CW3. Assisting is Nancy Kinsella (wife) with CW3 Hubert Marlow looking on. (25 Feb. 1976)

CW3 Hubert Marlow and Major General Albert R. Escola, Commanding General USACIDC, who was on a three-day visit to Fort Gordon, GA. (1975)

Lieutenant Colonel Douglas W. Scott, one of the finest and most capable officers ever to serve with CID, CW3 Hubert Marlow and Major General Albert R. Escola (1975)

Operations Officers conference, Third Region, USACIDC, Fort Gillem, GA. Left to right, front row: Colonel Ackerman, Commanding Officer, Third Region, CW3 Butcher, CW3 McLellan, CW4 Vespini, CW2 Copeland, CW3 Marlow and Col. Boden. Back row: CW3 Kirk, CW4 Barkley, CW2 Larry, CW3 Blake, CW4 Cain, CW4 Graham, CW4 Roll and CW4 Gladle. (10 Sep 1975)

CIDAA Reunion, Atlanta, GA. Three old friends, who served together at the Fort Gordon Field Office, USACIDC, during 1974-76, meet again. Retired Agent Eddie Jackson, Harry Nelson and Herb Marlow. (September 1990)

Top photo: Criminal Investigator Hubert Marlow at the beach, Cam Ranh Bay, South Vietnam (1970)

Bottom photo: A little relaxation on a South Vietnamese pilot boat, Criminal Investigators Hubert Marlow and Robert A. Cappuccio, at Cam Ranh Bay, South Vietnam. (1970)

Front row, L to R: Criminal Investigators Herb Marlow, Matt Moriarty, CW3 Jim Rawlings, Officer in Charge of Can Ranh Bay Field Office, Criminal Investigator Bob Cappuccio and Carl Coleman. Back row: CW3 Glenn Gladle, Operations Officer, Det. B, 8th MP Gp (CI), Criminal Investigator Ben Grotts, Captain Robert M. Hawk, Commanding officer and Criminal Investigator Tony Korey. (1970)

Old friends meet again at Cam Ranh Bay, South Vietnam during 1970. Left to right: CW2 Matthew E. Moriarty, LTC James D. Smith and CW2 Hubert Marlow. LTC Smith commanded the 142nd MP Co (Svc) as a 1LT and CPT during 1957-60. Moriarty and Marlow were members of the unit during that time.

Captain Robert M. Hawk, Commanding Officer, Det. B, 8th MP Gp (CI), Cam Ranh Bay, South Vietnam, and CW3 Glenn Gladle, Detachment Operations Officer. (1970)

Our Living Quarters at Cam Ranh Bay, South Vietnam. (1970)

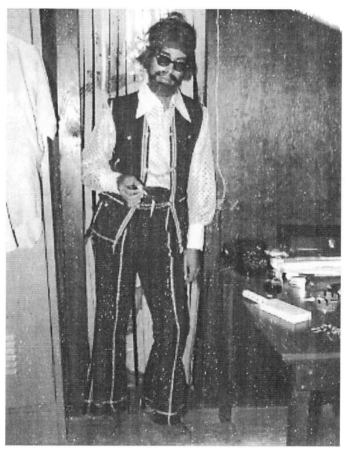

Criminal Investigator William C. Ward, my roommate at Cam Ranh Bay, South Vietnam, dressed like a gypsy. (1970)

A reunion with an old friend, Sgt T.U. Yi, CID, Republic of Korea Army, White Horse Division, at Cam Ranh Bay, South Vietnam. Yi was assigned to the U.S. CID Office, Hialeah Compound, Pusan, South Korea, during the author's tour of duty in Korea (1964-65). The photo was taken at Cam Ranh Bay during 1970.

Establishment known as "so Chin Linda's," just off Cam Ranh Bay on Highway 1, Su Chin, South Vietnam, located in front of which Criminal Investigator Leroy E. Halbert was fatally shot on 31 Dec 70. (photo 1 Jan 71)

Center building, was crime scene of a fragging at Bao Loc, South Vietnam. Subject placed a hand grenade, with 32 rubber bands around the handle and a few drops of lighter fluid on the rubber bands, on the sand bags, ignited the lighter fluid, and ran from the scene. The grenade exploded 21 seconds later, injuring a Master Sergeant seriously. (1970)

Damage to mess hall, at Cam Ranh Bay, South Vietnam, done by the tail end of a Typhoon (1970)

Home of a South Vietnamese Military Advisory Group (VMAG) officer, just on the perimeter of the U.S. Army compound, blown up by the Viet Cong durin the period of the fragging, negligent homicide and drug investigations, conducted by Criminal Investigator Hubert Marlow, at Bao Loc, South Vietnam (1970)

While in Saigon, on an investigative lead, Criminal Investigator Hubert Marlow meets his former co-worker, William E. Lowry, both were assigned to the CID at Ft. Sheridan, IL, during the period of 1965-67. (1970)

CID Investigators from the Republic of Korea White Horse Division, Cam Ranh Bay, with CW3 Rex Schulz who replaced CW2 Hubert Marlow (author) as the Officer in Charge of the Cam Ranh Bay Field Office. (1970)

Major Carl J. LeBourdais, Commanding Officer, Det. B, 8th MP Group (CI), Cam Ranh Bay, South Vietnam, presents CW2 Hubert Marlow (author) with the Bronze Star Medal. (Jan 71)

L to R: Warrant Officer in charge of the Korean CID, CW2 Hubert Marlow (author) and two Korean CID Investigators came to say farewell at the airport to Marlow, upon his departure from Cam Ranh Bay, South Vietnam, to return to the United States. (Jan 71)

USMC CID Chief Investigator Kozlowski and Criminal Investigator James Benson, Jr., making plaster casts of tire tracks at a crime scene. (Official USMC Photograph) (1960s)

USMC CID Criminal Investigator James Benson, Jr., dusting wall locker, of larceny victim, for fingerprints. (1960s).

Marine Corps Air Station, El Toro, California – Far left Criminal Investigator James Benson, Jr., USMC CID and unidentified Secret Service Agent (with sunglasses) – guarding President Lyndon B. Johnson and Governor Brown of California. (1960s)

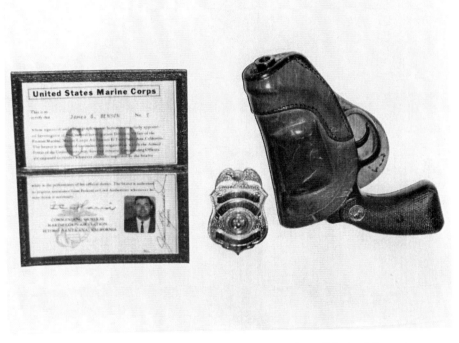

USMC CID credentials, badge and sidearm issued to Criminal Investigator James Benson, Jr.

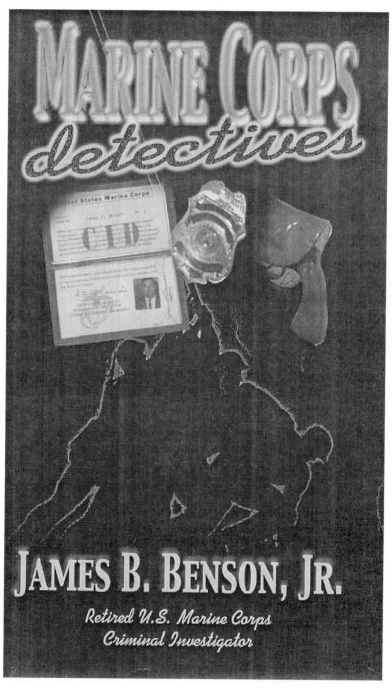

Book cover of book written by Criminal Investigator (Retired) James Benson, Jr.

Visiting my brother Karl-Heinz in Hamburg, Germany, (on the Elbe River) during 1989.

Brother Peter visiting Elmhurst, IL. His first visit to the USA (1996)

Visiting East (Communist) Berlin, Germany, to meet with mother-in-law. The Four Powers Agreement required that U.S. Military personnel be in uniform. L to R: Monika, Michael, and Adrian Marlow, Kaethe Lehmann (Author's mother-in-law) and Hubert Marlow (author). Standing in back is Dieter Marlow. (1972)

My twin brother Carlo as a member of the U.S. Army Ordinance Corp, in South Korea (1956-57)

Special Agent (Retired) presents a portrait of General Berry to General Berry. The portrait was painted by Casey Siewierski, an old friend of Herb Marlow.

Twin brother Carlo Marlow, General Leutnant (Major General) Adolf
Galland, famous WWII Fighter Ace and General of the Fighter Arm of the
Luftwaffe, and Hubert Marlow (author) at Chicago, IL.

Special Agent (Retired) Hubert "Herb" Marlow presents a CID Agents Association Certificate of Membership to USMC CID Criminal Investigator (Retired) Francis "Ace" Arciaga at Villa Park, IL.

USMC CID Criminal Investigator (Retired) Francis "Ace" Arciaga pulled a big surprise on Herb Marlow by presenting an Honorary USMC CID Criminal Investigator's badge to him. Marlow is the only person in the U.S. Army to be so honored and only the fourth person to be so honored by the USMC CID.

CHAPTER TEN

Japan

Tokyo

Criminal Investigator Shigeshi "Shug" Madokoro
Investigations during the Occupation of Japan

Criminal Investigator Shug Madokoro was assigned to the 23rd MP Detachment (CI), in Tokyo and it was a fairly large office by CID standards. The commanding officer was Captain Jack Hansford. The 23rd still had the WWII mix of investigators, consisting of civilian investigators former, Secret Service and FBI agents, city detectives and cops, and enlisted as well as warrant officer criminal investigators. So one could say the office had experienced investigators.

All smart criminal investigators know the value of informants, or "snitches" as they were called, and most of the time they did not come from high society types but from prostitutes and petty thieves or someone who had been caught for a minor violation and been given a break. It was no different with Shug Madokoro, who had developed some pretty good informants amongst the prostitutes. At the beginning of the occupation there were regular brothels in Tokyo, however; it was not too long before complaints from the States forced the closing of the brothels and they were placed off-limits to the troops. The worst thing about this was the fact that this forced the girls out of rather well run regulated establishments and into the street as streetwalkers.

It was chaotic for a time and the military police were instructed to pick up any Japanese girl seen with a soldier, load them on a two one half ton truck and take them to the Yoshiwara hospital for a VD examination. It did not take the girls long to organize themselves and stake out their territories, usually centered around railroad stations and military bases, in easy reach of their GI customers. Each area was ruled by a "queen bee" (madam) who ran her girls with an iron hand. All of the queen bees had gotten to know Investigator Madokoro, who spoke Japanese well enough to communicate, and they would call him, even in the middle of the night, if they were in need of help. They would tell him that one of their girls had gotten into trouble – mostly claiming one of their girls had been raped, which in the end would be a case of not having been paid for services performed. In other instances the Japanese police had picked up one of their girls for black marketing. The queen bee would call Investigator Madokoro and tell him the name of the girl that had been picked up and what police station she had been taken to. Madokoro in turn would have his interpreter call that police station and he would then learn that the girl had been apprehended for illegal possession of American cigarettes, which were worth more than gold at that time. The police would inform Madokoro's interpreter that they had seized the illegal goods from the girl, and would release her in the morning. Now Shug Madokoro knew how to take advantage of this situation, he informed the queen bee that her girl would be released in the morning; she in turn thought that this had occurred because he had used his powers as a CID Investigator by instructing the Japanese police to release the girl. Eventually this would pay dividends to him because the prostitutes became his eyes and ears since they were out on the streets at all hours of the night, at locations where the GIs hung out, and saw and knew everything.

The Murder of an Army Chaplain

Father Peter McGuinnes (not his real name) was an Army Chaplain and had been murdered near the Sugamo Prison, famous for being the place where the war crimes trials were being held. The murder of the chaplain had been assigned to two investigators who had received information indicating that two Koreans had killed the chaplain, but a month went by with no progress on the case. Brigadier General Charles Ferrin, the Tokyo provost marshal, was starting to feel the heat, because the murder of a chaplain was not taken lightly by the big brass and politicians. Criminal Investigator Madokoro had a good reputation as a sharp investigator and for that reason was called into the front office and informed he would take over the investigation. Shug Madokoro was presented with all the evidence collected to date, and statements taken so far, which included one statement taken from one GI, Private Harry Sloan (not his real name), who was placed near the scene of the shooting on the night it had occurred. Investigator Madokoro, after reviewing the statements, soon determined that the statement taken from Pvt Sloan was inconsistent with the statements taken from other witnesses in the area and this was a good lead to pursue further. This would be the time when the queen bees could come in handy.

No sooner said than done and Shug Madokoro contacted his queen bee in the Sugamo Prison area. Amazingly she told him that Private Sloan's girlfriend, Yoko, a prostitute, was with him the night he shot the chaplain. It did not take Madokoro very long to locate another prostitute, Sume, who had also witnessed the shooting. Investigator Madokoro picked up the two prostitutes and took them to the CID office where he took a detailed sworn statement from each then locked them up in protective custody. Now the fact that the two ladies were prostitutes presented one small problem in that Madokoro knew their testimony would be seriously challenged by the defense. For that reason he had both ladies polygraphed by detectives of the Tokyo Metropolitan Police Department. Of course the polygraph instrument of that time was not very sophisticated. Detectives also administered truth serum (sodium pentathol), and the results of both tests supported the truthfulness of their statements.

Investigator Madokoro soon determined the reason Sloan had murdered Father McGuinnes. Father McGuinnes was a one-man crusade in the Sugamo Prison area, chasing GIs out of off limits establishments and telling them to stay away from prostitutes. Madokoro learned from Yoko, Sloan's girlfriend, that the good chaplain had caught them together and had told Sloan to stay away from her. He gave Sloan a couple more warnings, when he again caught him in the company of Yoko, but Sloan paid no attention to that. When he again caught them together he told Sloan that he would write to his parents, who apparently were very religious and strict, and that he would tell them about his (Sloan's) activities. After all these warnings, Father McGuinnes again caught Sloan with Yoko, about 11:00 P.M. of the fateful night, and when he said to Sloan "I am going to write to your parents", Sloan had pulled out a .25 caliber pistol and shot and killed Father McGuinnes.

One night during the investigation, Criminal Investigator Kajiwara, a tough Hawaiian Nisei, was Investigator Madokoro's partner. Kajiwara, Yoko, Sume, a Japanese police woman assigned to watch the two prostitute witnesses, and Madokoro returned to the crime scene. It was approximately 11:00 P.M., the same time the murder had occurred, and they were at the crime scene to do some checking, when a drunken sergeant approached Madokoro and demanded one of the girls. He told Madokoro, "There are three girls and only two of you (guys)." When Madokoro told the good sergeant, "move on!" he became very agitated, smashed a whiskey bottle he had in his hand, and came straight at him with the jagged, broken bottle. Madokoro heard Investigator Kajiwara shout, "Stop!" as he drew his weapon. Knowing Kajiwara, he knew he would not hesitate for a moment to shoot, and all Shug could think of was what a helluva time he would have writing a report if Kajiwara shot the good sergeant. Shug shouted in a loud voice, "Don't Shoot!" That stopped both Kajiwara and the sergeant, to the great relief of Madokoro.

Investigator Madokoro briefed his commanding officer, Captain Jack Hansford, on his findings and Hansford and he then proceeded to the Sugamo compound, which also housed the GI prison guards. They contacted Sloan's commander, briefed him on the investigation, and asked him to bring Private Sloan, who was one of the prison guards, to them. He did, and Hansford placed his hands on Sloan's shoulder and informed him that he was under apprehension for the murder of Chaplain McGuinnes. Sloan was subsequently charged with murder, court-martialed, found guilty, and sentenced to many years imprisonment. Madokoro turned the drunken sergeant over to his commanding officer who took appropriate non-judicial action for his improper behavior as a non-commissioned officer.

Criminal Investigator Shug Madokoro
The not so smart Bank Thieves

After the surrender, and during the occupation, the Japanese were required to turn in all their precious metals and jewels, such as diamonds, and they were held by the occupation forces in seized vaults. This was when Corporal. Ken Sipes (not his real name) came up with a really bright idea; at least he thought so. Sipes and a Korean buddy, who was a resident of Japan, went to one of the Japanese banks in Tokyo, and informed the bank officials that they were from the provost marshal's office. They told the bank officials that they were there to investigate a report that the bank was illegally holding gold bullion in their vaults, and that they were there to confiscate the gold. The bank officials informed the two men that they were not holding such contraband, since it was forbidden by the occupation troops. Next the two mini-gangsters threatened to close the bank until such time that they produced the illegally-held gold. Now closing down a bank was serious business in Japan, because of the damage this would cause to the reputation of the bank. This could cause a run on the bank (people coming and withdrawing all their money) which of course would have a tremendous negative effect on the bank's funds. The bank officials then offered Corporal Sipes a large bribe in yen (Japanese currency), which he readily accepted and he and his Korean buddy then departed the bank. Bank officials thought about the incident for a while and then decided to call the Japanese police and report the incident because of the fact that an American soldier was involved. The Japanese police in turn notified the provost marshal's office of the incident.

Investigator Madokoro took Detective Ogawa, one of the detectives from the Tokyo metropolitan police assigned to the CID office, with him and proceeded to the scene of the crime, the bank. Madokoro and Ogawa learned from bank officials that the soldier (Sipes), as yet unidentified, and his Korean buddy had initially arrived at the bank on foot. After a discussion lasting about forty-five minutes, the two men had left, only to return shortly thereafter at which time, after some more discussion, the bribe was paid and the two departed in the jeep. Madokoro and Ogawa came to the conclusion that the soldier must belong to some unit stationed not too distant from the bank. They knew there was a signal battalion about a mile from the bank, and so they proceeded to the battalion motor pool and asked if anyone had checked out a jeep on the date of the incident and the approximate time provided by the bank officials. The dispatcher told them that Corporal Kenneth Sipes had indeed checked out a jeep during that time frame, it seemed Madokoro and Ogawa had hit pay dirt.

The two investigators proceeded to the unit orderly room and requested to see the commanding officer, they then informed him of the incident and requested to see Corporal Sipes, whose name was not known to them up to that point. Sipes was brought to the orderly room, and wouldn't you know he fit the description of the culprit as provided by the bank officials. Sipes' was placed under apprehension and taken to the bank, where he was positively identified as the culprit to whom they had paid the bribe. During interrogation Sipes told Investigator Madokoro that he had given most of the money (the bribe) to his Korean buddy for safekeeping. Madokoro and Detective Ogawa proceeded to the home of the parents of Sipes Korean buddy and searched their residence, recovering some of the bribe money. Madokoro told the Tokyo police to look for the Korean suspect since CID had no interest in him. Sipes was charged with theft, court-martialed, found guilty, reduced to Private, dishonorably discharged from the army, and sentenced to five years confinement.

Now you would think this was where this story ended, but not so. It was 1954, and Shugi Madokoro was assigned as an instructor at the CID school, Fort Gordon, Georgia, when one fine day his wife, June, went to the dentist at the post hospital. A dental assistant noticed her name and asked her if she knew a CID man by the name of Madokoro. June proudly proclaimed to him, "That is my husband," the dental assistant then said, "He is a friend of mine." He then informed June that he had been given a dishonorable discharge and confinement at hard labor for five years. He informed June that when the Korean war (excuse me, "Police Action") started, he took full advantage of an offer made to certain confined soldiers, which gave them the opportunity for a full pardon, providing they volunteered to serve in a combat unit in Korea. He had accepted the offer and was once again a soldier in good standing. You guessed it, it was none other than the former Corporal Kenneth Sipes. Yes, and this world is small indeed.

Criminal Investigators Shug Madokoro and George Keithan
The Rape of a Ten Year Old Japanese Girl

It was the fall of 1950, and the Korean War (excuse me "Police Action") was in full swing with new troops being brought to Korea. The famous 1st Cavalry Division, up until that time based in Japan, was in the process of being shipped to Korea. Two soldiers from the Division, Private first class Peter Long and Private first class. Fred Timmer (not their real names), had lucked out and gotten a pass to visit Tokyo for the purpose of picking up a pistol they had left at a gun shop to have engraved. The two picked up this pistol and then observed little ten-year-old Kazuko Tojo (not her real name) playing. Long and Timmer enticed the girl to get into their car, a Ford four-door sedan driven and owned by Long, by offering her a Coca-Cola, which was a big thing in those days. The two GIs then drove into a secluded area and both raped the ten-year-old child. In the process both got blood on their pants which gives you an idea what trauma the little girl went through. After they had raped the little girl, Long and Timmer noticed that their clothing was bloody and so the two, with Kazuko still in the car, drove down to a river and attempted to wash the blood out of their clothing. The two criminals at that time released Kazuko and went into a bar. While at the bar, the two became very rowdy and brandished the pistol they had picked up from the gun shop. The proprietor of the bar became a little scared and called the military police.

In the mean time, some Japanese men noticed Kazuko, while she was stumbling down the street with her clothing and body all bloodied and crying profusely. The men took the little girl to the Japanese police station where she told the police officers that two American soldiers had done bad things to her. Of course the police officers determined that the little girl had been raped and immediately notified the provost marshal's office. The desk sergeant was apprised of the incident and immediately alerted all military police patrols to be on the lookout for the two GIs.

The MPs arrived shortly after the proprietor of the bar had called, and when they observed Long and Timmer, and the condition of their clothing, it did not take them long to put two and two together and figure out that these two GIs must have been the ones who had raped the little girl. They arrested the duo and transported them straight to the CID office.

Criminal Investigator Keithan was the duty agent that night and Shug Madokoro was helping him with the case. George Keithan was a former secret service agent, and at one time had been on the presidential security team, guarding President Roosevelt, so he was a man of experience. First things first, so Keithan confiscated all of the clothing from Long and Timmer and then pulled a handful of pubic hair from both of them, and placed them in the cellblock. Criminal Investigator Shug Madokoro, who was fluent in Japanese, and Detective Ogawa talked to little Kazuko and took a full statement from her, as Shug said "she was a sharp little girl." They also took possession of Kazuko's clothing and found some pubic hair in her panties. Next Madokoro and Detective Ogawa held a lineup and without the slightest hesitation Kazuko identified her two assailants.

Investigators Keithan and Madokoro had all the evidence they needed to convict Long and Timmer. The specialists from the CID crime laboratory did their job well, they found Kazuko's fingerprints on the Coca-Cola bottle, with which Long and Timmer had enticed her into the car. They also found her fingerprints on the back door of the car. Examination of the clothing resulted in identifying Kazuko's blood type on the trousers of both Long and Timmer, amazingly and to the detriment of Long and Timmer all three persons involved in the crime, the two subjects and the victim, had different blood types. Examination of pubic hair of one of the two criminals matched pubic hair recovered from Kazuko's clothing.

The crime occurred in late 1950, so by this time the polygraph instrument had been perfected, and was no longer the crude system used by the Tokyo Metropolitan Police four years earlier. Investigators Keithan and Madokoro used the talents of Investigator Barton Imminger of the Office of Naval Intelligence (ONI), who was known to be one of the best polygraphers. Not only that, he was an extremely talented interrogator and only used the polygraph as an aid to his investigation, to let him know if he was going in the right direction with his line of questioning. Private Long was confronted with the physical evidence but never confessed and declined to give either an oral or a written statement. ONI Investigator and Polygrapher Imminger polygraphed and interrogated Private Timmer in the presence of Investigator Madokoro. Imminger shifted the blame onto Long by telling Timmer that it was Long who drove the car and stopped, enticing the girl to get into the car. It was Long who first raped Kazuko and then urged Timmer to do the same, so Long was mainly to blame for the situation he got him, Timmer, involved in. Playing on Timmer's emotions, by appearing sympathetic toward him worked. He would not write a statement but did agree to sign a statement if Investigator Madokoro wrote it out for him. Madokoro was more than happy to oblige him and Timmer initialed several corrections in the statement, which would prove that he had read the statement and knew its contents.

Both Long and Timmer were court-martialed and the staff judge advocate lawyers wanted Kazuko to testify at the trial, and identify Long and Timmer, but her parents objected saying doctors were working with Kazuko to help her forget the terrible incident. When Investigator Madokoro explained to them, in Japanese of course, how important it was for Kazuko to identify the two criminals at the court-martial, in order to get a conviction, and that this would be the last time they would impose on them, they relented. Kazuko was a very brave little ten-year-old girl, when she stood up in the courtroom and firmly pointed her finger at Long and Timmer. After the court-martial several members of the court approached Investigator Madokoro and thanked him for a well-prepared case. Both Long and Timmer were convicted and received long-term prison sentences.

Criminal Investigator William C. Ward
Proving Innocent Someone who Appeared Obviously Guilty

We in CID have always been taught, and pledged not only to solve a case by identifying the criminal, but also to prove someone innocent of a crime, if that was the case. This was exactly that type of case Criminal Investigator William Ward worked. Two soldiers paid a visit to the NCO Club, and both had been drinking. One of the two was quite drunk and in possession of a Spanish made "Starr" revolver. Being denied entry to the club, due to their intoxicated condition, the drunker of the two decided he would shoot his way into the club. The two men struggled, the pistol discharged, and a witness saw one man standing with the weapon in his hand, as the other fell to the ground. Murder right? Not so fast. The projectile had entered the deceased's neck from the upper right side of his upper shoulder, traveling down through his heart and doing the fatal damage. The suspect swore he had not fired the weapon, but there did not appear to be any way the victim could have held the weapon in his right hand and fired the shot into his shoulder. Since it appeared to be an open-and-shut case, Ward was advised to close the case and let the courts decide the outcome. A check of the Autopsy Report and re-examination of the body indicated no way the wound could have been self inflicted.

Investigator Ward, based on a "gut feeling" did not give up, but obtained a similar pistol from the rod and gun club, and had two MPs of the same height, weight, and build as the suspect and victim, reen-act the "crime" as described by the suspect and witness several times. Ward discovered that with the pistol held in the right hand, and someone forcibly pushing the hand back and up, it would cause the pistol to swivel around, with the thumb entering the trigger guard, and when forced back the pistol would discharge in a position that could have caused the fatal wound. The MP acting the part of the vic-tim complained the hammer spur kept striking him at the base of his ring finger. A quick check at the morgue disclosed an indentation at the base of the victim's ring finger matching that of the hammer spur. The suspects contention that he had attempted to disarm his intoxi-cated friend, when the weapon discharged, was correct and the sus-pect was proven innocent, thanks to a job well done by a good CID Criminal Investigator. When his tour of duty in Germany came to an end, Ward had planned to retire and requested a terminal assignment to Japan. He was informed that he would be permitted to retire at his point of debarkation, New York or he could accept an assignment to Vietnam and then pick his terminal assignment. Ward accepted and was assigned to the Cam Ranh Bay field office, Vietnam, and became the author's roommate (a good one at that), eventually ending up as the OIC of the field office. Ward returned from Vietnam to Fort Mac Arthur, California, in December 1971, and retired from the U.S. Army in February 1972.

Criminal Investigator Russell M. Dunn

Eyewitness Descriptions
A Valuable Lesson He Never Forgot

Fifty years ago the ink had hardly dried on Criminal Investigator Dunn's credentials, when he learned a valuable lesson that he never forgot. He also learned that sometimes the key to bringing an investigation to a successful conclusion is a good break.

In the year preceding Investigator Dunn's active duty military career he was a patrolman on a small town police department. He was also a member of a reserve CID unit that was called to duty for the Korean war (excuse me "Police Action"). After attending military police school, CID school, and a short assignment in the states, Dunn was assigned to the 7th CID, Kokuro, Japan, with duty assignment to a two-man sub-detachment at Sasebo, Japan.

Early one morning Investigator Dunn got a call from the Japanese authorities notifying him that they had found the body of a Japanese prostitute whose last known customer was alleged to have been an American soldier. When Dunn arrived at the site of the discovery, a house of prostitution, he was shown the body of a young woman lying on a bed. Her body showed numerous wounds that appeared to be teeth marks and there were several puncture wounds in her pubic area that had possibly been made by a sharp, pointed, "rat-tailed" comb that was lying nearby. A handkerchief was tied tightly around her neck. Later it was determined that strangulation was the cause of death. Criminal Investigator Dunn interviewed the occupants of the house and the madam who told him that the victim's last customer had been an American soldier who had paid for an all- night stay. Her description led Russell to believe he was probably assigned to the Sasebo replacement depot in a casual status awaiting shipment to the United States after having served in Korea. The most significant part of the madam's description of the suspect was that he had red hair. The suspect had also asked if there were any girls who had resided there eighteen months earlier. The madam informed him that none of the current girls had been there back at that time. Dunn contacted the commanding officer of the replacement depot and within two hours Russell's witnesses and he were on the parade grounds viewing a lineup of over three thousand soldiers. The witnesses failed to identify anyone as a possible suspect. Over the next few days they also looked at all the military personnel boarding ships headed for the United States.

During all these lineups Investigator Dunn was totally focused on finding a redheaded subject. Dunn learned that a tour in Korea was for eighteen months for personnel who transferred to Korea from an assignment in Japan as opposed to a twenty four months assignment for personnel coming directly from the United States. This might be relevant in locating a suspect who had been assigned permanently to the area before going on to Korea. And, the suspect had reportedly asked if there were any girls available who had been there back eighteen months earlier. With this new lead Investigator Dunn started a process of checking old transfer records against current locator files. Back then there were no computer records and cross-checking was a slow hand process. Dunn had asked Japanese authorities to try to locate some of the earlier occupants of the establishment. They identified one girl at a house on Japan's northernmost island of Hokkaido. She remembered a redheaded man named "Johnny," who was a regular customer at the house in Sasebo. She reported that on one occasion Johnny, and three of his friends had caused a disturbance at the house and were arrested by the military police. Dunn retrieved all the old MP blotters and after meticulously searching through them found the names of four soldiers who had been arrested as reported by the witness. Further checking revealed that one of these soldiers was stationed at the replacement depot on the date of the murder. But he was one jump ahead of Investigator Dunn–he was aboard ship enroute to the United States. To add to Dunn's consternation his name was not Johnny and Dunn later learned he was not redheaded. Was Dunn on the wrong trail?

Nonetheless, Investigator Dunn pursued this lead. He was able to identify the unit where the suspect had been assigned back a year and a half ago. One of his friends was able to provide Dunn with a small snapshot of him and several others. The madam of the house positively identified him from this picture. With this identification the CID at Fort Lewis, Washington, took him into custody as he debarked the ship in Seattle, Washington. He was returned to Japan, where he subsequently confessed to the crime. He was later court-martialed and sentenced to confinement for thirty five years. How to account for the suspect not being redheaded? The subject had light brown hair, but when Criminal Investigator Dunn took him back to the crime scene and stood him where the madam had talked to him, the overhead amber fluorescent light showed his hair to be bright red.

One other most significant incident occurred at the time of the initial lineup of three thousand men. After the witnesses had viewed this one company of personnel an officer had come to Investigator Dunn and stated that one of his men was extremely nervous when the witnesses passed in front of him. He then went on to say that this person was not redheaded so Dunn had disregarded this bit of information, continuing the search for "Johnny with the red hair."

During one of the interrogations of the subject after he had been returned from the United States Dunn asked him about the lineup. He admitted that he was the person who had been referred to by the company officer. He said that he had wanted to run out and say he had done it but he also wanted to get home to see his family. So he stayed in place, nervous and frightened, and somewhat relieved when he was not identified. Dunn could have solved this case in hours instead of weeks if he had only questioned the eyewitness's identification. A most valuable lesson which stood Investigator Dunn in good stead in the years ahead.

Criminal Investigator E. "Buck" Ballow
Robbery and Homicide on Okinawa

The morning after the murder, the case was assigned to Criminal Investigator Jearl E. Ballow and Gene Bolton. A young U.S. Air Force serviceman had been found in the back streets of Koza, Okinawa, and rushed to the Ryukyus general hospital in Sukiran where he lived only long enough to say "A brother got me." He had been fatally stabbed during an armed robbery.

Unfortunately by the time Criminal Investigators Ballow and Bolton got the case the crime scene had been destroyed. By canvassing the area, the two investigators were able to track the airman to a nearby hotel and by searching his hotel room, identified him and determined he was on leave from Thailand. The only lead Ballow and Bolton had was the modus operandi used in the robbery.

For some time, about a dozen robberies had occurred in and around Koza where the victims were approached from the rear; a knife was held to the victim's throat; they were ordered to turn over their billfolds, and then ordered to lower their trousers. Investigators Ballow and Bolton's victim had two small, but fatal, slashing knife wounds on the neck, his trousers were around his ankles, and his billfold was missing. Ballow and Bolton made the assumption that if they solved the robberies they would solve the murder.

Investigators Ballow and Bolton pursued the case for two months and developed almost no information on the murder or the robberies. Then one Monday morning they had a visitor in their office, Private Bernadotte R. Gaines. He was a friend of the CID (of sorts) in that he would occasionally pass on minor bits of information. While Ballow and Bolton were talking to Gaines, a young marine, one of the robbery victims, passed their open doorway, stopped, and shouted, "That's the guy that robbed me!" pointing directly at Gaines. Investigators Ballow and Bolton quickly separated the two and had one of the other criminal investigators take a statement from the marine victim.

Investigators Ballow and Bolton began to interview Gaines, who offered to give them a statement, but when almost finished with the statement, decided that he had better get legal counsel. Ballow escorted him to the staff judge advocate (SJA) office, located next door to the CID office. Criminal Investigators Ballow and Bolton typed up Gaines' statement and they both signed it showing that the information therein had been subscribed to them after advising him of his rights, but not sworn to as the interview had been interrupted when Gaines requested counsel.

That afternoon Gaines returned to the CID office and said he wanted to talk to both Ballow and Bolton. They both told him they could not discuss the case with him since he had requested counsel. But that there were some other cases they needed to clear up and Investigators Ballow and Bolton proceeded on a plan, which would probably be illegal today.

Criminal Investigators Ballow and Boltin told Gaines of one of the other similar robberies, advised him of his rights, and when he declined counsel they interviewed him and solicited his confession. They did this systematically over the next few days, always going on to a new case and never reverting to any previous case about which he had already been interviewed. In that way, plus having a line-up, viewed by all of the victims, they were able to clear up twelve robberies. While all this was going on, Ballow made repeated calls to the SJA regarding getting Gaines legal counsel, to no avail, with each call recorded in his case activity summary. That would later prove to be crucial testimony in the case. Gaines was placed in pre-trial confinement and two days later attempted suicide by slashing his writsts. He was taken out of the stockade and placed in a hospital ward where he could be guarded at all times.

One afternoon Investigator Ballow received a call from Gaines asking that he and Investigator Bolton come to see him that night. He had something he wanted to get off his chest. Ballow and Bolton visited Gaines, and without prompting him, he confessed to the murder. Bolton wrote out the confession to the murder of the visiting airman, including the advising of his rights, on a notepad, and Gaines signed the confession. Gaines was tried by court-martial, found guilty of the offense of murder, and sentenced to life imprisonment at the Fort Leavenworth military prison. After the trial, Ballow met the judge at the "Little Club" and over lunch he lauded Investigators Ballow and Bolton for their efforts to get legal counsel to protect Gaines' rights. He also stated that the way they had gone about getting the confessions was probably the "neatest piece of legal chicanery he had ever witnessed," but it would hold up upon review. Another job well done.

CAMP ZAMA

Criminal Investigators Bunyan Johnson and William L. Garner
The Big Bully Wouldn't Confess

Criminal Investigators Johnson and Agent Garner (CID School classmate of the author) were members of the 521st MP Detachment (CI), Camp Zama, Japan, located near Tokyo, Japan, during the Fall of 1965, when they interrogated Specialist four McDonald, a strong suspect in a larceny case involving the theft of money. Sufficient evidence had been gathered placing McDonald at the crime scene, however it was not enough to get him convicted. During the interrogation

McDonald emphatically denied stealing the money from the footlocker of a fellow soldier, or being involved in the theft in any manner. Investigators Johnson and Garner, from years of experience, were convinced they had their man. No matter how hard they tried, or what technique they used, McDonald just would not confess. After some time had passed without success, Garner decided to apply an investigative technique he had successfully used in the past to obtain confessions from reluctant suspects willing to take a polygraph examination (that so-called lie detector). So with a certain amount of confidence Garner said "Are you willing to take a polygraph examination to prove your innocence" (right on). McDonald gave him a very simple reply "No." So much for proven techniques. Garner then stood up, made eyeball to eyeball contact with McDonald and said "Mac, I think you are a liar and a thief." McDonald, a fine specimen of a male at six feet eight inches and two hundred fifty pounds, rose to his feet and said "You know, Mr. Garner, I think you are a slob, how do you like them apples?" After McDonald had risen to his feet and made his remark, Investigator Johnson wasted no time in defusing the situation. He rose to his feet and said to McDonald "Mac, I know you are big, but we have equalizers for big guys like you." At that point McDonald became as meek as a kitten and sat down. Investigators Johnson and Garner never got a confession from McDonald, and the evidence they had was not sufficient to charge him. Investigator Johnson asked McDonald, before they dismissed him from the CID office, "Mac, what did you plan to do to Mr. Garner?" and he replied "Mr. Johnson, if it had not been for you, I was going to throw him out of that window." Not a pretty picture since the interview had been conducted on the second floor of the CID office. At the conclusion of the interview Investigators Johnson and Garner briefed the Operations Officer, Jim Moran and the Assistant Operations Officer, Jess Burdick, of the investigative results, and both thought the incident comical, especially Burdick.

Criminal Investigator Bunyan Johnson
A Criminal Investigator Got an Undeserved Ass Chewing

During the summer of 1966, Criminal Investigator Johnson and his counterpart in the Japanese police planned a joint raid due to the high drug and black market activities in the Camp Zama area involving

U.S. Forces personnel and Japanese nationals. The raid was to take place in the evening with search and seizure action to be done at a bar known for drug and black market activities and at several local residences of Japanese nationals and military personnel. About seven CID investigators and twelve to fourteen Japanese police officers conducted the raid. The raids were successful in that a large amount of drugs of all types were confiscated. In addition all types of U.S. liquor, such as Johnny Walker Red and Black, and both U.S. military scrip (currency) and Japanese yen were confiscated. Several U.S. servicemen and Japanese nationals, a total of about twenty subjects, were arrested and prosecuted. The unfortunate thing about the entire matter was that one of the CID special agents, who shall remain unanimous, became "the butt of the joke" because someone had forgotten to mention that a big mean german shepherd dog called one of the residences his home. When the Investigator entered that residence the dog, without hesitation or warning, bit him in the ass (ouch). Needless to say, the poor investigator not only had to feel the pain of the canine bite, but additionally had to suffer the indignity of much harassment from his fellow criminal investigators.

CHAPTER ELEVEN

Korea

Uijongbu

Criminal Investigator Oscar Michaud
A Bad and Racist CID Polygrapher

It was 1957, and combat had ended in Korea four years earlier. Criminal Investigator Oscar Michaud was assigned to the CID Sub-Detachment at Corps Artillery and very close to the Demilitarized Zone. It was a hot summer and the weather caused Michaud some problems in that he became very ill as a result of dehydration, resulting in his being hospitalized for two weeks at the field hospital in Uijongbu, which was also the location of the 19th MP Detachment (CI). After finishing his hospital stay, Investigator Michaud flew to Japan for a two weeks rest and recuperation (R and R) period. Upon his return to Korea, he did not return to the Sub-Detachment, but instead was assigned duties as the operations officer of the 19th MP Detachment (CI).

After his return Michaud did not have to wait too long for work even though he was the operations officer, he still worked cases to help out. He was the duty agent when he received a report from the military police (MP) that a burglary had occurred at the local post exchange (PX), and that several valuable items had been stolen.

Criminal Investigator Oscar Michaud was informed by the MPs that they were detaining a black soldier, Private first class Tom

215

Murray, whom they suspected of being the culprit. *First things first,* thought Oscar, and proceeded to the crime scene to determine how entry had been gained to the PX, what had been stolen, and what crime had actually been committed. Examination of the crime scene disclosed no signs of a forced entry, so it appeared that the offense was larceny.

Having completed his crime scene search, Oscar proceeded to the MP Station and picked up Private first class Murray, the suspect, to determine his involvement in the crime if any. Oscar had learned a long time ago that being a suspect does not necessarily make one a subject or guilty party. Being in the wrong place at the wrong time can make anyone a suspect. Investigator Michaud took Murray to his office and began to interrogate him in his usual mild manner, never raising his voice, but asking pertinent questions and treating the suspect as a human being. Oscar had learned a long time ago that you catch more flies with honey than vinegar, the key to success was to ask the right question at the proper time. Michaud questioned Private first class Murray for about two hours, and during that time, unknown to Michaud, his commanding officer, Captain Ken Halloway (Not his real name), had been listening in on his interrogation and subsequently told him that he was very pleased with his method of questioning. Investigator Michaud was still new in 19th MP Detachment (CI), and getting acquainted with his new commanding officer and fellow investigators. Halloway said to Michaud, "Have Moore give Murray a polygraph test." Bill Moore (not his real name) was a fellow warrant officer in the office and the polygrapher. CID polygraphers are criminal investigators and normally individuals who have worked as a "street agent" (working cases) and at some point decided to attend the CID Polygraph School (now the Defense Polygraph Institute) and then specialize in that field. Other criminal investigators opted to work in specialties, such as fingerprint examiner, crime scene and laboratory photographer, chemist etc. at the CID Crime Laboratory. Oscar Michaud was one of those criminal investigators who did not place too much value on the polygraph but preferred to use his interrogation skills to determine the facts of a crime. It should also be remembered that the polygraph is an investigative tool, an aid to the investigator, but not a substitute for good interrogation or questioning of a suspect, victim, or witness. A polygraph examination is also not admissible in court as evidence against an accused. Oscar, after completing his interrogation of Private first class Tom Murray, determined that Murray had been on guard duty at the PX, and prior to the alleged burglary had made a thorough check of the interior of the PX. All appeared to be in order at that time, in that he observed nothing out of order, at least from his vantage point. Murray told Investigator Michaud that he had not stolen anything from the PX, nor was he aware of anyone else who might have during the time he was on guard duty at the PX.

Investigator Michaud was convinced that as a result of his interrogation he had obtained the facts and that Private first class Murray did not commit the crime. Michaud was against giving Murray a polygraph test but at the insistence of his commander, Captain Halloway, he finally agreed to ask Murray if he was willing to undergo a polygraph examination. Murray, who had told the truth and after being informed how the polygraph worked, felt he had nothing to fear but only something to gain by undergoing the polygraph examination.

A few days after Michaud's interrogation of Murray he was given a polygraph examination by Polygrapher Moore. After completing the examination Moore informed Michaud that Murray had failed the polygraph test. Investigator Michaud was very much surprised but did not feel that his investigation was now complete, that the guilty party had been caught and all he had to do was to write his final report. Instead Investigator Oscar Michaud went to the PX and started to question some of the Korean employees of the PX. Funny how things sometimes turn out, because Oscar determined that a Korean PX employee, whose job it was to clean the bathrooms and other areas of the PX during the day, had failed to show up for work. Now it is not unusual for an employee not to show up for work at times but Oscar figured he might as well record the personal data on this particular employee, a Mr. Kim Sung Je, Kim being his last name.

Next Investigator Michaud got together with the Korean detectives assigned to his office providing the information on Kim to them. It took only about two days for Oscar's case to be solved. The Korean detectives arrested Kim while he was attempting to sell some of the stolen PX items on the black market and they subsequently got a confession from him that he in fact had stolen the items from the

Uijongbu PX. The Korean detectives determined that Kim had hidden in the PX at closing time, and after everyone had departed, stole several items and departed through the rear exit of the PX. How could this be compatible with the polygraph test results? Oscar was asking the same question and headed straight for Moore's office with whom he had a not-so-pleasant conversation. Oscar confronted Moore with the facts of the investigation, which of course now included some physical evidence that supported Michaud's original contention that Murray had not committed the crime. To the best of Michaud's recollection, Moore replied with words to the effect of "I don't give a shit, He's a God damn ... (Using a racial slur). Investigator Michaud reported the matter to Captain Halloway, who did not seem to care about Moore's remarks, apparently another racist. We can only be happy that it is rare to find characters like Halloway and Moore in the CID and normally they are found out sooner or later and kicked out of the CID. We all know that each police/investigative Agency has some bad apples that need to be disposed of. Unfortunately they sometimes succeed in doing harm to a "good guy" because he did not go along with their way of doing business. If Halloway and Moore had behaved in that manner after CID became a separate command, and the CID was no longer under the jurisdiction of the local provost marshall, disciplinary action against them would definitely have been taken.

About a day or two later, Investigator Michaud was notified by the colonel in charge of the MPs and CID, that his wife was ill and had requested Oscar's return home. The army would not approve his return and fortunately his wife's health soon improved. Criminal Investigator Michaud no longer had the desire to work for and with the likes of Captain Halloway and Chief Warrant Officer Moore, and managed to get a transfer to one of the CID units on Okinawa, Japan, with the assistance of the good colonel. This meant that his wife and four children would be able to join him on Okinawa. Korea did not have accompanied tours of duty for CID (meaning that the wife and children could not join a soldier). Little did Oscar know of the vengefulness of his former commander Captain Halloway.

Investigator Michaud arrived on Okinawa and thought all would be fine now and went about doing his job. About sixteen months into his tour on Okinawa Oscar Michaud received the surprise of his life, when he received a letter, dated 9 Oct 57, from Brigadier General David P. Shorr (the acting provost marshal general), office of the provost marshal general, Washington, D. C., informing him that if he continued to receive low efficiency ratings his days in CID would be over. In the General's own words "I sincerely trust there will be no recurrences of the previous instances of declining efficiency." Needless to say Oscar was in a state of shock, because he had always received above average ratings, either excellent or superior. Apparently this low efficiency report had been written by none other than Halloway, a case of vindictiveness you might say. When Criminal Investigator (CWO) Oscar Michaud's efficiency report was reviewed at OPM (Office of Personnel Management), Officer Branch, the not-so-good efficiency report came to light.

The review by OPM was done to determine if an officer or warrant officer was eligible for consideration to be promoted to the next higher rank, or should be included in a future RIF (Reduction In Force). In a RIF an officer or warrant officer would be discharged from the Army or revert to his prior enlisted rank. Fortunately this vindictive act did not harm Oscar but was taken care of in the proper manner.

Criminal Investigator Carl C. Craig
KN, KP, K9, HAWK Fiasco
Stolen Missile Guidance System

The following account of a potentially serious compromise of the Hawk Missile program, specifically in Korea but with implications throughout the U.S. military worldwide, highlights, once again, the importance of an investigator acting on intuition and following his gut-feelings which go beyond the teachings of criminal investigative procedures. This is one of those memorable "war stories" of Criminal Investigator Carl Craig.

Investigator Craig was assigned to the famous 19th CID Detachment, at Uijongbu, Korea, during the period August 1963 through October 1964. The 19th CID covered everything from Seoul north to the Demilitarized Zone. During this tour Craig also had the unpleasant duty of having to make physical security surveys of the classified MSA and tactical Sites north of Seoul.

Early one morning Craig was awakened in the "hooch" (quarters) and directed by the operations officer (the boss) to get down to the aviation Detachment and catch a chopper (helicopter) ride to a specific tactical Site to investigate the break-in of a Hawk Missile launcher van. The initial report indicated that the highly classified "guidance system" of the Hawk Missile had been removed from its secured console and was presumed stolen.

Now Investigator Craig was not one to add superfluous data to this incident, however; the irony of the matter was that the ride on the "bubble" two-seater chopper (like the ones you see in the TV Series MASH) almost ended in disaster. It seemed that in their haste to depart, the pilot had told his maintenance crew to "get a move on," at which time they evidently left a drain or bleeder valve loose on the hydraulic system they had been working on. Halfway to the Hawk tactical site the hydraulic fluid evidently leaked out and as a result the chopper couldn't be steered manually. The pilot auto-gyrated down to a nicely filled rice paddy where they sat for about thirty minutes before Craig was rescued by a Dust-Off (medevac) Huey chopper from the 406th Medical Battalion and taken on to his destination. On arrival at the Hawk site, virtually on top of a mountain, the commanding officer and numerous subordinates were awaiting Criminal Investigator Craig's arrival. They were totally puzzled over the fact that someone had gained access to a Hawk Missile launcher which had been up and running in the launch mode. The CO was totally bewildered that someone had shut it down and removed the guidance console which was the only top-secret component of the entire missile. The irony of it was the fact that this missile was being guarded by two supposedly ferocious German shepherd military guard dogs.

Entry to the van had occurred between midnight and 4:00 A.M. and was discovered in the "down mode" by a member of the missile crew and the dog-handler. An immediate alarm was given and all members of the site were summoned and accounted for. Interrogations had already commenced by the furious commander and his immediate subordinates. There were only about twelve U.S. military personnel on the site. Investigator Craig commenced interviewing them in backward order to establish the name of individuals and when they were last on duty.

The CO stated that he was suspicious, at first, that one of the men was playing a prank on another, but when everyone was confronted it was obvious that this was not the case. This was very serious business. At this juncture in the military situation in South Korea, the Hawk missile sites were on standby alert twenty four hours a day, year round. This missile was on the ready and would have instantly sounded an alert should its antennae have received enemy radar impulses. It could have been fired within minutes, but not this one. It was "dead," and the commander was visibly shaken. His career was on the line. Investigator Craig sensed that all of the military personnel were truly shaken by this matter. Craig realized that he would have to take them all back to Camp Red Cloud, one by one, interrogate them and run polygraph tests. He knew he was not dealing with a bunch of recruits. All of these personnel had "Crypto" and higher security clearances because the "tips" on those Hawk missiles were "very potent." Eighth Army was buzzing and the generals were now aware that the theft of the Hawk Missile guidance system, critical to the first line defense, placed the U.S. Forces in Korea in jeopardy and peril. This information sent alarms and shock waves all over the Far East Command and back to the Pentagon. Craig realized that as the CID investigator on the scene he was in the hot seat too! About two hours into his interviews, Craig discovered that the site had a mess hall. It was run by one U.S. sergeant and several Korean cooks and KPs. The last Korean cook or KP would normally have departed just after midnight after feeding the shift on duty. Since this was a twenty four hour operation, meals were served four times a day, around the clock. The mess sergeant had left earlier the night before and returned to his unit. Craig does not know how he conjured his next steps in the pursuit of the dilemma he was facing, but he felt that he had to try something else. He asked the sergeant in charge to get him the dog-handler. When he came forward Craig asked him to bring the two dogs that were guarding the missile. He and one other handler brought both dogs back to the scene on leashes. Investigator Craig asked the commanding officer to have all of the men who were on the site that night to assemble behind a building out of sight of the dogs. Craig then asked him to have one man at a time approach the dogs and to come as close to them as possible, making sure that the dog-handlers would not allow the dogs to actually attack the men. Craig was running a "familiarity test" between the dogs and each soldier on the site. As each man approached them, the dogs went into a frenzy, lunging as hard as they could at the men. Craig was thinking to himself, "Well, so much for this investigative technique." By now it was mid-day and all of the Korean cooks and KPs were on duty. The Mess Sgt. had also returned. Investigator Craig asked him to get all the Koreans together and one by one they were required to approach the dogs, which lunged furiously as each approached them. Craig's ploy was not producing any spectacular results. At this point Craig learned that there was a straggler amongst the Korean KPs, and when he was ordered to approach the dogs he expressed much reluctance to do so. Craig asked the dog-handlers to lead the dogs toward the KP. As they neared him they didn't react at all and never made a sound. Both dogs tugged gently at their leashes ambled over to the Korean KP and licked him on the hands. It was obvious that Investigator Craig had his man. Craig had the ROK (Republic of Korea) CID agent attached to the 19th CID flown in immediately and the KP was interrogated in the usual Korean manner which would normally cause any suspect to confess, whether he was guilty or not. The Korean KP confessed to feeding the dogs and entering the missile van on the night in question around 1:00 A.M. He emphatically stated that he had no idea whatsoever how to shut it down. He just "turned some knobs and switches" and it quit making noises. He then turned two latches on a metal cabinet and pulled out a console with all those transistors, thermistors, and instruments in view. He then decided to steal the component and sell it on the black market for whatever it would bring. He led the Korean police, ROK CID, and Investigator Craig to a Korean radio shop in the city of Tongdu-Chon, where he had sold it for the equivalent of fifty U.S. dollars. Little did he know that what he had sold for fifty dollars had probably cost Uncle Sam several hundred million for its development and production. The Korean radio shop owner had already partially disassembled the guidance control system but about ninety percent of it was recovered intact. Any one who served in Korea, then, or at another time, knows that once something is stolen its identity disappears within a matter of minutes for small things, and in just a matter of hours for a ten ton truck to be disassembled and dispersed. Or as we used to say in Korea, "Slicky boy can steal a radio and leave the sound behind." Needless to say, the immediate commanding officer and those all the way back to the Pentagon were relieved at the quick solution to this case. None were happier than Criminal Investigator Carl Craig. The big picture was that if the guidance system for the Hawk had been truly compromised to foreign agents it would have been detrimental not only for national security reasons, but untold millions of dollars would have been required to retool its radar and guidance systems to keep our adversaries from homing-in with their missile radar on our Hawk sites all over the world. The ROK Counter Intelligence Agency (CIA) took custody of the KP. Investigator Craig was confident that they soon knew when he was conceived, who conceived him, and what his great-grandparents ate for breakfast on July the 4th one hundred years ago. Of course there is an official case number, however, agent Craig refers to this case as his "KN, KP, K9, HAWK Fiasco" (Korean National, Kitchen Police, K-9 Dogs and HAWK Missile).

Failure to Pay
Special Agent Richard A. Denoo
The Wisdom and Good Training of a CID Agent

One night Special Agent Denoo was the duty agent and responded to the scene of an assault upon a Korean national female. Witnesses indicated that the perpetrator was thought to be an American soldier.

The crime scene was a blood-soaked bed and blood-smeared walls. The victim had been removed to a local hospital with her throat cut. Several Korean National Police were taking pictures of the crime scene. As agent Denoo watched, one of the Korean police officers began to climb onto the bloody bed. The bedclothes had not yet been taken from the bed for evidentiary purposes.

Investigator Denoo interrupted the police and very diplomatically offered to take the pictures with his state of the art crime scene camera and informed them that he would provide excellent copies for their use. They readily agreed and he had thus been able to stop them from totally contaminating the crime scene. Subsequently Denoo was able to obtain palm prints, which eventually led to the arrest of the soldier responsible for the vicious assault.

A carpet knife was found to be the weapon with which he had cut her throat. Due to the curved shape of the blade the knife had ridden over the neck tendons without cutting her major arteries. The victim survived. The soldier was sentenced and imprisoned in a Korean prison, which you might say is double punishment. What had provoked this vicious assault? As you might have surmised, not love, not money, but sex–or rather a failure to pay for services rendered.

Special Agent Robert F. Coucoules
A Pleasant Assignment Interrupted
Undercover Again, this time at Yongsan, Korea

What happens when you, as a CID agent, do a good job in certain types of investigations? You guessed it, you get selected again, and that is exactly what happened to Special Agent Robert F. Coucoules.

During 1973, he was assigned to the 6th MP Group (CI), Fort Lewis, Washington, and was happy with his assignment, thinking it would be his last post before his retirement. However, he was mistaken, because he was given an undercover assignment that he did not welcome.

Someone at USACIDC decided that Agent Coucoules should proceed to Korea as an assumed staff sergeant with a postal MOS (Military Occupational Specialty) with an assignment to the 16th Base Post Office located at Yongsan, Korea. Coucoules was to investigate suspected mail thefts occurring there. The U.S. Post Office Department was complaining about the excessive claims for undelivered insured mail that was emanating from the APO (Army Post Office) at Yongsan.

Coucoules proceeded to the Fort Lewis Logistic Center where he was issued uniforms and sergeant's stripes. Fictitious records and travel and assignment orders were also issued. It was decided that Agent Coucoules would pose as an alcoholic sergeant and that he would not be allowed to reenlist because of his alcohol problem.

When Agent Coucoules arrived at Yongsan, he reported to the 16th BPO (Base Post Office) first sergeant, who informed him that he was sorry, but he had no place for him to bunk at that time. Coucoules was left to fend for himself. He lived out of his duffel bag for the entire time he was there. He slept either on the floor or in any bunk which was unoccupied when someone was gone overnight. He was not too well respected, particularly by the first sergeant, as evidenced by the welcome he gave Coucoules upon his arrival.

Coucoules had to act like he was an alcoholic and not motivated, on the job or otherwise. He soon learned who the clique members and leaders were, and began to hang out with them as much as he could, especially in downtown Seoul where the stolen items were fenced and sold on the black market. Even though Agent Coucoules outranked the group members as a sergeant they thought of him as an equal.

Meanwhile, two U.S. postal inspectors, one from San Francisco and the other from Seattle, arrived in Seoul and took up residence in a hotel. Periodically Coucoules would make contact with them and provide whatever information he had developed.

Agent Coucoules stayed undercover for about one month and then on the appointed day, he went to his BOQ (Bachelor Officers Quarters), also located at Yongsan, and changed into his uniform wearing his rank of chief warrant officer (W3). Coucoules then met with the commanding officer and first sergeant and informed them of his true identity and mission. He then proceeded to walk down the length of the post office building so that all could see who he was. Many of the postal workers believed that he knew more than he actually did, always a plus for a CID agent.

Unfortunately, Agent Coucoules had never witnessed any thefts. When interviewed, some of the personnel admitted to things that Coucoules was not even aware of, but since almost all the violations had occurred before Agent Coucoules' arrival, and there was insufficient evidence to prove any of the cases, no charges were brought. It is significant to note that after his identity became known, and that he had been on an undercover assignment the rate of claims was drastically reduced, so the efforts were not a total loss after all.

Agent Coucoules later learned that the unit was renamed because of the stigma involved. Coucoules' days as a specialist in APO undercover investigations came to an end with his retirement on 31 July 1975 with more than twenty seven years of active duty.

Special Agent James E. Mercer
Good CID Agents Hate Crooked Cops
Justice Prevails

From the beginning of a CID agent's career it is instilled in him that "it is better to allow ten guilty persons to go unpunished than to be responsible for convicting one innocent person". This moralistic principle was a guiding force in countless investigations that Jim

Mercer conducted over the many years he served as a CID special agent. As Special Agent Mercer's career was drawing to an end, he was assigned to CID Command and assigned an investigation that would test and reaffirm the wisdom of this philosophy.

The Military Court of Appeals questioned the authenticity of a statement given by a soldier in Korea who had been convicted of murdering another soldier. The statement consisted of about a one-paragraph confession, which appeared to have been typed on one of the lousy portable typewriters in use at that time. The preprinted statement form required that the suspect be advised of his rights, under Article 31, Uniformed Code of Military Justice (UCMJ), and set forth what offense he was suspected of having committed. In this case "Murder." However, the word "Murder" was visibly darker and in bolder print than the remainder of the statement and appeared, even to the untrained eye, to have been typed on a different typewriter.

The statement was sent to the CID crime lab in Tokyo, Japan, and it was determined that the word "Murder" was not in vertical and horizontal alignment with the balance of the typed statement, indicating that the statement had possibly been taken out of one typewriter and placed in another to insert the word "Murder." This placed in question what the suspect had been advised of as to the nature of the crime he was suspected of when questioned. This prompted a review of the initial investigation and the matter was referred to the CID Command to resolve. The two CID agents who had conducted the initial investigation were still stationed in Korea.

The Court and Case file records were reviewed. It appeared that both the agents could have perjured themselves when they testified under oath that the suspect was advised that he was suspected of having committed murder, and that the word "Murder" was typed on the statement as part of the confession that the suspect signed.

Agent Mercer traveled to Korea to interrogate the two agents. One of the agents refused to talk to him without his attorney being present. The attorney would not permit his client to render a sworn statement regarding the issue. The second agent was on leave in Germany. He agreed to be interviewed and was given a polygraph examination. The results of the polygraph examination were inconclusive.

It was obvious that there had been some serious infractions during the conduct of the initial investigation in Korea. The validity of the initial investigation was further questioned when it was made known that the suspect had passed a polygraph test administered in Korea during the course of the investigation. It was the opinion of the polygraph examiner that the suspect was not deceptive in his denials of having killed the victim, who in this case was also his friend.

The suspect, a Native American, volunteered the following information, without objection from his counsel: On the evening in question he and his buddy had been at a Korean bar drinking. They engaged in some loud drunken discussions. When they left the bar he was too drunk to remember anything until he woke up in the hospital badly beaten and bruised.

The next thing he recalled was two CID agents interviewing him in the hospital and advising him that his buddy was dead. The agents told him that they knew it was an accident and that he didn't mean to do it, and that if he cooperated and gave a confession he would likely only be charged with aggravated assault. After repeated denials that he didn't recall what had happened he finally gave a statement.

The suspect acknowledged that he had been advised of his rights under Article 31, but denied that he was ever advised that he was suspected of "Murder". Since this was the key issue involving possible perjury charges against the two CID agents, the suspect was requested to take a polygraph examination. The suspect and his counsel agreed.

Robert A. Brisentine, Polygraph Examiner, was summoned from his job at the CID records repository in Maryland to conduct the polygraph examination. While the test was being conducted at the Fort Leavenworth prison, Agent Mercer received a phone call from his office at CID Command, informing him that they had just received word from Korea that two Korean suspects had been arrested and had confessed to the murder for which the American soldier had been convicted and was now serving time at Leavenworth.

It was one of the greatest pleasures Agent Mercer had ever experienced to inform the convicted soldier, that he would be released from prison in a few days, paid back pay, restored to his rank and be permitted to return to active duty if he so desired. He apparently was in a state of shock, because the only words that Mercer recalled him saying were, "Thank God, I didn't kill my buddy." Mercer has often wondered how the two agents who were responsible for this innocent person being convicted lived with themselves.

CHAPTER TWELVE

USA

Fort Belvoir, Virginia

Special Agent Henry H.G. Mungle
A Finance Clerks Error could have ruined an Officer's Career

A captain at Ft. Belvoir, Virginia was accused of travel fraud from several TDY (Temporary Duty) trips. Special Agent Mungle had a good relationship with the defense counsel at the staff judge advocate (SJA) office and on the day before the general court- martial was to begin counsel came to agent Mungle for a test as a last ditch effort to clear her client. Agent Mungle reviewed the investigative results and ran a polygraph test. The good captain was solid-no deception indicated. This result, in the face of the investigative facts, did not add up. So Agent Mungle took it upon himself to go to the finance office. Agent Mungle interviewed the finance clerk who had handled the accused's vouchers. Agent Mungle discussed the issues with the clerk and made him go back through the documents and prove to him that a false claim had been made. During this process the clerk discovered that he had made accounting errors and other administrative mistakes. Based on this new information, and the results of the polygraph test, the captain's counsel was able to have the commanding general drop all charges and clear his name on the morning that his general court-martial was to begin. So you see, sloppy work on the part of one person (the finance clerk) could have caused great grief to the captain, and good work on the part of another person (Agent Mungle) saved his day.

So in Agent Mungle's own words "Getting a confession gives great satisfaction. However, clearing someone accused of a crime is most rewarding, especially when the case facts show they did it."

Fort Totten, New York

Criminal Investigators
Walter "Walt" F. Junkins and Jack Whalen
Two Types of Polygraph Instruments
and the Phony Polygraph Examiner

In 1948, Leonard Keeler patented what became popularly known as the "lie detector", now known as the polygraph instrument. This law enforcement tool received widespread publicity and Criminal Investigators Walter F. Junkins and his CID partner, Criminal Investigator Jack Whalen, both members of the 17th CID, Fort Totten, New York, readily recognized its practical application. They were investigating a larceny of a "Hi-Fi" recorder stolen from the Service Club. They developed a suspect, a street-smart kid, who was quite evasive during his interrogation.

Investigators Junkins and Whalen discussed the newspaper article about the lie detector with their suspect and then asked him if he was willing to take a lie detector test. He agreed. Junkins and Whalen set about constructing and using their own version of a lie detector instrument. In collusion with the Operations Officer, Joe Kelly, Investigators Junkins and Whalen obtained an orange crate, covered it with green cloth and mounted a red light bulb in the center of the box. They then attached two strings to the bulb fixture- the second functional (or let's say Phony) "Lie Detector" was complete. They then placed their lie detector in the interrogation room, seated the suspect in front of it and instructed him to hold one string in each hand. They informed him that if he told a lie the bulb would light. They asked him his name, address and age, and of course the bulb did not light. Next they asked him, "Did you steal that "Hi Fi" recorder?" When he replied in the negative agent Whalen, the phony Polygraph Examiner activated the light. He readily confessed and took Investigators Junkins and Whalen to the pawnshop where he had disposed of the stolen property.

This story might have been titled: "The Criminal Had Connections, Saw The Light And Pulled Some Strings With CID" Investigators Junkins and Whalen often wondered if they could have been famous had they registered their invention with the U.S. Patent Office.

Fort Bliss, Texas
Special Agent Robert L. Cherry
Nothing Unusual Happened During My CID Career,
I Just Worked Normal Cases

Matters of the Heart

Matters of the Heart, but not in the romantic way you would normally associate with that remark. On 30 November 1973, a date Special Agent Cherry will never forget, he was involved in one of two ongoing operations being conducted by the Fort Bliss, Texas CID, aided by several military police investigators (MPI). One operation was a narcotics investigation, the other, to which agent Cherry was assigned, was an attempt to identify and arrest the subject of several robberies and aggravated assaults, which had occurred on a bridge leading to the main gate of Fort Bliss.

The CID had set up a plan enabling them to block off the bridge once the subject was identified, and this was done with one of the participants acting as a decoy. Sure enough the subject took the bait and robbed the decoy, whereupon, with the investigator in the lead, they converged on the subject. A scuffle ensued and Agent Cherry was stabbed in the heart but he was unaware that he had been wounded. The amazing thing is that immediately after the scuffle Agent Cherry subdued and handcuffed the criminal. He then began having problems breathing and grew faint. As he touched his chest he felt that it was wet and for the first time realized that he was injured.

Lucky for agent Cherry the military police immediately rushed him to William Beaumont General Hospital, Fort Bliss, and only minutes away from the crime scene. Agent Cherry credits the fact he is still amongst us to the skills and excellent work performed by the medical staff on duty. Agent Cherry recovered after an extensive stay in the hospital and is thankful that his guardian angel was watching over him.

Colonel Henry Tufts, Commander USACIDC, at the time, wrote agent Cherry a letter in which he said, "Although we all realize that our special agents face inherent dangers in their daily performance of duty, we rarely appreciate the extent of this hazard until it actually occurs; this is why I wished you to know of our concern for your welfare."

Just think, Agent Cherry was the one who said to the author, "Nothing unusual happened during my CID career; I just worked normal cases." Special Agent Cherry, what is a normal case?

Fort Lewis, Washington

Special Agent Courtland D. Bradbury

A Naked Woman in the Woods-Another Rape Investigation

While stationed at Ft. Lewis, Washington, Special Agent Bradbury was the duty agent, when he received a call about 4:00 A.M., this was about 1975 or, 76, from the MP desk informing him that some guards had reported finding a woman hiding in the woods without a stitch of clothing on her. It was in the middle of winter and snow was on the ground. Agent Bradbury arrived at the scene and found a woman that was just about ready to be taken by ambulance to the hospital. She was blue from the cold and unable to talk. She did manage to tell one of the guards that found her that she had been driven onto the post by a guy she met at the bar where she worked, that he had taken a shot at her and raped her. He had also tied her to a tree with her clothing but that she managed to escape when he apparently went back to the car to get his gun.

Agent Bradbury had another CID agent accompany the victim to the hospital to initiate the rape kit process, and to obtain as much information and details as possible about the rape.

Agent Bradbury, his fellow agents, and the MPs were not sure if the suspect was still in the area, and the guard could not recall observing a car leave the area. Agent Bradbury, his fellow agents, and the MPs searched for hours, and did find the spot where the victim had been tied up, with her clothes still at the tree. They also found the spot where the vehicle had been parked and some footprints. A crime scene was established, prints lifted, and photographs were taken.

By this time the victim was able to recount some of the incident to the other CID agent, enough so we had some leads to work on. The local police found the car of the suspect at the bar where the victim worked, there was a bullet hole inside the vehicle, and the police had a lead as to the identity of the suspect, by name and address. Agents from his office, FBI, and local Police went on a mission to apprehend the culprit. Agent Bradbury, on the other hand, tired as he was, interviewed the victim in detail and had his secretary take down the statement in shorthand.

The victim gave the following account to Agent Bradbury: She worked at this bar in Tacoma, Washington, and the suspect was a regular customer. During his visits to the bar she would engage in conversation with him and she knew that he was in the army. On the evening of the crime, the subject asked her to do him a favor, he told her he needed to take a gun from his off-post residence (where he was cohabiting) to someone on post who was going to buy the gun, and that he would pay her for her time. He convinced her to do this.

The victim drove the subject to his and his girlfriend's residence, and he picked up a 45 caliber semi-automatic pistol. She then drove him on to the post, where subject had her park her car on a back road, in back of the barracks, telling her he didn't want to be seen by the guards. She bought his story, and parked her car in a dark, secluded area, and waited for him while he went into the barracks to sell the weapon. Shortly thereafter, he returned and told her the person who was going to buy the weapon was not there. The next thing she knew was the subject holding a gun to her head and telling her to start giving him "a blow job." She of course told him no, and for him to get out of her car. At that instant, the Subject grabbed her, and in the process the gun went off with a round going over her head. Any fight in her suddenly left her, and she did as instructed. The Subject raped her, committed anal intercourse, and forced her to commit oral sodomy. After he was unable to get further erections, he forcibly took her into the woods, and took the few clothes she had left and used them to tie her to a tree, and made her perform oral sex once more. When he could not get an erection anymore, he got angry, and said something about getting his gun. He left her immediate area, and it was then that she had been able to get her hands untied and escape from the criminal. She ran very hard and had no idea where she was; she just knew she had to get away from the subject and did not even bother to pick up her clothes. The criminal was apprehended and convicted. He had left so many clues that a blind man could have followed him. It could well have ended up a murder case, had the victim not managed to escape.

Murder
Special Agent Courtland D. Bradbury
A Headless Corpse

Fort Lewis, Washington, 1976 and Special Agent Bradbury was the back-up duty agent, and would only be called if the duty agent received more than one call at a time. It was a nice afternoon on a weekend, when Agent Bradbury received a call from the MP desk, requesting that he respond to an area between Fort Lewis and McChord Air Force Base. It seemed that some human bones had been found and they might have located a body. Agent Bradbury arrived at the crime scene within thirty minutes, to find the duty agent and several MPs standing around what appeared to be a gravesite. Agent Bradbury observed two arms sticking out of the ground, mostly bones with fingers missing, most likely done by animals. One pressing item was to create a larger, secure crime scene, which had not yet been done, and since darkness was setting in, it was requested that the fire department provide some adequate lighting at the crime scene. Since this was still on government property, we felt it was within the jurisdiction of the army and therefore CID. Bradbury called the local county coroner and requested he stand-by while he and some of the MPs dug up the body. They had some shovels and very carefully started to dig and exhume the remains. The ground was soft and digging was easy, and when Agent Bradbury got to where he believed the head would be, judging by the position of the exposed part of the body, he was unable to get a shovel into the ground in that area. Bradbury and his assistants continued though, and exhumed the decomposed, headless body of a male, still wearing U.S. Army fatigues. A thorough search of the gravesite and area failed to disclose the head.

Agent Bradbury figured that someone had removed the head and fingers on purpose, to hide the identity of the victim. A check of the pockets of the victim's fatigues found the victim's military ID card in his shirt pocket; his nametag was still legible and identical with the name on the ID card. He determined that the individual most likely was a soldier that had been reported as AWOL (Absent Without Leave).

After some great investigative work on the part of agent Bradbury and his fellow agents, it was determined that the murder involved a drug deal gone bad. Three suspects, all black army soldiers, were involved when the incident occurred, but all had already been released from active duty. For that reason the FBI assumed case jurisdiction, and with the assistance of Special Agent Bradbury and his fellow agents, they arrested all three suspects. One of the suspects was still in the Fort Lewis, Washington, area, residing off- post, and he still had the victim's head in his freezer. CID never got the straight facts on why the head had been removed, but one of the subjects admitted that they were trying to hide the identity of the victim. They obviously were not too smart or they would have removed the victim's ID card and nametag. The subject that had the head in his freezer never disclosed why he had kept it. Another successful investigation conducted by the army's finest.

"Fort Carson, Colorado"

Criminal Investigator William C. Ward
A Convinced Recruit - The Case of the Barracks Larceny

It was 1964, at Ft. Carson, Colorado, and the 5th Infantry Division had just been reactivated and the post was crawling with troops fresh out of basic training. Criminal Investigator Ward was the duty agent, and received a complaint of a barracks larceny at one of the units. Now we all know how difficult it is to solve barracks larcenies with forty two suspects per bay. A wallet had been stolen from the wall locker of one of the recruits. Investigator Ward became an actor, who could compete with the likes of John Wayne. He did not just go about lifting the fingerprints quietly but made a big show of it, lifting the prints not only from the victim's locker, but also from some other lockers, all the time keeping up a little chit-chat with the victim about how easy this was going to be. Of course he talked loud enough for all the other recruits to hear him. Ward said "All I have to do is compare these prints with those of everyone in the bay, and I will have my man!" Of course all the troops around him heard this and also Agent Ward's reassuring the victim with "This is a piece of cake."

After lifting several prints with lifting tape, placing them on a three by five cards, showing them to the victim and commenting on what good clear prints they were, Investigator Ward closed his clipboard with a snap. He then turned his back towards the troops and said "Alright, the guy that took that wallet come with me"! Ward then walked out of the troop bay and, you guessed it, a very sorry looking recruit followed right behind him. Talk about bluffing people. When Ward got to the hallway he stopped, read his suspect his rights and asked him if he understood them, the suspect replied "Yes sir, and I'm sorry I took the wallet." Case solved.

To Disturb a General is Not a Good Idea
Special Agents Courtland Bradbury and Merle Kuhlman
The Late Shift on a VIP Protection Assignment

Fort Carson, Colorado, 1970 and a time when there were many anti-Vietnam war demonstrations. The biggest traitor of them all, Jane Fonda, was visiting Colorado Springs, Colorado, with the intention of marching on Fort Carson, Colorado. The post commander, a major general had received threats and of course CID was assigned to perform VIP security.

Special Agent Courtland Bradbury and Special Agent Merle Kuhlman were pulling the 2400 hours to 0400 hours watch and sitting in front of the general's quarters. They were sitting in one of those beautiful baby blue 1964 or 1965 model Fords that had seen its better days. On this particular vehicle the dimmer switch functioned as the siren switch (remember when cars used to have the dimmer switch on the floor?}. Unfortunately Agent Bradbury was sitting in the driver's seat trying everything to stay awake, when sometime around 0200 hours Agents Bradbury and Kuhlman heard this sick sound of a siren wailing. They couldn't figure out from where it was coming, and it took Agents Bradbury and Kuhlman about a full minute before they realized it was the siren on their own car. Agent

Bradbury apparently had accidentally stepped on the dimmer switch and activated the siren. They began throwing switches on the dash; Agent Bradbury had not driven one of these museum pieces for some time since the CID office had a lot newer model cars. Finally they managed to silence the siren but by that time the general was calling the MP desk wanting to know what was going on. Agent Bradbury had to endure a lot of harassment about this for some time.

What Powder?

Special Agents Courtland Bradbury and Ron Freudendahl
A Smart Ass Suspect

Fort Carson, Colorado, during the early days of Special Agent Bradbury's career as a CID agent, while an apprentice agent longing for the day when he finally would get his badge and credentials. Special Agent Ron Freudendahl was teaching Special Agent Courtland Bradbury the art of patrolling and being observant. They once again were checking the area around the "Corral Club" (enlisted club), when agent Freudendahl spotted what looked like a drug deal being made. Agents Freudendahl and Bradbury pulled up, and Agent Freudendahl got out of the car and walked up to the suspect and asked him what he'd just purchased from that other soldier. The suspect said nothing, and Agent Freudendahl identified himself as a CID agent and asked the soldier to empty his pockets. There was a small bundle that Agent Freudendahl took possession of and proceeded to open. When he had opened the bundle it revealed a small amount of white powder. Agent Freudendahl asked the suspect, "What's this?" and without blinking an eye, the suspect leaned forward and said "what powder?" at the same time he blew as hard as he could dispersing the powder. Fortunately Agent Freudendahl had been holding the bundle over the hood of the CID car and enough of the powder landed on the hood for Agents Freudendahl and Bradbury to scrape up and use as evidence. Understandably Agent Freudendahl was not too gentle when he placed the handcuffs on the suspect.

Stupid, Stupid, Stupider

Special Agents Courtland D. Bradbury and Ron Freudendahl
As close as being a Hippie as you can get and still be in the Army

Special Agent Courtland Bradbury was with the CID at Fort Carson, Colorado, and it was 1969 or 1970, when he was not yet a "full grown" agent, but an apprentice agent and the proud carrier of a letter with his photo on it introducing him and informing everyone that he was legitimate, you might say, and cleared to investigate.

Agent Bradbury was working with Special Agent Ron Freudendahl, and they had a quiet day and were driving a pale blue Ford, not exactly what you would call the pride of CID, and anyone looking at it would say, "Poor GI, can't afford anything better". Be that as it may, the Ford did have a police radio, a whip antenna, and a sticker on the dashboard telling the driver which button turned on the sick siren. It was the middle of the day, cold outside and agents Bradbury and Freudendahl were just riding around the post, for lack of doing anything better. Agent Freudendahl had a kind moment, and stopped the car and picked up a young man hitching a ride on post. This guy was about as close to being a hippie as you can get and still be in the army. He was carrying a backpack. After he got into the car, agent Freudendahl struck up a conversation with him, and the kid determined that agents (unknown to him) Bradbury and Freudendahl were alright guys, and so he wanted to sell them some dope. Agent Freudendahl being the cool person he was, told the kid that he was short of money, but that he could stop by his barracks and get some. That was cool with this dude, he had some pot that he wanted to sell and he needed the money. Now Agent Bradbury was sitting in the car taking all this in and really having a hard time not to burst out laughing.

Agent Freudendahl pulled the car up at the north end of the CID office; a two story building, with about six windows facing the parking lot they were sitting in. A big sign proudly announced that this was the 6th MP Group (CI), with the letters big enough that even an almost-blind person would have no need for Braille.

Agent Freudendahl got out of the car, left Agent Bradbury with this character, and walked into the CID office, with Agent Bradbury still having a hard time believing what was happening, with his six month's of CID experience. Agent Bradbury while looking at the CID office suddenly noticed that all the Agents were looking out of the windows at him, and Agent Bradbury could see they were breaking up. The "army hippie" seemed to be in "Never-Never Land" because he did not have a clue what was going on. Agent Freudendahl returned to the car, and told the kid that he could not find any money but he had found this instead and with that he pulled out his badge and credentials. Unbelievably, the dude still did not have a clue what was going on until agent Freudendahl put the handcuffs on him. That was when he finally realized that he had screwed up badly and was under arrest.

Never Mess with a Cool Headed CID Agent

Special Agents Courtland D. Bradbury and John Nettie What Are You Going to Do About This?

Special Agents Courtland Bradbury and John Nettie, while assigned at Ft. Carson, Colorado, pulled duty they referred to as "Goon Squad Duty." So they would drive around certain trouble spots and look for groups that might be asking for trouble, and it was their job to break it up before it began. One night, while on "Goon Squad Duty," Agents Bradbury and Nettie were walking past the "Corral Club" (enlisted club), when three black soldiers approached them, and one of then pulled a knife and held it to Agent Nettie's neck, saying words to the effect of "What are you going to do about this?" Agent Nettie calmly pulled his weapon, placed it at groin level of this wise guy, and calmly said "What are you going to do about this?" The black soldier turned white, dropped the knife, pissed in his pants, and Agents Nettie and Bradbury thought he was going to have a heart attack. He was arrested and punished.

Fort Polk, Louisiana

Criminal Investigator Weeden R. Nichols
Dumb, Dumb, Dumber

One cool winter night in early 1968 at Fort Polk, Louisiana, Criminal Investigators Denny Walsh and Weeden Nichols had the duty, and things were slow–a rarity. Walsh was a Cook County (Chicago, Illinois area) sheriff's police officer (with whom the author is well acquainted) who had been drafted and had been given non-school apprentice status in CID for his period of the draft (a program briefly used during the Vietnam war, to quickly increase CID manpower from the normal strength of one thousand two hundred to one thousand four hundred agents, called CAS–Civilian Acquired Skills).

Investigators Nichols and Walsh decided to go to agent Nichol's home, off-post (there was no post housing) for supper. When they got back about an hour later they found that there had been an armed robbery a half-hour before, only a half block from the CID office. The victim was a lawyer or CPA from St. Paul, Minnesota, who was taking his National Guard training at Fort Polk. The incident had occurred near a small enlisted men's club (EM club) located in the block across from the CID office. The trainee had been on his way to visit a friend and had gotten lost.

The victim described the perpetrator as tall, dark-haired with dark mustache and facial scarring, and wearing a gray sweatshirt. The weapon was a small black handgun with a white grip. Investigators Nichols and Walsh walked into the EM club and asked, "Anybody know the tall guy with the black mustache, wearing a gray sweatshirt, who was just in here?" Somebody said, "Oh, you mean Virgil Goasa. He just left. He's in the third barracks that way." Nichols and Walsh thanked the helpful individual and picked up Virgil. Virgil was a Specialist four back from Vietnam with a Silver Star, more than one Purple Heart, skin grafts that showed, and probably more that did not show. He was from Greenwood, Mississippi. Nichols enjoyed talking to him. He was a pretty honest guy, in his own limited way. Virgil denied everything. Next day Investigators Nichols and Walsh recovered the victim's wallet under the cement steps of a nearby barracks. Investigator Nichols dusted the plastic dividers for fingerprints. It contained no clear finger-prints, only smudges. He then wiped the dividers clean and applied his own prints, which he then lifted–very nicely.

Criminal Investigators Nichols and Walsh then summoned Virgil to the CID office again, showed him the wallet and the lifted fingerprints. Nichols explained to Virgil that he was going to roll his fingerprints and send them, together with the lifted fingerprints from the wallet, to the CID Laboratory where the examiners either would or would not iden-tify the lifted prints as his. Virgil then confessed and got a starting-pis-tol out of the crawl space over his bunk. Nichols walked him over to his orderly room, explained to his commanding officer what he had done, and added also how cooperative he had been.

Two days later Investigator Nichols was in the dayroom of the CID office playing a hand of pinochle during lunch, when one of the clerks told him someone was up front to see him. There was Virgil, hat in hand. Virgil told Nichols, rather apologetically, "Mr. Nichols, I don't think I should have confessed. I just remembered I was wear-ing gloves when I took that wallet"

Virgil got his discharge, just as scheduled. The victim got his money back and Investigator Nichols was happy, Investigator Walsh was happy, the victim was happy, and the army was happy.

"Fort Knox, Kentucky"

Special Agent Robert N. "Bob" ZaZa
Getting the Last Laugh-A Most Embarrassing Moment

Multiple break-ins had occurred at the enlisted men's golf course, Ft. Knox, Kentucky. The perpetrator(s) was using the golf course club-house like an ATM machine. On one of the break-ins it was learned from a witness that the suspect drove a 1956 Ford.

One night, while on duty, Special Agent Bob Zaza checked the golf course parking lot, and found a car that fit the description of the suspect's vehicle. No one was in sight, so in order to prevent the sus-pect from eluding apprehension Agent Zaza let the air out of one of the tires on the suspect's car. He then went to catch him in the act.

It is not known if the suspect saw Agent Zaza coming or if they managed to miss each other in the dark. What is known is that when the suspect saw his flat tire and the CID sedan parked nearby, he returned the favor by pulling the ignition wires on Agent Zaza's sedan. He then drove off in his car leaving a very frustrated Agent Zaza in the parking lot.

Agent Zaza had returned to the car when he heard the suspect start up his car, but was unable to pursue him in his now disabled CID sedan.

The story had a happy ending though. When it got light Agent Zaza followed the rubber marks and then scars from the wheel rim on the pavement as the tire disintegrated, right to the suspect's residence. The FBI was called, as the suspect was a civilian not under the jurisdiction of the CID, and an arrest was made. A few years later, at a reunion of the Criminal Investigation Agents Association (CIDAA), at Colorado Springs, CO, Special Agent Dick Slisz while telling war stories, asked Agent Zaza if he remembered when a fellow named Royal Jones had disabled his CID sedan and escaped. Agent Zaza's only reply was "God, not only do you remember one of my most embarrassing moments, but after thirty years you still remember the jerk's name." That's alright though, Agent Zaza made up for the embarrassing moment when he was assigned and worked the My Lai massacre case to a successful end.

Fort Jackson, South Carolina

Criminal Investigator Carl E. Craig
Aggravated Assault and Severe Identification Crisis

During the build-up to the Cuban Missile Crisis, (1961-1962) Criminal Investigator Carl E. Craig was assigned to the 89th MP Detachment (CI), Fort Jackson, South Carolina. Thousands of Spanish speaking men, supposedly to invade Cuba, were undergoing basic and advanced infantry training there. They were all volunteers; Cuban exiles, Puerto Ricans, and other Caribbean Islanders.

Just like any military town, there were numerous "beer-joints" at that time along Columbia's Main Street, patronized mainly by military trainees. The average young GI has a perceived theory that he has just got to project that "macho" image, and these Hispanic troops were no different! One weekend while Investigator Craig was on duty, he received a call from the MP desk to proceed to the post hospital ER where a Hispanic male trainee was being treated for serious stab wounds. Craig discovered that a soldier named Rodriquez (Not his real name) had been stabbed several times in the left side of his chest (missing his heart amazingly), and that he had suffered a multiply pierced left lung. He had lost quite a lot of blood, his left lung had collapsed and he was suffering from severe shock. He was in a semi-comatose state and almost totally incoherent.

Investigator Craig quickly summonsed a Hispanic MP sergeant and through his interpretation, discovered that Rodriquez had been stabbed by a soldier named Sanchez (Not his real name), somewhere outside a bar in downtown Columbia, South Carolina. Craig realized this could technically translate to a "Dying Declaration," as the attending doctors told him that Rodriquez might not live to make a written statement. Investigator Craig fully identified everyone present who had heard him verbally respond that a soldier named Sanchez was in fact his assailant. Craig pulled out all stops in attempts to identify Sanchez. In the interim period he received word from the city MP detail that a young female who worked at a bar on Main Street might shed some light on the matter. She was interviewed and stated that she had been seeing a young trainee by the name of Sanchez. On the same night in question this same Sanchez had come to the bar. He was intoxicated and had expressed himself very angrily. In a boastful manner, he told her that he was going to all of the local bars in search of a trainee by the name of Rodriquez. He produced a stiletto-type knife from his pocket, and stated that he was going to kill this Rodriquez individual, if he found him. Here's where things got tangled up to the degree you would not believe. This Sanchez did in fact wind up in a brawl in a nearby alley, and took a pretty good beating himself. He did not stab or cut anyone. Some of his buddies took him back to his unit dispensary and had him patched up. His clothes were torn and bloody. One of his unidentified buddies allegedly found the knife in his pocket, and threw it away. It was never recovered.

Over the next few days, Rodriquez showed signs of recovery (He did in fact fully recover). When he was interviewed at length, the whole story came into perspective. Rodriquez had got into a fistfight with a different trainee, whom he knew by the name of Sanchez, who did in fact stab him several times in the chest. He didn't know the first mentioned Sanchez existed. When the first mentioned Sanchez was interrogated, he readily admitted that he was just being "macho" and was trying to impress his girlfriend when he said he was going to kill someone by the name of Rodriquez. By freak coincidence he had just made up the name Rodriquez. He had no idea whatsoever that in reality, a trainee named Rodriquez had in fact been stabbed by another trainee named Sanchez, several blocks away from the affray that he was involved in. (What are the odds on something like this? Investigator Craig said, "I'd wager that winning the lottery would be a close second!")

The real (subject) Sanchez who actually stabbed Rodriquez was subsequently apprehended. The knife that he used was recovered from his personal belongings. He had cleaned it, however there was enough blood residue to establish a match with the blood type of Rodriquez. He confessed to stabbing Rodriquez, received a general court-martial, and was sentenced to five years confinement at the Fort Leavenworth Military Prison. Think about this! If in fact Rodriquez had died, the _first Sanchez_ would have logically been charged with murder, based on his statement to the girl and other circumstantial evidence, including the fact that the foreign blood on his clothing matched the "blood type" of the victim, Rodriquez! (No DNA checks back then). With this much evidence, Investigator Craig would not have had any reason to look for the second Sanchez

Army War College–Carlisle Barracks, Pennsylvania

Criminal Investigator James E. Mercer
Jump Starting Subject's Memory with Booze

Criminal Investigator Jim Mercer was the investigator in charge (AIC) of the CID office at Carlisle Barracks, Pennsylvania, during the late 1960s when his office had received several complaints regarding break-ins (offense: burglary) at the post exchange (military store) and mess hall. During one of the break-ins at the PX an orange-colored comb was recovered as evidence from on top of broken glass at the point of entry. The comb was identified as belonging to one of the soldiers assigned to the garrison. Numerous items of jewelry had been stolen from the PX.

Initial interrogation of the suspect failed to produce a confession nor did it lead to the recovery of any of the stolen merchandise. Another disappointment was the fact that the CID crime lab was unable to make a positive comparison identification of short black hair samples from the comb, with known hair samples from the suspect.

A few weeks later the PX was again burglarized and this time items of civilian clothing were stolen. Investigator Mercer and his fellow investigators were able to determine the size of the items of clothing stolen, because of the empty spaces on the clothing rack. There seemed to be an empty space in one of the areas (you know the typical identifying tags, small, medium, large etc.) Once again it was time to pay a visit to their burglary suspect, and as luck would have it Mercer and his partner found the stolen items of clothing in the suspect's locker. There was only one problem, when the suspect was asked to try on the coats recovered from his locker they were about two sizes too big for him. His explanation was "I like loose fitting clothes."

A relentless interrogation of the suspect by Investigator Mercer, got results when the subject finally admitted that he had broken into the PX and stolen the jewelry. The subject informed Mercer and his partner that he was willing to cooperate in returning the stolen property. He then informed them that there was a slight problem in obtaining the stolen property in that he could not remember where he had hidden the loot. Subject continued by explaining to Investigator Mercer and his partner that when he drank alcohol he would go into a trance and muster strength and vitality beyond that of a normal person. This was partially substantiated by the fact that when he stole a field safe from the messhall, he had broken a heavy chain which had secured the field safe to a steam pipe in the mess hall.

Mercer and his partner went along with the subject's fairy-tale explanation, and agreed to take him to a local drinking hole (bar) and buy him a few drinks. Of course Mercer and his partner were confident they would be able to recover their expenses out of the CID 0.15 Fund (Confidential Fund).

Now the subject was no dummy, he figured he might as well go first class, and so he said to Investigator Mercer and his partner "I might be able to remember a little quicker if I have a couple of shots of whiskey!" They were promptly served to the subject. Sure enough that worked! He finally lit up like a Christmas tree and told Mercer and his partner that he remembered he had hidden the money, jewelry, and other loot in "Promised Land." Since he was not sure where "Promised Land" was located, and Mercer and his partner did not want the subject to lose his train of thought, they quickly purchased a six-pack of Colt 44 and left the bar. The subject directed Mercer and his partner to a hollowed-out tree on post. After arriving at the designated tree, he stuck his hand up the hollowed-out part of the tree, and "Bingo" out came a wool glove insert filled with money. "Man, that's great" Mercer and his partner told the subject, followed by "Now where is the rest of the merchandise?" At this point the subject was in need of a memory refresher in the form of a Colt 44 beer, which was promptly supplied him by the two investigators. Not only did they supply him with the beer but also had the courtesy to open it for him. Subject then guided Mercer and his partner to an area under one of the barracks, however the search was negative. Subject was distraught that he was unable to recover more of the loot and remarked "Someone Done Stole from Promised Land."

Next Investigator Mercer, his partner and the subject moved on to the hallway of the barracks in which the subject resided. The army was in the process of replacing the old wooden footlockers with upright metal wall lockers, and for that reason the old wooden footlockers had been stacked up in the hallway, until they could be picked up and stored in a warehouse. The subject looked in a couple of the footlockers and "Bingo" he pulled out the stolen jewelry. Mercer and his partner were now happy, because not only did they get a confession, but now they also had recovered the stolen property and had hard evidence in that they had made nearly a full recovery of the stolen property.

Another successful investigation was completed. Subject was discharged from the Army under Section 8, as a "Nut." Now came the easy part, right? Just submit the paper work and get reimbursed for expenses from the .015 fund. Wrong, Mercer's boss told him "You must be out of your mind, if you think I'm going to reimburse you from the .015 fund for getting the subject drunk and obtaining an illegal confession." Investigator Mercer pleaded with his boss, telling him "The confession was obtained before we got the subject drunk! It was only the merchandise that was obtained under somewhat questionable circumstances." Mercer's pleading fell on deaf ears, his argument was to no avail, this meant he and his partner had to pay for the subject's booze out of their own pockets. Still, Mercer said, "It was some of the best spent-money I've ever donated!"

Ft Irwin, CA

Criminal Investigators Bunyan Johnson
and Maurice "Matt" Dillon
The Trading Post

Now Fort Irwin is one of the smaller army bases, located in the middle of the Mojave Desert and there is no big city life on hand. One day during the spring of 1965 Criminal Investigator Johnson went to the post photo lab to get some photos developed for one of his cases. The non commissioned officer in charge (NCOIC) of the photo lab wasted no time in informing Investigator Johnson that the base had a "wife-swapping club" in operation. He suggested that the military police or CID do something about this immoral action and violation of the law, before someone got hurt.

The NCOIC informed Criminal Investigator Johnson that many of the women were getting into big fights, pulling out each other's hair and threatening each other with knives because it seemed that they were fighting over one particular man (husband), an Italian gentleman, the "Italian Stallion." Apparently, in their opinion, he had the best equipment, provided the best service, and greatest pleasure.

Having been duly informed of a violation of the law, and illegal immoral behavior which could give the army some bad publicity, Investigator Johnson could not let it go in one ear and out the other, so he reported this matter to his boss, Major Murphy, the provost marshal (remember this was before CID command was created). Major Murphy, to the dismay of Investigator Johnson, came to the conclusion that it would be a good idea if he, Johnson, investigated the matter since he had gotten the information.

Criminal Investigator Johnson was in charge of this investigation, but got help in that Criminal Investigator Matt Dillon was instructed to work on the case with him. Since Fort Irwin was such a small and isolated post it was very difficult to infiltrate and conduct surveillance of any activity on the base, because everyone knew the CID investigators on base, and Investigator Johnson was the only black CID Investigator on base. To make matters worst, Johnson found out that one of the female participants was a co-worker of his wife's at the post exchange. This particular female spotted Johnson during one surveillance when he unsuccessfully attempted to duck in the CID car. The CID cars also stuck out like sore thumbs, because they were all the same type of car and all were painted white.

After Investigator Johnson was spotted the "lady" minced no words, approaching him and addressing him in language which, if printed, would soil this paper. The investigation was a success in that the allegations were substantiated based on statements of witnesses, however; no confessions were made. Those involved in the "trading business" were all non commissioned officers (NCO) and the co-worker of Investigator Johnson's wife was married to a first sergeant. All involved were identified reprimanded, transferred or moved off Post. The surveillance took place at the NCO club where the participants would gather and pull the key to their next lover's residence from a hat. Rumors had it that the same type of activity was taking place at the Officers' Club, which apparently came to a stop as soon as they became aware of the ongoing CID investigation.

The Presidio of San Francisco, California

Criminal Investigator Robert R. Meier
Assault Consummated by a Battery or was it Police Brutality?

During May 1955, while assigned to the 13th MP Detachment (CI), Augsburg (Bavaria), Germany, Criminal Investigator Robert R. Meier received orders assigning him to the 60th MP Detachment (CI), Presidio of San Francisco, California, with TDY enroute, to attend the CID school at Fort Gordon, Georgia. Now Meier had been accredited as a CID criminal investigator during Feb 1954, after graduating from the U.S. Army Europe (EUSAREUR) intelligence, military police school, and special weapons school, Oberammergau, Germany. He just had not attended the CID course at the provost marshal general's (PMG) school, for some reason a must during those times, even though the Oberammergau course was just as good. His experience and attendance at the Oberammergau CID course, prior to attending the PMG CID course paid off, because he graduated as the honor student of his class.

Meier arrived at San Francisco early in July 1955, and had never met his new commanding officer until he reported for duty to him. He got anything but a warm reception from Captain Robert E. Kruger; to the contrary, the first words out of his mouth were "So you're the honor student of the CID course!" Then he said, "You're late reporting in and you are out of uniform–you're now a specialist first class, not a sergeant first class.

In those days all enlisted CID criminal investigators, after attending the CID school, changed from NCO ratings to specialist ratings. Just as four years later, when the super grades of first sergeant (E8) and command sergeant major (E9) came out the system again changed and the former Specialist three (E4) rank became Specialist four (E4), Sergeant (E5) became Specialist five (E5), Staff sergeant (E6) became Specialist six (E6) and Sergeant first class (E7) became Specialist seven (E7) in CID. This was changed again a few years ago and today the only specialist rank left in the Army is Specialist four (E4), all other ranks are NCO ratings

So it was not a pleasant beginning for Investigator Meier and it appeared that someone with whom Meier had a brief encounter some time before, had not taken it too well and this individual had apparently poisoned the mind of Captain Kruger to the detriment of Meier. After some discussion, Meier finally convinced the good captain that with travel time and authorized leave, he had actually reported to the unit a couple of days early, not late. Meier also informed him that his rank was still sergeant first class and not specialist one because he had not yet been issued official orders converting him from sergeant first class to specialist one. This was the beginning of a short stormy relationship between him and Captain Kruger, and to the detriment of Investigator Meier. Not the type of relationship a subordinate wants to have with his superior, especially if that superior is his commanding officer and thereby in a position to cause much grief to the subordinate. Meier practiced being a covert investigator by staying out of the way of Captain Kruger as much as possible.

One morning, around the middle of September 1955, Chief Warrant Officer James T. Flower, the operations officer, called Investigator Meier into his office, and handed him an MP complaint report which indicated that a female civilian had reported an off-duty military policeman (MP), an enlisted man, for kicking her cat; "police brutality?" Meier, as any normal investigator would have, laughed and tried to return the complaint form to Mr. Flower, but Flower declared that Captain Kruger had instructed him specifically to give the complaint to Investigator Meier for investigation.

A little befuddled, Meier returned to his office and handed the complaint to his partner, Criminal Investigator (SP2) Sam Lister. Sam was just as dumbfounded as Meier had been, and asked him, "what are we going to do?" to which Meier replied "Investigate."

Meier and Lister interviewed the accused MP, who readily admitted having kicked the cat. He explained that he was dating the complainant's roommate. On the evening in question he had escorted his date back to her apartment, as a gentleman would, and while they were standing inside the door, the cat had approached him and rubbed against his ankle in what appeared to be a friendly act. Thinking the cute cat wanted some affection and to be petted, he had reached down to pet it. The cat turned on him, by clawing his hand and drawing blood. Impulsively, he gave the cat a swift kick and transported her through the air and out of his vicinity. He willingly provided a sworn statement, which indicated he acted in self-defense.

The military policeman's date and her roommate, the complainant, were also interviewed and statements were taken. The owner of the siamese cat stated that she had taken her cat to a veterinarian, who determined the siamese cat had sustained no injuries as a result of the incident. Criminal Investigators Meier and Lister asked the complainant for a copy of the veterinarian's report, which she gladly provided.

All attempts by Investigators Meier and Lister to interview the cat were unsuccessful as she would only reply with "meow" in Siamese and no cat interpreter was available. Having completed the investigative portion it was now time to write a draft case report. Now let it not be said that Investigator Meier had lost his sense of humor, the question would be "does Captain Kruger possess any sense of humor?" Meier would soon find out.

In the spot were normally the CID report number appears, Meier put "KAT" and in the offense block he put "Assault Consummated By a Battery", with the MP's name appearing in the "subject block" and the cat appearing in the victim's block of the report. As I stated, Meier had not yet lost his sense of humor and so he reflected in the "substantiation" portion of the report "The victim was not interviewed due to the lack of a Siamese interpreter." Sam Lister, his partner, who had been assigned to the unit for some time and was more familiar with Captain Kruger, adamantly declined to have his good name appear on the draft report and, as it turned out, for good reason.

Meier soon found out that the good captain grossly lacked any sense of humor. Meier gave the draft report to Mr. Flower, who immediately passed it on to Captain Kruger. It did not take long and Meier was informed that the captain wanted to see him. He entered his commanding officer's office and soon found himself standing at attention, feeling bite marks in his rear end as Kruger commenced to chew his ass. That was not the end of it, not only did Meier get chewed out, but the good captain accused him of insubordination and relieved him of his badge and credentials.

About twenty minutes later Meier was ordered to report to the provost marshal, Lieutenant Colonel Saxon. When Meier arrived at the PM's office, Captain Kruger was already there and the good colonel was reading Meier's draft report of investigation. Needless to say Meier expected the roof to come crashing down on him. After Lieutenant Colonel Saxon had finished reading the report he asked Meier "Did you write this report?" and Meier replied "Yes sir." Meier then felt great relief when the good colonel, who obviously possessed a sense of humor, said "This is the funniest thing I have read in a long time. May I keep this?" Being somewhat in a state of shock, and at the same time feeling relief, Meier replied once again "Yes sir." Lieutenant Colonel Saxon then turned to the humor-lacking Captain Kruger and instructed him to return the badge and credentials to Agent Meier, and in the future, to assign only criminal matters to his investigators. This of course did not do anything to make the captain like Meier any better than before.

Criminal Investigator Meier's enlistment was due to expire the following month, and having seen the handwriting on the wall, he figured it was time to escape from the claws of Captain Kruger into friendlier territory. He took his discharge on 24 October 1955, drove to Washington D.C. with intentions of getting out of CID and re-enlisting for helicopter school, but found out he could not re-enlist for that school, but that entering the school was on a competitive basis. While in DC he talked to Major Al Carbone, chief of CID for the Transportation Corps who offered him a job with CID at Fort Eustis, Virginia or Brooklyn Army Terminal. Meier decided that he was going home to Rochester, New York, first and go hunting with his dad. He did just that and went to Canada with his dad, where they did some duck hunting. Lieutenant Colonel Thomas Guidera had been Meier's boss during 1951, as a Major, when he was the provost marshal at Fort Meyer, Virginia. Guidera talked Meier out of leaving CID and he then accepted the assignment at Fort Eustis, and re-enlisted on 7 December 1955. Meier was promoted to warrant officer during October 1960 and retired as a chief warrant officer (W4) on 1 July 1979.

Schofield Barracks, Hawaii

Criminal Investigators Robert J. Woods and Alex Freitas
You might say this wife really screwed him

It was a nice sunny day in "Paradise" in 1971, and Criminal Investigator Robert "Bob" Woods was thinking how lucky he was to be stationed in "Paradise." It was time to go to work and so he proceeded to his office, at the 102nd MP Detachment (CI), Schofield Barracks.

Bob had been working on a larceny case and as all CID Investigators had his informants. On this occasion he had a meeting with a prominent local prostitute, known to him as Linda Smith. Linda provided Bob with some good information on his larceny case and then like a gentleman Bob escorted her off-post. That finished his contacts with Linda for a while, or so Bob thought, but he was in for a pleasant surprise and in this case Linda most likely became an unwilling supporter of his investigations.

It was about a week after Bob had talked with Linda regarding his larceny case, when another informant tipped him off that a certain Staff Sergeant John Slickey was living in an apartment in Waipahu and was receiving the temporary lodging allowance (TLA). Further that his wife was not with him in Hawaii, a "no no", because in order to be authorized to receive the TLA, a service member must have his family with him in Hawaii or any other place in regard to the TLA rules.

Investigator Woods thought it might be a good idea to pay Staff Sergeant Slickey a visit and find out if the informant was bullshitting him or if Slickey in fact was committing the offense of fraud against the U. S. Government. No sooner said than done and Criminal Investigator Wood with partner Criminal Investigator Alex Freitas were on their way. They arrived at the apartment before noon, and announced themselves by knocking on the door. Boy, was Bob in for a surprise when the door opened; it was none other than Linda Smith. She said, "Hello," calling the investigators by their names, and then asked what the occasion of their visit was, or in other words, what did they want. Bob told Linda "I'm looking for Staff Sergeant Slickey," and Linda replied "He lives here, but he is not home right now." However she did say that she expected him home in a few minutes. She then asked Bob and Alex if they would like a cup of coffee, and wait. Of course Bob and Alex agreed.

A few minutes later the door opened and in walked the totally unsuspecting John Slickey. He looked at the two strangers in his home and Bob at that time introduced himself and his partner. The uninformed Slickey underestimated the knowledge of the two CID Investigators in his home and said "I'm glad my wife gave you some coffee." Had his real wife been there she would most likely have poured hot coffee over his head. Bob did his thing by advising Slickey of his rights, who then asked, "What is wrong?" Whereupon Bob informed him that he was suspected of the offense of fraud against the U.S. Government. Bob then told Slickey that he knew Linda Smith quite well and that he had several contacts with her at Schofield Barracks. At that point Slickey got a shocked look on his face and just said "Oh."

Investigators Woods and Freitas informed Slickey that he was under apprehension and that they were going to take him to the CID Office at Schofield Barracks. Faced with such clear evidence against him Slickey made a full confession in the form of a written statement, and was then released to his unit. Slickey's commanding officer was informed that he was being charged with the offense of fraud against the U. S. Government and that a CID report of investigation would be forthcoming. Slickey was given a general court-martial (the highest military court). He was found guilty as charged, reduced to the grade of private, and sentenced to two years confinement at Leavenworth. All that for the privilege of calling a prostitute his wife.

Schofield Barracks, Hawaii

Special Agents Robert J. Woods and Ron Ammon
A Fatal Traffic Accident, a Conspiracy, Larceny and Fraud—
All in a days work

It was the Spring of 1972, and Special Agent Bob Woods was still stationed in "Paradise," but by now the CID had been centralized with the establishment of USACIDC, and Bob had gotten used to his new title of Special Agent. Special Agent Ammon was not Bob's regular partner, but he had worked well with him on several prior cases. This time they would leave the island of Oahu and head for the big island of Hawaii to investigate a fatal accident that had occurred just outside the Pohakaloa training area (PTA). Ron Ammon had been told irregularities were suspected in the way the military clubs were being managed on the big island, and this normally meant someone was stealing from the system in one form or another. It seemed like a good time for Agent Ammon to go along to the big island since he could use the fatal accident as a ruse to cover his real intentions of looking into the club management.

Off they went, via TWA (in this case "Teeny Weenie Airlines" in the form of an Air Force L-19 aircraft from Wheeler Air Force Base, Hawaii.) They arrived on the big island during the afternoon and immediately went to work investigating the fatal traffic accident. An M-151 (better known as a Jeep), with a 90 mm recoilless rifle mounted on it had rolled over, killing one soldier who was riding in the back. It was determined by the doctor on duty at PTA, that the soldier had died of a broken neck. Agents Woods and Ammon questioned the sergeant riding in the vehicle that was following the accident vehicle, and he told them that as his vehicle came over a hill he had observed the overturned jeep. He stopped and ran to the most seriously injured soldier (the deceased) and attempted to clear his breathing by moving his head around, not a good idea with someone who has a broken neck. Possibly the soldier could have survived if he had been handled properly at the scene of the accident, but the sergeant meant well and Agents Woods and Ammon did not have the heart to tell him what the cause of death was.

Agents Woods and Ammon finished their work in regards to the accident and then asked if there was a good place to get something cold to drink, and they were directed to the NCO club on post. Both proceeded to the club and sat at the bar and told the four bar tenders on duty that they were on the island to investigate the fatal traffic accident, and that they just wanted to relax for a while before working on the accident case some more.

They swallowed the story and Woods and Ammon had a free hand to observe any and all irregularities that occurred at the club right in front of their eyes.

During their presence at the club, over approximately the next three hours, they observed the bartenders run a slush fund (in other words bypassing the official cash register), pre-pour drinks and then dump them in the sink when no one ordered what was poured. They also got a number of bottles of whiskey from the storeroom with absolutely no accountability, and sold cigarettes and other bar items with absolutely no recording of the sales being done. Agents Woods and Ammon asked the bartenders where the club manager was, and they were told he would be in later. When they told the two agents the manager's name, Ammon was not surprised to hear the name of a club sergeant he had busted previously, when he was managing an NCO Club at Fort Shafter, Hawaii, for promoting prostitution in the club. When the sergeant finally came, the bartenders told him that the two agents were just relaxing after working on a fatal traffic accident investigation, but I'm sure his heart was beating a little faster.

The good club managing sergeant tried to get on the good side of Agents Woods and Ammon by telling them to stick around because he had arranged for some girls to come in later. Ammon thought *Gee, I wonder what type of girls he is going to bring into the club this time.* The two agents left and the club closed as it normally would at the end of the day. Special Agent Ammon submitted his CID report of investigation and the good sergeant was relieved of his duties as club manager and did not manage another club on Hawaii thereafter. A complete audit was subsequently conducted by HQ, U.S. Army Support Command, Hawaii (USASCH).

Special Agents Bob Woods and Ron Ammon left the club in their rental car for their motel at Hilo, to get rested up for the next day. The next day they were on their way to the Kiluea Military Camp (KMC), a joint services (Army, Air Force, Marines and Navy) rest and recuperation (R and R) camp, currently under the command of an army major. The first thing Bob and Ron tested was the liquor sales package store. They entered the store and were told by the manager that only authorized military personnel were permitted to purchase alcohol (per regulation), which of course was considerably cheaper there than in the local economy. I guess he thought that explanation would take care of things and the two agents would be on their way, but he underestimated CID. Bob and Ron positioned their rental car about a block from the package store, in an inconspicuous manner, and directly behind the unsuspecting camp commander's office. They got out the binoculars and 35mm camera with telephoto lens and, not really to their surprise, began to observe some interesting activities. It seems the store manager had lied to them when he stated only authorized military personnel were permitted to make purchases because a good number of known civilians were entering the store and exiting with bags full of merchandise. Bob and Ron made notes and took photographs.

That evening Agents Woods and Ammon went to the club at the R&R center and sat at the bar. The bartender on duty was very meticulous in running the bar, but had one bad habit; he was overcharging the customers who purchased cigarettes and cigars. Bob and Ron asked the bartender, "When do you have "happy hour" at this club" and were promptly informed that there were no "happy hours" at that club. Now this was very odd and raised the suspicions of both agents because they knew that all clubs had "happy hour" on designated days and at designated hours. Being familiar with the process of "happy hour" the two agents paid the local liquor distributors a visit on the next day. They were told that it was their practice to provide both the club and package store, with free cases of whiskey and other beverages, with the number of free cases being based on the number of cases the club/package store purchased. Bob and Ron of course knew that the free whiskey was used to offset the cost of "happy hour," and was also used for lower prices on special and promotional sales at the package store. Needless to say their suspicions were raised to a higher level. For the next three days, without interruption, the two agents continued their surveillance of the package store, made notes and took additional photographs without apparently raising anyone's suspicions, that is until the fourth day. On the fourth day a major came out of the back door of the headquarters building and approached the two agents, and introduced himself as the camp commander. Bob informed him that he was Mr. Woods and his partner was Mr. Ammon, and that they were both with the CID. The major asked "Can I be of help to you?" to which Bob replied "No, we are only watching some illegal purchases being made at the camp package store." The major then requested that the two agents come with him to his office. Agents Woods and Ammon told him they would see him a little later, this of course was done for psychological reasons, not to let the major think he had any type of command power over the two agents. About an hour later the two agents waltzed into the major's office. He indicated to them that it was not possible that anything illegal was going on at KMC since he ran a tight ship. He must have thought the two agents were blind because his ship obviously had a few bad leaks.

Special Agents Woods and Ammon informed the major of their observations and instructed him to bring in the managers of the bar and the package store, and to inform them to bring along their inventory and purchase records. In the presence of the two agents the good major summoned the two managers and instructed them as requested. After both managers had arrived, the major had another surprise in store for himself, when he and the managers were advised of their rights by the two agents.

A check of the inventory records from the package store failed to reflect any entries that the package store had received any free whiskey or other liquor from the distributors, nor was there any listing in the bar records to that effect. Funny, since the distributors had informed the agents that free whiskey had been supplied to the bar and package store. What did they do with the free whiskey? In particular since they did not have a "Happy Hour." You might suspect that at that point all three, the major and the two managers, after being advised of the conversation the agents had with the distributors, were having a very "Unhappy Hour." The two sergeants indicated this by stating that they had nothing more to say. Agents Woods and Ammon dismissed the two managers and continued their conversation with the major. He asked both if they would like to have some coffee, they said, "Yes please" and the major called for a carafe of coffee to be brought to his office. When the major attempted to pour the coffee into the cups, he was shaking so badly that he spilled coffee on his leg, which was far from the cups. He excused himself, to go to the rest room, and told the two agents that he had had a bad night. Agent Ammon replied "It's not half as bad as this day is going to be for you!" When the good major returned, the two agents continued to question him about his sergeant managers. He indicated that they were very thrifty because one of them drove a brand new Lincoln Continental, the same as he drove, and Bob thought *Sure paid with money from the free whiskey.* When both agents just looked at the major he became really nervous and asked that they end the conversation, since he had nothing further to say. The package store was closed, and the bar did not reopen until a full audit was conducted by HQ, USASCH.

The two agents prepared a CID report of investigation listing the camp commander (the major) and both sergeant managers as subjects for the offenses of conspiracy, larceny, and fraud. Another job well done and true to the CID motto "Do What has to be Done".

Ft. Benjamin Harrison, Indiana

Special Agent Albert F. "Al" Kaan
Two Officers and Not Such Gentlemen

Special Agent Al Kaan was assigned to the CID Office at Fort Benjamin Harrison, Indiana, at that time the Army Finance Center and Personnel Training Center. Now Fort Benjamin Harrison was a very small post by army standards.

It was during the summer of 1982, while Al was the duty agent, when he received a call from Captain (CPT) Mary Jones (Not her real name), who was employed at the Equal Employment Opportunity (EEO) office on the post. She was one unhappy lady, because she could not find her precious diamond ring, which not only was very valuable but also had great sentimental value for her. The good captain could not say if she had taken the ring off in the bathroom while washing her hands, or if it just had slipped off her finger without her noticing it. Of one thing she was sure, that she had worn the ring when she went to work at the EEO office that day and now it was no longer on her finger and she had no idea where it was. After listening to Captain Jones, Al said to himself, *why am I here? There appears to have been no crime committed so there is no reason to open a CID case regarding this incident.* However, due to the value of the ring, which was in the neighborhood of about five thousand dollars, and the possibility that Captain Jones had taken the ring off in the bathroom or in her office, had laid it down and someone had then stolen it was real. Al thought it prudent to at least assign a CID sequence number, so the situation could be monitored.

Now any CID agent will tell you that it is not smart for any crook to leave or send notes, because they have the nasty habit of turning into evidence. Several days after Agent Kaan had talked to Captain Jones, she called Al and told him that she had received a note–constructed of letters cut out of a magazine–stating that the return of her ring would cost her two thousand five hundred dollars. She was instructed to respond by placing an ad in the personal section of the Indianapolis newspaper. Al knew the note came from the real thief, because it described the ring in detail-and the design of the ring was very unusual. Now Agent Kaan had good reason to open a CID investigation, since the offense was not only larceny but also extortion. As requested by the thief a response was placed in the newspaper with the request that the thief provide a photo of the ring (which might possibly contain the fingerprints of the thief), and it was stated that the owner of the ring would pay the two thousand five hundred dollars in return for getting her ring back. A photo was indeed received a few days later and it reflected a true image of the beloved ring.

The notes and responses were all placed under the windshield wiper blades of the victim's car in the parking lot at her office. Agent Kaan figured if that was the way the thief was going to communicate, it might be the trap that would slam down on the mouse's head. So a continuous surveillance of the victim's vehicle was established from a building closest to her car, which at the same time would give the agent on surveillance a good view of the parking lot and the victim's car. Unfortunately the nearest building to the car was still a few hundred yards away from it. It didn't take long before an individual was observed placing a note under the windshield wiper blade of the victim's car, and Agent Kaan thought, *now we will know who the thief is.* Unfortunately he was to be disappointed, because the photos of the person depositing the note snapped by the surveillance agent were not sharp enough to identify the messenger and possible thief.

258

As luck would have it, one evening it was Agent Kaan's turn at surveillance, and since the last photos turned out a disappointment, he came better prepared in that he brought a much better camera than had been available at the beginning of the surveillance. Kaan observed an individual whom he knew to be a commissioned officer, but not such a gentleman. It was none other than Captain John Snead (Not his real name). Agent Kaan knew this because he had previously apprehended and interrogated Snead concerning an unrelated incident. Captain Snead approached the building and met another commissioned officer, who worked in this building, along with the victim and both entered the building. Since this meeting had occurred after hours it appeared significant. Al Kaan suspected that the thief and extortionist was someone who worked in the building, and who knew the victim. This was based on the circumstances under which the ring was stolen and on the contents of the initial extortion note.

During the course of the next six weeks several communications and responses were exchanged, but CID was never able to identify the criminal(s) positively. Specific instructions for the exchange of the ring for money were received by the victim and the criminal(s) clearly indicated they would not do this on post, instead they chose a parking lot at a nearby SafeWay store. Agent Kaan decided that he would have to use the victim to make the exchange, because using a CID agent or someone else would cause the deal to go bad. Agent Kaan was pretty sure the criminal(s) knew the victim and would recognize her at the agreed upon exchange location, and would also suspect a trap if someone else showed up. An agent was secreted in the victim's vehicle and heavy security–consisting of both CID agents and deputies from the local Sheriff's Department–was established in the area where the exchange would take place.

The surveillance team was equipped with both video and still photo camera equipment, and all the members had to do was just have patience and observe. Finally an individual approached the victim's car. The individual talked with the victim for several minutes and she gave the long-awaited signal that she had seen the ring. The co-conspirator then walked away from the car without having made the exchange of the ring for the money. It should be mentioned that the CID command had denied the use of funds from the .015 fund (confidential fund) for this purpose. This did not stop agent Kaan; he just got inventive and took some of his own money, cut green paper, and covered it with real bills to make it look like a bundle of money. The suspect had not walked away from the victim because he had discovered the dummy cash, however. This was a great cause of concern to Agent Kaan.

As soon as the co-conspirator had gained some distance, between himself and Captain Jones's vehicle, Agent Kaan and a deputy sheriff approached the co-conspirator, and flipped their badges at him. As soon as he saw the law enforcement badges, he threw his hands in the air and spilled his guts. He told Agent Kaan and the deputy what his involvement was with the ring. It was soon determined that this fine gentleman had just recently been released from the big house (state prison). He was gainfully employed at a local pizza place as a delivery man and was a co-worker of Captain Snead. Snead was the individual whom Agent Kaan had observed, entering the building where the victim's office was located, after duty hours and meet another captain during the surveillance of the victim's car on post. This wonderful specimen of an officer had recruited the ex-con to be his delivery boy, for pay of course. The ex-con was supposed to meet the Captain at a local restaurant and turn over the money to him. The first thing Agent Kaan did, of course, was to secure the ring from the ex-con.

The captain was subsequently identified by the ex-con, and it was none other than Captain Snead. He was apprehended in the restaurant when he met with the ex con, and taken to the CID office. He was the same Captain Snead whom Agent Kaan had apprehended some time prior to the theft of the ring. On this prior apprehension Captain Snead, who was a student attending the officer's advance course, had to be in compliance with the army weight program to complete the course and also prevent being discharged due to overweight. Snead had a big problem with excess baggage (by being significantly overweight), so he came up with a brilliant plan; at least he thought so, by offering the first sergeant a bribe to alter the records of the weigh-in, so that he would appear to be in compliance. The first sergeant was outraged that Snead had dared even to think of bribing him, and had reported the incident to his superiors. As a result a CID case had been opened and Agent Kaan had interrogated Snead, who then confessed to attempted bribery. He appeared before the post commander who, under the provisions of Article 15 of the Uniform Code of Military Justice, had given Captain Snead a punishment, which was non-judicial punishment. The Article 15 punishment effectively ended his career as an army officer because it would have stopped him from getting promoted, so apparently he had sought employment at the pizza place that also employed the ex-con. You might say Snead had been burned and become interrogation-shy as a result of his first confession to Agent Kaan.

As a result of interrogating the ex-con, and the fact that tell-tale documents were found in the wallet of Captain Snead, Captain Smith was identified as the one who actually stole the ring. Captain Smith was a friend of Captain Snead, and had stolen the ring from the bathroom of the EEO office, where the victim had taken it off while washing her hands and had forgotten it. It was also Captain Smith who had set the extortion scheme in motion. This thieving captain was a co-worker of Captain Jones and had previously admired her ring, and had been a suspect from the beginning, but at first there was no evidence to link him to the theft. Captain Smith was also apprehended and declined to answer any questions, as did his cohort, Snead.

Justice was served, because both, Captain Snead and Captain Smith, were tried by general court-martial, the highest type of court in the military, and both were dismissed from the Army. Both appealed their case to the Military Court of Appeals and lost.

What made the investigation difficult was the fact that Fort Benjamin Harrison was a very small post by army standards and everyone seemed to know everyone else. The primary thief in this case, Captain Smith, was married to a lieutenant who was the aide to the post chief of staff. For that reason great secrecy about the investigation had to prevail and the local command was not briefed until the thieves had been bagged.

Fort Hood, Texas

Special Agents Richard W. Smith and Jack Mize
The Saga of the Break-in, or how Agent Smith's Career almost ended in two weeks

It was December 1977, and Agent Richard Smith was attending the CID basic course at the military police and CID school, Fort

McClellan, Alabama (now located at Fort Leonard Wood, Missouri), and in a matter of days he could call himself a "graduate". It was not an easy school, but he had overcome the first hurdle when he had been accepted into the CID program, providing he successfully graduated from the CID school, which he did a few days later. He went home to California on leave to spend Christmas with his wife and children and his parents. It was a well-deserved vacation after the difficult days of trying to make it through CID school, and his pride was showing when he got home. He was now officially a United States Army "apprentice" CID agent, and soon would be in receipt of a set of credentials and a brand new shiny CID badge to prove it.

Agent Smith was assigned to Fort Hood, Texas, not exactly a place where he could just ease into his new career. Fort Hood was the home of the 1st Cavalry Division and the 2nd "Hell on Wheels" Armored Division, additionally there were several other major units in Fort Hood, totaling about forty two thousand troops and their dependents, which came to around eighty thousand citizens. You could say it equaled a good-sized town. To take care of police matters there was the 545th MP Company, assigned to the 1st Cavalry Division, the 502nd MP Company, assigned to the 2nd Armored Division which would deploy with their respective divisions if called upon. And of course there was the Fort Hood military police, which controlled the military police station and came under the post provost marshal. All three MP units worked together as a team and had their hands full on weekends and paydays. Agent Smith was assigned to the Fort Hood CID district office, with an authorized agent strength of forty agents. Unfortunately the authorized strength had nothing to do with reality because normally, at any given point there were only twenty-five agents present for duty, due to temporary duty (TDY) commitments, leave, and school attendance.

Agent Smith reported to Master Sergeant (MSG) Vic Deavers, a CID agent with years of experience and the chief of the investigative support section, Fort Hood CID district office, Sixth Region, USACIDC. Master Sergeant Deavers asked Agent Smith "What is your CID sequence number?" Now what kind of a question is that? thought Agent Smith and so his reply to Deavers was "Huh," This really impressed Deavers, who got on the phone and called someone at CID command, with whom he obviously was very familiar. Agent

Smith only picked up Deavers side of the conversation and heard words like "dummy" and "rookie agent" that hurt. A few minutes later, Master Sergeant Deavers wrote a number on a piece of paper and told Agent Smith to engrave it in his brain because it was like his "CID Social Security Number." He then instructed Smith to go and see the operations officer, Chief Warrant Officer (W4) George Cain, who wasted a total of about thirty seconds on Agent Smith, just enough time to inform him that he was going to be assigned to the Housebreaking/Larceny Section. He instructed him to report to the boss of that section, Special Agent David Glenn. Now you would think that Glenn was going to receive Agent Smith with open arms, after all he was gaining another special agent in his section, but Smith was going to be disappointed, because all he could decipher was something to the effect of "another damn rookie agent." He did not even have the courtesy to call him by his official title of "Apprentice Special Agent." Agent Smith soon found out that Agent Glenn's section consisted of only two experienced agents, Glenn and Special Agent Freddie McBride; the rest were all apprentice agents.

Special Agent Smith had been at the CID office about two weeks, gaining experience you might say in cleaning the duty agent's room and making coffee for the wheels (experienced agents). However he had not been to a crime scene yet, because that was reserved for the duty team, and as a "rookie" he was not fit for that job yet.

One fine afternoon his immediate boss, Special Agent Glenn, called him into his office in the presence of Special Agent Freddie McBride and Jack Mize, Jack having attained the status of experienced apprentice agent, with three months of experience under his belt. Agent Smith was aware of the fact that Mize had been working on a series of housebreaking incidents in the Comanche Village housing area on post. He had succeeded in identifying the culprit, a teenager, Donnie Brakes, the son of Staff Sergeant Johnny Brakes, assigned to one of the 1st Cavalry Division units. Unfortunately Staff Sergeant Brakes was in the field a lot, and therefore doing little in the form of discipline when it came to "junior." According to his mother, Donnie was her baby who "could do no wrong." This "junior gangster" had been picked up by the Military Police and CID as a strong suspect, but it always seemed there was either not enough physical evidence or it was a case where no action was taken. This kid was driving residents and the law enforcement folks on post nuts with his escapades.

Once again a housebreaking was reported and the CID duty team responded and processed the crime scene. This time it seems luck was on the CID's side, because at the crime scene they recovered a piece of sheetrock that had been kicked out by the culprit, which had a beautiful perfect impression of a tennis shoe on it. The duty team also found out that the son of Staff Sergeant Brakes, Donnie the "junior gangster," had been observed in the area where the crime had occurred.

The case was assigned to the Burglary/Housebreaking Section, and Special Agent Dave Glenn assigned it to Agents Jack Mize and Dick Smith, with a combined CID experience of three months and two weeks, wow. Now Jack Mize was no dummy and figured that if he could get Donnie Brakes's tennis shoes, the case would be solved. He was sure of this because the tennis shoe impression on the sheetrock was of such magnificent quality that it would be a cinch for the crime lab to match it to Donnie Brakes's tennis shoes. Good idea, now all they had to do was to get the tennis shoes.

Special Agent Glenn thought it a good idea if both Agents Mize and Smith worked on the case, to gain some valuable experience as to how a good CID case is worked and solved, and also so he could check off another block on both apprentice agents' monthly evaluation report. This would go on for one year, the required period a new agent had to serve in CID on probation as an "apprentice special agent." If he made it he would become a full fledged CID agent and get his real credentials, without the word "Apprentice" on them. Agent Mize, the senior of the two agents, instructed Agent Smith to return to the CID office at 1900 hours (7:00 P.M.) and they would then proceed to Staff Sergeant Brakes's quarters and attempt to confiscate Donnie's tennis shoes as evidence. But first they would both go home and eat supper; after all it was easier to think on a full stomach. Agent Smith went home for supper and was really excited that he finally would get the chance to do some real detective work.

No sooner said than done, and Agents Mize and Smith were on their way to Staff Sergeant Brakes's on post quarters. While enroute the two agents discussed their course of action, and Agent Mize told Agent Smith about his prior contacts with Donnie. Mize told Smith he was hoping they would get sufficient evidence, physical and through interviews of witnesses, to nail the "junior gangster," and with a little luck have the entire family kicked out of their on-post quarters, thereby preventing further crimes in the future.

It was around 1915 hours (7:15 P.M.) when the two agents arrived at Staff Sergeant Brakes's quarters. Mize knocked on the door, and Staff Sergeant Brakes opened it. The two agents identified themselves, not that Mize really needed to because he was already familiar to the Brakes household, and entered the quarters. Brakes was still dressed in his fatigue uniform (field uniform), and the name of the uniform matched his mood and appearance. He obviously was fatigued from the constant training cycles his unit was going through, and now he had the pleasure of a visit by two army CID agents in his living room to end another perfect day for him.

Agent Mize explained to Staff Sergeant Brakes that Donnie was suspected of having committed the offense of housebreaking and that evidence found at the crime scene had the impression of a tennis shoe on it. He wanted Donnie's tennis shoes, so he could prove that Donnie was responsible for the housebreaking or prove that the imprint was not that of Donnie's shoes, thereby clearing him of any wrongdoing. Staff Sergeant Brakes was agreeable and told Donnie to go upstairs and get his tennis shoes. This is when all the "fun" started. Donnie obeyed his father and went upstairs, however when he came back downstairs he was not carrying the tennis shoes, but was wearing them. Agent Mize said to Donnie, "You have to take the tennis shoes off," and Donnie reacted by dashing towards the front door. Agent Mize grabbed Donnie and the fight was on. Staff Sergeant Brakes stepped in front of Agent Mize, which enabled Donnie to duck behind his mother and she moved out of the way. Agent Smith attempted to grab Donnie when Donnie's sister, Mary, grabbed him around the waist. Now the waist of a CID agent, adorned with his pistol, is dangerous "off-limits" territory to infringe upon, and Smith, thinking Mary was attempting to grab his weapon, smacked her in the face with the result of a bleeding nose. At that point Staff Sergeant Brakes came charging at Agent Smith, and in addition to that problem the family dog, apparently hungry, attempted to take chunk of meat out of Smith's lower leg by attaching his teeth to it. At this point Staff Sergeant Brakes made a big mistake by taking a swing at Agent Smith's face. He reacted in 007 fashion by pulling his weapon and telling everyone, except Mize of course, to "freeze;" and he did not mean for them to get the shivers. Donnie and his mother ignored Agent Smith's command. Smith managed to get to the telephone, and call the military police desk sergeant who started to go through his routine telephone answering drill. Agent Smith just about had enough and yelled at the desk sergeant to send some back-up. The desk sergeant asked Smith "where are you?", a good question that he could not immediately answer, but it came back to him and he screamed it out at the desk sergeant. While all of this was going on, Staff Sergeant Brakes was giving Agent Smith dirty looks and the impression that at any moment he was going to pounce on him. All this time the family dog was still attached to Agent Smith's leg. Smith managed to shake the dog loose from his leg and he handcuffed Staff Sergeant Brakes. Agent Mize got his wish and had Donnie under firm control, while Agent Smith used Mize's handcuffs to adorn the wrists of Mrs. Brakes. At the same time he instructed Mary to sit down on the living room floor, she complied apparently thinking one bloody nose was enough for one day.

Finally, while all this was going on, the MP duty officer, First Lieutenant Jones, a military police reserve unit officer on his two weeks annual active duty, in civilian life a police officer with the El Paso, Texas police department, just outside Fort Hood, had arrived at the scene, along with two MP patrols. Staff Sergeant Brakes wasted no in time complaining about what had occurred, and accusing Agents Mize and Smith of having used excessive force and police brutality. He expressed his desire to file an official complaint against the two agents. First Lieutenant Jones listened to Brakes's complaint, and being a cop in civilian life, said to him "As far as I'm concerned, these two gentlemen are federal agents, and they had the right to shoot not only you but your whole family!" Agents Smith and Mize thought *this is just what we need, someone with a can of gasoline pouring it on the fire.* Agent Mize instructed the MPs to transport the entire Brakes family to the MP station and detain them there.

While Agents Mize and Smith returned to the CID office they discussed the incident and made sure they would both relate the same facts of the incident. After arriving at the CID office, they informed the duty agents of what had occurred and called their immediate boss, Special Agent Dave Glenn. A little while later Special Agents

Glenn and McBride arrived at which time Mize and Smith informed them in detail of what had occurred.

The next thing that happened was what we would call the "domino effect" and "cover your ass" because Staff Sergeant Brakes contacted his commanding officer, complaining about the "police brutality." His commander called his superior, and he in turn called the brigade commander— the "domino effect." Now comes the "cover your ass" effect, because the first thing the brigade commander did was to contact the commanding officer of the Fort Hood district office, Lieutenant Colonel (LTC) Jon W. McFarland who arrived at the office along with the operations officer Chief Warrant Officer (W4) George Cain. Based on Staff Sergeant Brakes's complaint of "police brutality," Lieutenant Colonel McFarland and Chief Warrant Officer Cain deemed it appropriate to initiate a "commander's inquiry" regarding the actions of Agents Mize and Smith at Staff Sergeant Brakes's quarters. By now it was 0200 hours (2:00 A.M.) and Agents Mize and Smith were starting to feel the heat when they were advised of their legal rights. They had gone from special agent to "suspect," not a good feeling. Both Mize and Smith had a funny feeling in their stomachs and were somewhat scared to say the least. However, they felt they had done nothing wrong, they had conducted the investigation properly, and that it was Staff Sergeant Brakes and his family members who had caused the problem. For that reason both of them provided sworn statements to a couple of seasoned CID agents from their office. After that they both went home and to bed, it took Agent Smith a while before he fell asleep, because now he was worried about getting bounced out of CID, or worst, possibly going to jail, not a pretty thought.

Four hours later they were back at the office, ready and willing to start another day as special agents doing their job. Agent Smith assisted Agent Mize in preparing the laboratory request forms in hopes that the end result would be a laboratory report that clearly stated the impression of the tennis shoe on the sheetrock was made by the tennis shoes they had confiscated from their suspect Donnie Brakes. They turned over the laboratory request, the sheetrock and the tennis shoes to the CID evidence custodian, so he could forward it to the criminal investigation laboratory at Fort Gillem, Georgia. In the meantime telephone calls were made to Third Region Headquarters, at Fort Gillem, Georgia, and to CID headquarters at Falls Church, Virginia reporting the apparent misbehavior by the two "rookie" agents, who really did not want the publicity at that stage of their career.

For the next several weeks Agents Mize and Smith felt as if they had been afflicted with leprosy, and they were on pins and needles. It seemed almost as if they had become "persona non grata" in the office, because hardly anyone had the desire to converse with them or be seen with them. But relief was just around the corner in the form of a laboratory report, which finally arrived clearly stating that the tennis shoe imprint on the sheet rock matched the tennis shoes confiscated from Donnie Brakes. Both Mize and Smith breathed a little relief but felt they were not completely out of the woods. But further good news arrived from the staff judge advocate (army lawyer) at Third Region, who after careful review of all facts presented him stated that in his opinion neither Special Agent Jack Mize nor Special Agent Richard Smith had done anything illegal during the course of their investigation at Staff Sergeant Brakes's quarters. On the contrary, he recommended that charges be filed against Donnie Brakes and Staff Sergeant and Mrs. Brakes. The commanding officer of Staff Sergeant Brakes wasted no time in taking action against him and the post commander directed that Staff Sergeant Brakes and his family vacate their on post quarters.

Agents Mize and Smith felt redeemed, and a funny thing happened, they were instantly cured of their leprosy, and people in the office became friendly again. Such is life.

Forty Year Old Mystery

Criminal Investigator Carl E. Craig
He still followed the CID motto "Do What Has To Be Done"

You have heard the U.S. Marines say "Once a Marine Always a Marine." I suppose the same is true for CID agents, "Once a CID Criminal Investigator/Agent, always a CID Criminal Investigator/ Agent" and it seems they never stop being true to the CID motto "Do What Has To Be Done." CID Criminal Investigator (Retired) and South Carolina State Police Lieutenant (Retired) Carl Craig did just that.

On 11 April 2001 South Carolina's leading newspaper *The State* ran a front page article that is seldom heard of: "Forty Year Old Mystery—Retired Cop Breaks 1961 Murder Case." The featured retired cop was none other than CIDAA long-time member and retired U.S. Army CID Criminal Investigator Carl Craig of Columbia, South Carolina, who is also a retired lieutenant (criminal investigator) from the South Carolina State Police System.

On 1 March 1961, while Criminal Investigator Craig was assigned to the 89th MP Detachment (CI), Ft. Jackson, Columbia, South Carolina, a "State Cab Company" driver was reported missing, after failing to come home the night before. The cab driver was a retired former mess sergeant at Fort Jackson, South Carolina. His cab was found abandoned on a downtown Columbia, South Carolina, Street. There was blood on the back of the driver's seat, and remnants of his wallet strewn about the back seat and floor of the taxi. The cab's meter showed a very long trip had been made. This scenario was indicative of an apparent robbery and probably grievous bodily harm to the driver.

The Columbia, South Carolina city police processed the cab, assuming that this would be in their area of jurisdiction. Two days later, as a result of an organized search, the body of the cab driver was located about thirty miles south of Columbia in rural Richland County. At that point the Richland County sheriff assumed jurisdiction and opened a homicide investigation.

An autopsy of the cab driver revealed that he had been shot in the back of the head at close range. The single projectile had fragmented into three pieces, and entered his brain. The fragments were retrieved and taken to the state police crime lab. The ballistics examiner rendered a conclusion that the bullet was copper-coated lead, and was fired from a 32. caliber H&R revolver. Carl remembered this case well, but had not been actively involved in assisting the sheriff and his investigators at that time.

On or about 5 March 1961, the sheriff came to the Fort Jackson CID office seeking assistance in locating a soldier who had purchased a .32 caliber H&R revolver on the afternoon of 28 February 1961 at a local pawnshop. A CID investigator accompanied the sheriff to the unit where the soldier was supposedly assigned, and discovered that the soldier in question was AWOL. This fact alone gave rise to the soldier in question being a logical suspect.

On 29 March 1961 the soldier, Edward Freiburger, was apprehended for hitchhiking by the Tennessee State Police. Upon being searched he was found in possession of the .32 caliber H&R revolver that he had purchased the day before the cab driver was murdered. The AWOL soldier was remanded to the custody of the military police at Fort McPherson, Georgia.

The sheriff retrieved the H&R revolver directly from the Tennessee trooper who had apprehended Freiburger. The revolver was taken to the state crime lab. The examiner rendered a verbal report the following day that he had made a 90 plus percent match, however, as we are all aware, ballistics is a 100 percent science, so the examiner was reluctant to render a solid conclusion that the weapon the soldier purchased on 28 February was the actual murder weapon. The sheriff attempted to have the FBI reexamine the revolver but they declined. The bureau (FBI) at that time, and probably now, refuses to make second examinations of firearms.

In the interim period, attempts were made to have Freiburger transferred from the Fort McPherson stockade to the Fort Jackson stockade. The staff judge advocate declined to honor that request.

The sheriff was able to interview Freiburger at the Fort McPherson stockade about two months after the crime was reported. He failed to elicit any statement whatsoever from the suspect. Freiburger was tried for being AWOL and for other offenses, and was sentenced to one year and one day to the U.S. Army prison, Fort Leavenworth, Kansas. The sheriff re-interviewed the suspect six months later and secured an eighty two-page statement. The contents of that statement were very damaging to the subject.

The sheriff had ironclad evidence that Freiburger had in fact bought the revolver on 28 February. He did admit to buying the revolver, but lied emphatically about the date he had bought it. The sheriff had a solid circumstantial case, but apparently chose not to take the case to a South Carolina grand jury to seek an indictment. With all the evidence the sheriff had, Investigator Carl Craig was totally surprised that the sheriff did not take the case to the grand jury.

Criminal Investigator Craig remembered that when he had left Fort Jackson for the 19th MP Detachment (CI) in Korea in August 1963, this case had not been resolved. Craig retired from CID on 1 September 1969 at Columbia, South Carolina, and had totally forgotten about the case. After serving another twenty two years as a criminal investigator for the State of South Carolina, he retired again.

In 1996 Investigator Craig actively involved himself in the election committee of the current sheriff. During the campaign Craig and the sheriff talked about the thirty-six unsolved murders in Richland County over the past forty years and the need to establish a cold crimes squad. Investigator Craig agreed to volunteer his services on a *pro bono* basis in this effort. Investigator Craig's candidate won the election. Six months later Craig was on the job working two days a week, reviewing specific cases that showed some potential for being solved. Investigator Craig's first case was assigned by the sheriff and he resolved that it had in fact been a suicide, and not murder as originally suspected.

In September 1999, one of the current lieutenants in the sheriff's investigation division, who had known Craig for over twenty five years, casually asked him if he remembered a case in the 1960s when a taxi driver had been killed. Craig responded that he certainly did and gave the lieutenant the name of the victim.

The lieutenant stated that he attended the same church as the two remaining relatives of the cab driver, and asked Investigator Craig if he would be willing to take another look at the file. Craig agreed and was astounded at what he discovered. The case jacket had been stored for almost forty years and was virtually falling apart. After careful handling, he was able to reproduce the entire file.

After about three months of backtracking every element of the case, it was discovered that every person who was involved in this case was now deceased: the sheriff, coroner, medical examiner, ballistics expert, and the two investigators. Another two weeks work into the background of the suspect revealed that he now resided in Indiana. A request for his criminal history and current background was made to the Indiana State Police. Retired Agent/Lieutenant Craig and his actively assigned sheriff's investigator proceeded to Indiana where they interviewed the suspect, Edward Freiburger. Freiburger feigned total loss of memory about his time in the army and at first denied ever being at Fort Jackson or the Fort Leavenworth army prison. His demeanor was fully that of a solid suspect, and while he made no confessions, it was highly evident to Investigator Craig that he was attempting to cover up his misdeeds of 1 February 1961.

Unbelievably, the suspect murder weapon was found in pristine condition, along with the three bullet fragments, in the evidence vault of the state police firearms lab. Realizing that the first examiner had made a close match with 1961 forensic equipment, Investigator Craig decided to locate a present day criminalist who was familiar with the specific type of ammunition involved in this murder. In March 2001, the revolver and fragments were sent to a nationally certified, highly qualified firearms examiner who had very sophisticated equipment. The examiner was a former CID lab firearms examiner, a Chief Warrant Officer (W4) CID reservist and a current state chief criminalist. His re-examination of this revolver revealed that the projectile that killed the cab driver was fired from the same revolver that Freiburger had bought on 28 February 1961, which had been taken from his person on 29 March 1961 by the Tennessee state trooper. Predicated on this evidence, a warrant was issued for Edward Freiburger who voluntarily drove from Indiana to South Carolina, surrendered to the sheriff on 9 April 2001 and was booked on the charge of murder, and remanded to the Richland County Detention Center. He was arraigned on 10 April 2001 and held on a fifty thousand-dollar surety bond.

Investigator Craig made a very profound statement about this matter: "I could be anywhere I want to be at this juncture in my life. I'm almost seventy two years old, in fairly good health, and basically financially secure. I'm doing this work without compensation of any kind, for self-satisfaction, and closure for the victim's families. I truly believe this is a case of "Destiny," or "Divine Intervention."

"After having retired from the investigative business twice, and still being around at this juncture doing this kind of work is very rare. The real irony in the case is the fact that I became involved in something that I remembered from forty years ago." Investigator Craig said he pinched himself and asked what the odds are that he would have been present on a particular day when the lieutenant asked him to have another look at this case? Had he not been there, doing what he was doing, the case file would have rotted in the archives, and the subject would have gone to his own grave with the blood of the victim on his hands.

Carl is reportedly very close to resolving two other unsolved murders. His motto is still the CID Motto "Do What Has to Be Done."

An investigator can't get much better training than that is offered in the U.S. Army CID school, now located at Fort Leonard Wood, Missouri. No wonder the United States Marine Corps sends its CID investigators to the U.S. Army CID school.

Edward Freiburger, now 59 years of age, considered a model father, grandfather, and church member was released on bond from the Richland County jail. On 1 August 2002, a jury in Columbia, South Carolina, handed down a unanimous guilty verdict on the charge of murder. Freiburger was sentenced to life in prison. Under sentencing guidelines at the time of the crime Freiburger will be eligible for parole in ten years.

Ft. Gordon, GA

Special Agent Hubert Marlow
My Last Assignment in CID

Operations Officer of the Ft. Gordon Field Office, and Retirement from the Army

My next, and last, assignment was as the operations officer of the Fort Gordon field office, 3rd Region, USACIDC, Fort Gordon, Georgia, from January 1974 until my retirement on 01 May 1976. I had received orders assigning me to HQ, USACID, and had received a letter from Colonel Henry Tufts welcoming me to headquarters. I was not to crazy about spending my last two years before retirement in the Washington, D. C., area due to its high cost of living. I managed a change of assignment and instead relieved Chief Warrant Officer (W3) Harry DeJongh, who was scheduled to attended polygraph school, as the operations officer. The Commander at my arrival was Major M. Thomas Fairris, one of the best commanders I ever had, followed by Major James W. Macolly, a real politician. After our annual inspection by the inspector general, USACIDC, he made the following comment to the region commander: The Fort Gordon field office has the most efficient operation that he had seen worldwide throughout USACIDC. This resulted in a letter of commendation from Colonel Albert A. Ackerman, 3rd Region commander. While I was the operations officer of the Fort Gordon field office,

Major Fairris decided he was going to attend the CILMOC (CID Logistics Management Course — which covered logistical operations and fraud) at Fort Lee, Virginia. This occurred during the period when Major General Albert R. Escola came to Fort Gordon to visit the field office, the crime lab and the MP school. I was the acting commander and thus his sponsor for three days.

I have often wondered if Major Fairris did that on purpose. Here was I, a Chief Warrant Officer (W3), seated next to Major General Escola with a number of colonels and lieutenant colonels at the table, but such was the protocol.

Shortly after Major Macolly took over as the commanding officer of the Fort Gordon field office, the chief of my narcotics section, Chief Warrant Officer (W2) Rick Matherly, one of the best agents any operations officer could ask for, came to me with a little problem. Rick and one other man from the narcotics section had apprehended a soldier for the sale of marijuana. This soldier now accused Rick and his partner of drug involvement. It was clear to me that the soldier wanted to get the attention off himself, and what better way than to accuse the CID agents of drug use. I told Major Macolly to let us check this out before he called our higher headquarters, Third Region in Atlanta. I also told Major Macolly what would happen if he reported it to region headquarters before checking if there was any truth to the allegations. I told him that he would be spending a lot of his time calling region headquarters answering questions, and that he would be replying in writing, thus creating a lot of extra work for himself. The good major did not listen to me and what I told him is exactly what happened. Within a few days we were able to prove that the arrested soldier had lied, and as I said had done so to get the attention off himself. Needless to say I never had any more problems with Major Macolly after that, he would listen to me.

Being the operations officer was a very routine job; with little direct involvement in each investigation, other than to give guidance to junior agents. I recall one bad habit most new CID school graduates and apprentice agents had. They would come bouncing through the CID office with their newly assigned .38 caliber revolver strapped to their side and the coat hooked behind the revolver. Now this happened by accident of course, right on. Walking around the office they, of course, wanted all the suspects and visitors to know that they were armed and an agent, although there still was a little green behind their ears. I would pounce all over these youngsters, telling them if they wanted to be cowboys to go to Texas. I instructed them to either cover the weapon with their coat or take the weapon off and secure it. Inside, of course, I chuckled and was amused by their behavior which of course also had a touch of pride.

One other incident comes to mind. I had a tall muscular agent working for me. Chief Warrant officer (W2) Roger Mueller (not his real name) came into my office one day, and during his stay I instructed him to do something, to which he replied "I ought to punch you in the mouth!," not a smart thing to do to a superior. I was seated and got up and said to Roger "Go ahead, Roger. It will be my pleasure to attend at your court- martial!" Roger left and returned about thirty minutes later and apologized for his behavior. I could have easily relieved him of his badge, credentials, and .38 cal. pistol, but I knew my people pretty well and figured Roger had some other problems bothering him at the time.

Roger, after his retirement in the grade of Chief Warrant Officer (W3), some years after I had retired and was working for the Defense Investigative Service (DIS), also worked as a special agent for DIS in the Los Angeles, California, area. After a few years he resigned from DIS because he had a job offer with the Defense Criminal Investigative Service (DCIS). However; before starting in his new job, sadly he shot and killed himself. What a sad ending for an obviously troubled man.

While I was assigned to Fort Gordon first the military police school, then the CID school and finally the CID crime lab all moved. The place where I had started my career in law enforcement would also be the place I would end true law enforcement work.

CHAPTER THIRTEEN

Vietnam

Other Dangers, Besides Criminals, Faced by CID Agents
Special Agent Arcy W. Lyle

A Day in the Life of Special Agent Arcy Lyle
He Will Never Forget

This, his most memorable experience in Vietnam had nothing to do with his work as a CID agent, but rather had to do with the quarters he was assigned to, namely the Hotel Victoria in Cholon, a suburb of Saigon. Agent Lyle and a navy ensign shared a nice room, with bath, on the fourth floor, directly above the main entrance. No vehicles were allowed to stop directly in front of the Victoria. An American MP and a Vietnamese policeman, guarded the sole entrance used at all times. Barriers were also placed in front of the hotel so no vehicles could reach the front entrance. Intelligence reports indicated that the Hotel Victoria was on the VC's hit list, and a complete curfew, with few exceptions, was in effect between 0100 hours and 0500 hours.

April Fools Day, 1 April 1966, is a day Agent Lyle will never forget. At 0500 hours, he and his roommate were awakened by the sound of gunfire (carbine, pistol and shotgun). Wisely he and his roommate had worked out a course of action for just such an event. Agent Lyle and his roommate ran into the bathroom and lay flat on the floor. About two minutes later there was a small explosion and agent Lyle thought, *Gee, that wasn't so bad*, but when his roommate got up and started to leave,

Agent Lyle warned him that there should be another explosion. Previous attacks by the Viet Cong (VC) had almost always started with a big explosion, followed by an explosion of a claymore mine to harm those attempting to escape to safety. Lyle knew what he was talking about because within three or four minutes the second explosion occurred. It was a big one. Lyle was picked up from the floor about six inches and slammed back down. The wash basin was hanging by the pipes. The ceiling and floor above had fallen on one end, but fortunately Agent Lyle and his roommate had left the bathroom door ajar and it caught the ceiling. The entire room was a shambles, with the mattress from Lyle's bed hanging on the balcony railing outside their window.

Agent Lyle and his roommate escaped with a few minor cuts and bruises; others were not so lucky. One guy in the next room died later that day, his roommate was medically evacuated the next day. The MP and Vietnamese policeman, the hotel desk clerk, a young lady employed at the snack bar, the officer of the guard, and his driver were also killed. There were one hundred fifty seven wounded, some slightly, some seriously.

Murder
Special Agent Andrew A. Jackson
Camp Bearcat, Vietnam

The solution of a murder case with an "unknown" subject is often the product of dumb luck. This occurs in the CID as well as in civilian homicide investigations. In 1968 such an event occurred with Special Agent Andrew A. Jackson, then a newly promoted Chief Warrant Officer (W2) and chief of the 9th Infantry Division CID in Vietnam. For solving this homicide he was awarded a Bronze Star medal and much acclaim.

Sherlock Holmes Sure Didn't Have Anything on you Guys

About February or March of 1968 the 9th Infantry. Division was moving its base operations from Camp Bearcat, about ten miles from Long Binh, to Tan An, a village deep in the Mekong Delta, some fifty bone-jarring miles away, over bumpy dirt roads periodically laced with mines by Viet Cong sympathizers.

One enlisted CID agent and six Militay Police Investigators were under Andy's command. One MPI and a small number of MPs continued operations at Camp Bearcat. Andy reported directly to the 9th Infantry Division PM.

During the first week of the relocation, a grisly murder occurred in a little village adjacent to Camp Bearcat. An elderly Vietnamese man had been stabbed twenty seven times in an execution-style murder. Local villagers, primarily several prostitutes, reported that a young GI in uniform with the nametag of "Green" had been drinking and asking about Viet Cong (VC). He had also been seen in the vicinity of the home where the victim lived. It was strongly denied that the old man or any of the villagers were in any way involved with the Viet Cong.

Whether or not there was any substance to the denials of VC sympathy among the villagers, the killing was clearly an act of murder in an unauthorized foray by a lone American soldier in an off-limits location. Not only was there no evidence to support the notion that the victim was associated with the VC, there was no military authorization for the soldier to be in the village, let alone to carry out his own interpretation of wartime justice.

Agent Jackson and his fellow investigators worked the case as diligently as if the murder had occurred on the base. The interviewed Vietnamese witnesses, made a rough composite sketch of the suspect, photographed the body and the crime scene, a trail into bushes leading from the victim's home, and rounded up all soldiers stationed at Bearcat whose surname was Green, Greene, Greenwald or anything similar.

All were interviewed and most alibis verified. Those who could provide no verifiable alibi for the time period were photographed and photographic line-ups were conducted with several Vietnamese witnesses. None identified any of the people portrayed as resembling the suspected killer. Aside from a general agreement in height and build and that he was a Caucasian enlisted man in a uniform with the nametag, "Green," none of the witnesses could provide any further substantive information. Agent Jackson and his fellow investigators began to suspect that all Americans looked alike to the Vietnamese villagers.

The case was unsolved and destined for closure when the CID unit moved to Tan An. Agent Jackson left instructions for the Camp Bearcat MPs to notify the PM office or the CID at Tan An if any additional persons with a name of, or similar to, "Green" were located, and provided a list of those who had been investigated and cleared. Agent Jackson really didn't expect to hear any more about the case.

About a week later the remnants of Bearcat were packing to move when a call came from the Bearcat MP desk sergeant who remembered that the CID was looking for someone named Green. The call was transferred to the PM. The desk sergeant stated that he had a soldier named Green, an outsider from Long Binh, standing before him who was being held for CID. The PM called Jackson to his office and informed him that he wanted him personally to go to Bearcat.

The "Green" in question had been arrested for speeding and reckless driving in the Camp Bearcat compound. He was a courier delivering intelligence information from his command to the 9th Infantry Division. Upon leaving Bearcat he cut a few "wheelies" with his jeep and was driving recklessly. He had promptly been arrested. His response to being arrested and held for investigation was arrogance and indignation, insisting that the 9th Infantry Division had no right to detain him.

The prospect of making the arduous journey back to Bearcat to interview someone from another army command, whose only connection to the murder case was that he was unfortunate enough to be named Green, put a damper on Andy's whole day. He was even less enthusiastic about the trip when he found that all jeeps in the motor pool were in service or in repair. The motor sergeant, thinking he was doing Andy a favor, stopped a deuce-and-a-half (two one half ton truck) that was leaving for Saigon with a truckload of GIs enroute for Rest and Recuperation (R and R) departure. The rear of the canopied truck was crammed full, so Agent Jackson was wedged in the front seat with the driver and two other enlisted men. What absolutely capped the day for Jackson was the canvas top for the driver's section which was missing, exposing those in the front seat to the elements. Naturally it rained. Because it was the monsoon season it rained daily, and these were not gentle rains but downpours.

By the time Agent Jackson was dropped off at the Bearcat MP station, he was thoroughly soaked and in a foul mood. An irate first lieutenant who identified himself as Green's company executive officer met him. He began berating Jackson for harassing his man, an

outstanding Specialist four (E4) with a flawless record. He demanded that Jackson instruct the desk sergeant to release the man to him
immediately.

This fitted exactly with agent Jackson's mood. He told the lieutenant to take it up with his PM as Green was held at his orders and
that he had just traveled fifty miles in the rain to interview this man
about a murder case and he was going to do that before releasing him
to anybody. The young lieutenant protested some more and then
announced he wanted to be present if this man was interviewed to be
assured that he was treated fairly.

Jackson considered denying the request but he had to admit that
it had some legitimacy under the circumstances. He told the lieutenant that he could sit in during the interrogation, but he could not
make any comments or give Green any advice; one word out of him
and he would be ejected from the interview room. He nodded his
agreement.

Agent Jackson's investigator on duty at Bearcat was present and
standing by. An interview room was waiting. Jackson and the Military
Police Investigator were at the table with a chair reserved for Green
and the lieutenant was seated in back against the wall. Green was
brought into the room and his handcuffs were removed.

It was hard to imagine that this All-American appearing fellow,
about age twenty, had raised such a ruckus with the MPs. Now, in the
presence of an officer from his unit he was polite and docile. He
seemed to be mystified as to why he was being held for questioning
about a murder.

With his lieutenant present and taking notes, Agent Jackson was
careful to give Specialist Green a thorough advisement of his Miranda
rights, strictly by the book. He had no qualms about relinquishing his
rights against self-incrimination, insisting that he had no knowledge
of any murder.

After obtaining some preliminary background information
Agent Jackson asked him how often he went to this little village. He
denied ever having been there. Jackson asked if he had been there to
solicit a prostitute and again received a firm denial that he had ever
been to the village for any purpose. Jackson told him that there were
witnesses who had seen him or someone very similar to him just
before the murder and that he would take his photograph and have

a photographic line-up. If he was there the witnesses would pick him out, so he might as well say something in his defense about why he was in the village and why he had executed a helpless old Vietnamese man. Again polite denials permeated with "sirs," Agent Jackson was getting nowhere and his lieutenant was tapping his foot with impatience.

Agent Jackson sensed that while this young fellow was making a show of being open and forthright, he really wasn't. It was something in the quickness of his denials, the glib tone of his voice, and the lack of shock at being suspected of murder. Jackson decided to try a different approach.

Agent Jackson began talking in a more conversational tone instead of sounding accusatory. Jackson told him that he reminded him of his kid brother and he could understand how he could get carried away in a wartime situation so far from home. Jackson asked him where he was from. "Tennessee." "did his folks still live there?" "Oh yes", he beamed. His dad had a big productive farm. Jackson could see that he had reverence for his dad in the way he mentioned him, so he asked him to tell him about his father and his life at home. He related that he and his family were avid church members and that his father was a, "World War II hero who had killed fifty Japs."

Jackson felt that he was beginning to get somewhere and the motive began niggling at him. He let him ramble on and marveled with him at the man that his father was and said that he could see why he admired him so much. Then Jackson turned on his religious key. He reminded him that life is uncertain, that he could not be sure that he would return from Vietnam safe and sound. He said, "Someday you will have to account to your Maker for these deeds, as I will have to for mine. You may fool everyone, but you cannot fool God about what was done." Agent Jackson asked if he really wanted this on his conscience if it turned out that his fate was not to leave Vietnam alive. Then he asked what would his father think if he knew the true story?

As Jackson spoke, in the earnest tones of a sympathetic friend, he saw a tiny tear begin to well up in the corner of one eye. Jackson was already leaning across the table towards him and immediately leaned even closer to his face. He knew that he had somehow strummed the right chord. He continued without letting up the pace, emphasizing now the shock and disappointment his father, a true hero, would feel if he knew of his son's actions. Suddenly, Green blurted out: "I didn't mean to murder him." The lieutenant almost fell off his chair. Tears now streaming down his face, Green related how he had felt an obligation to be a war hero also, as was his dad. After drinking too much he had decided to find a VC to kill. Most of the villagers ran away from him but he stumbled into a shack where there was an old man all alone. Green took out his hunting knife and ordered the old man out of the house. He had pushed him down a trail a little way from the village and killed him.

He had rationalized that the old man was probably a VC and deserved to be killed but admitted that he was horrified after he realized what he had done. He blamed it on his drinking. Where was the knife now? At his barracks, hidden under his bedsprings. He would take me there and give it to me. Green seemed relieved that it was over and said that he had been unable to sleep because of his guilty feelings. Later it was learned that he had bragged to several of his buddies that he had killed a Viet Cong, but nobody took him seriously as he was a braggart who drank too much. The knife was recovered from his bedsprings, just where he said it was. He had cleaned, and hidden it right after the murder.

After the interrogation and confession, Green's lieutenant shook Agent Jackson's hand outside the interview room and apologized for his earlier hostility. Then he paid him and the CID Command the highest compliment he could think of, "Sherlock Holmes sure didn't have anything on you guys," he said.

Special Agent Robert F. Coucoules
Working Undercover in the Army Postal System
Phan Thiet, Vietnam

During his tour in Vietnam, in 1968, Special Agent Bob Coucoules was given an undercover assignment with an army post office (APO) unit located at the Phan Thiet fire base. The clerk running the post office was reportedly selling one hundred dollar postal money orders in large numbers to a Korean national who was apparently traveling around Vietnam by Air America the (CIA run airline).

Unknown to the clerk, but known to the base commander, Coucoules assumed the rank of a Staff Sergeant (E-6), newly assigned, and took over the post office from the clerk. He was billeted just across the hall from the door to the post office along with a sergeant assigned to a Bird Dog outfit.

Coucoules left his CID credentials, badge, and handcuffs with the local MI (Military Intelligence) located in a tent across the airstrip. His roommate was not initially aware of his true status. After Coucoules observed the clerk passing the money orders and pocketing his profits, he informed him that from then on he would sell the money orders to the Korean so that he would have some money to buy a new car when he returned to the U.S. During a two-to-three week period Coucoules sold numerous money orders to the Korean and received an additional ten percent of the price of the money orders for himself.

Coucoules had been advised that a CID agent, stationed in Hong Kong, monitored the money orders and determined that they were being deposited in a suspected communist account.

Then one day, knowing that the Korean was due back, Bob was told to terminate the investigation the next morning. That night the Korean national police and a CID agent landed at the fire base in General Abrams aircraft and went to the MI tent to stay the night. Coucoules recovered his credentials, badge and handcuffs from the MI office and informed his roommate who he was and what he was doing. His roommate agreed to stand by while Bob apprehended the subject in the morning and to assist him in case of a physical confrontation.

The following morning the Korean arrived on schedule. However, this time, after passing the money orders to him and receiving the money, Special Agent Coucoules apprehended him and cuffed his wrists behind his back. Bob had been advised that the Korean national police, who had arrived the night before, needed to arrest the suspect with the money orders on his person. Consequently Coucoules held on to the handcuffs and marched him over to the military police tent. While enroute the Korean offered to give Bob the money orders if he would let him go. When Coucoules walked into the tent, he identified himself as a CID Agent, and asked the desk sergeant to call the MI tent and inform them that the subject was in his custody. The Korean national police subsequently took the Korean into custody. Coucoules never found out what happened to him, but knowing the Korean system of justice, I'm sure he had some unpleasant days ahead of him. This was not to be Coucoules last assignment uncovering crimes in the Army postal system.

Bao Loc

Special Agent Weeden Nichols
Given a Second Chance, to No Avail

As did all special agents assigned to the Cam Ranh Bay field office (including the author, at a later date), Agent Nichols took his turn in going to a small compound at Bao Loc, Vietnam, to conduct investigations whenever required. Bao Loc was primarily the base for a battalion of the 173rd Airborne Brigade (Separate) and the aviation unit, which supported that battalion. It was Nichols's turn once again, and he proceeded to Bao Loc via UH-1D helicopter, the only safe way to get there. Among other things, Nichols had to investigate the near death, due to a drug overdose, of a young soldier.

Bao Loc was an inhospitable place (not entirely uncommon for Vietnam). It could rain all night long, fill the ditches with water, turn everything to mud and seem very cold at night. Then, before the sun was up for many hours, it would be hot with dust blowing.

The soldier who had nearly died from an overdose, probably of heroin, was a pale red-haired kid from Oklahoma. Agent Nichols never forgot the kid from Oklahoma, how he had interviewed the boy only the day after he was found in the ditch at night. It had been raining hard that night, and the kid was lying half in the water. It was amazing he had not drowned or died from the overdose. There had been almost no signs of life when he was found. The kid was lucky that day. The battalion surgeon, a captain, had been caught in the Vietnam-era medical draft. He had been commissioned into the U.S. Air Force. Later it was determined that the air force had too many doctors, and the army too few. The doctor, still technically in the air force, was assigned as a battalion surgeon to Bao Loc. Regardless of service identity, the good doctor worked over the red-haired kid for hours and, almost miraculously, brought him around. Even in Vietnam, that physician never forgot for a moment that he was supposed to be a healer.

As Nichols remembers the case, there were multiple layers of sadness, perhaps tragedy. The kid had been left in the ditch by some of his "buddies", who had shot him up with heroin, accidentally overdosed him, and then dumped him in the ditch. Obviously a life meant less to them than saving their own skins from drug charges. It was sad that the physician had been bounced around due to inter-service administrative glitches as though he were a mere thing. And Agent Nichols was particularly sad when he was informed two weeks later that the young man had died from another overdose of drugs. What Agent Nichols remembers most vividly about the kid whom he interviewed two weeks before the boy's death, other than that he would not "rat" on his so-called buddies, was how very respectful and straightforward he seemed, as his mother most likely had taught him. There were a lot of seemingly unnecessary deaths and a lot of seemingly wasted lives in Vietnam.

Song Pha, Vietnam

Special Agents Weeden Nichols and Alan R. Knowlton
Murder, an Innocent Soldier and an Angry Ally

It was late October 1969, on a Sunday afternoon at Cam Ranh Bay, when the duty agent at Detachment B, 8th MP Group (CI) received word that a member of the engineer battalion at Phan Rang, had reported the murder of a U.S. soldier. The GI had been murdered by an Army of the Republic of Vietnam (commonly referred to as ARVN) soldier at Song Pha, located part way up into the mountains near Phan Rang. Murder by an ally was a very touchy and sensitive matter and CID group headquarters wasted no time in directing the Cam Ranh Bay CID to respond fully and immediately.

One company of the U.S. Army Engineer Battalion, engaged in building a paved highway up into the mountains, was located at Song Pha and protection for the engineer company was being provided by a Vietnamese Rural Force/Popular Force (RF/PF), commonly referred to as "Ruff-Puff". Also located with the engineer company for road security was a detached platoon of an ARVN armored company, commanded by a lieutenant. The platoon had two V-100 armored cars, one commanded by the lieutenant, the other by a sergeant.

The job of investigating this murder fell upon Agents Nichols and Knowlton, who immediately gassed up the jeep, because you didn't want to run out of gas in the middle of territory inhabited by the Viet Cong (VC). As was policy Nichols checked out an M-16 rifle. Whenever travelling through areas known to be infested with VC, it was always the policy of the CID to have two agents travel together with one, as we would say, "riding shotgun." Nichols placed the M-16 rifle across the windshield, at his disposal immediately if needed. Agents Nichols and Knowlton traveled to Phan Rhang, with Knowlton doing the driving, and when they arrived they were met by the sergeant major (SGM) of the engineer battalion, with jeep and driver at the ready. You have heard the saying "There is Safety in Numbers" and this was certainly true in Vietnam. The sergeant major and his driver escorted Nichols and Knowlton to Song Pha and it was a case of "pedal to the metal" or "lead-foot" all the way. Upon arrival at Song Pha the first thing Agents Nichols and Knowlton did was to make a courtesy call on the old Vietnamese lieutenant colonel in command of the "Ruff-Puffs.

Merely being in the presence of the lieutenant colonel made it obvious that one was in the company of a good soldier. Agents Nichols and Knowlton found out the lieutenant colonel had soldiered since he was a teenager and had served as a paratrooper under the French. He displayed that restraint, courtesy, and air of essential kindness, coupled with an aura of unquestionable authority rendered only by the best of officers, no matter what army. Since neither Nichols nor Knowlton spoke Vietnamese, the good Colonel assigned them a master sergeant of the ARVN Intelligence Corps as their interpreter. Agents Nichols and Knowlton proceeded with the investigation over the next three days. Nichols and Knowlton determined that relations with the Vietnamese ally at Son Pha had been good. At least for the Americans, but probably for the ARVN's too, the center of social activities had been the combination bar and whore house in the village. The seed or root of the tragedy probably lay in white racism. The Vietnamese prostitutes had developed prejudices against all black Americans.

A black U.S. soldier, not assigned to or familiar with the area, had been sent on TDY (temporary duty) to the engineer company at Song Pha from battalion headquarters at Phan Rang. Off-duty he had all intentions of enjoying the same services as the rest of the U.S. soldiers in the area, and so he went with the other off duty GIs to the "social center" where he picked out a prostitute that appealed to him from several available. The problem was the prostitute refused to have anything to do with him and made it quite clear to him that it was because he was black. The rejected and embarrassed soldier then made the mistake of trying to force the prostitute to provide the desired service by manhandling her back to her cubicle. At this point the ARVN sergeant in command of the second V-100 armored car entered the area just in time to hear her protests and witness the ongoing struggle. To prove that chivalry was still alive, he came to the rescue of the damsel in distress, a big mistake because the black soldier proceeded to seriously and painfully trounce the much smaller ARVN sergeant. The ARVN sergeant gathered his V-100 crew about him and left the establishment in pain and humiliation. As they were walking from the entrance to the house of prostitution to their V-100, they met a very small white American GI on his way to the house of prostitution. The sergeant, "our ally," ordered his troops, all armed with M-16's, to take the American soldier prisoner, which they did. All who knew the American soldier, Vietnamese, American officer, and enlisted personnel alike, described the soldier as a "nice guy." The sergeant had the GI placed on the deck of the V-100 which then proceeded down the nicely paved highway, compliments of the U.S. Army engineers, and as the V-100 rounded a curve at a fairly high rate of speed, the GI either fell off or jumped, Agents Nichols and Knowlton were unable to determine which. As the GI departed from the moving vehicle he was shot and killed by the private who had been ordered to guard him by the sergeant. The poor GI was at the wrong place at the wrong time.

Agents Nichols and Knowlton developed one witness to the murder. A U.S. Air Force major, a forward artillery controller (FAC) flying over the V-100 at the time had observed the body of the American GI roll off the V-100 and lie lifeless by the road. Nichols and Knowlton had interviewed all available witnesses, either directly if they spoke English, or through the interpreter. They could not interview the Vietnamese sergeant or members of his V-100 crew involved in the murder. The ARVN, by design, had moved them to another station to place them out of reach of CID, even before Nichols and Knowlton had arrived at Song Pha. Nichols and Knowlton knew where the V-100 crew was but were never allowed to contact them, so much for our "Vietnamese ally." Agents Nichols and Knowlton, being fully aware how hot this case was, filed a final report of investigation the day after leaving Song Pha, with an action copy to the ARVN. No action was ever taken against the sergeant and the rest of the V-100 crew by the ARVN authorities, but I'm sure they had nothing to laugh at when the VC and North Vietnamese troops took them prisoner.

Criminal Investigator Hubert Marlow

My Tour of Duty in Vietnam
First as a Street Agent and then as the OIC of the Cam Ranh Bay Field Office

My tour with the 52nd MP Detachment was supposed to be a three year-tour, but came to an abrupt end after two years, when the army thought I was in need of a little warmer climate, and sent me to Cam Ranh Bay, Vietnam. Chief Warrant Officer (W3) James W. Rawlings was the officer in charge of the Cam Ranh Bay field office, and Chief Warrant Officer (W3) Martin J. Crean was the officer in charge of the Nha Trang field office, both subordinate to Chief Warrant Officer (W3) Albert E. Vanden Bosch and later Chief Warrant Officer (W3) Glenn E. Gladle, operations officers of Detachment B (Provisional), 8th MP Group (CI). The CO at the beginning of my tour was Captain Robert M. Hawk and at the end of my tour it was Major Carl J. LeBourdais. Members of the unit were: Criminal Investigators Robert A. Cappuccio, Carl D. Coleman, Benjamin J. Grotts, Matthew E. Moriarty, William C. Ward, Gary E. George, Ralph R. Wiest, Patton E. Joyner, Anthony L. Korey, Thomas C. Rich, Leroy E. Halbert Jr. (who was murdered on 31 December 1970), and Samuel J. Wilkinson. I worked as an investigator for about six months, and then became the officer in charge (OIC) of the Cam Ranh Bay field office, when Chief Rawlings departed. I was relieved by Chief Warrant Officer (W3) Rex Schulz on 28 November 1970 and departed in early January 1971.

The Saddest Day of my Tour in Vietnam
The Murder of Two CID Criminal Investigators

It was New Year's Eve 1970, about 2200 hours, when Criminal Investigator Ralph R. Wiest and Criminal Investigator Leroy E. Halbert came to me, as I was sitting outside our hooch (quarters). They said to me "Herb, you want to go with us? We have to go to So Chin (a village off the peninsula of Cam Ranh Bay) to check out some leads." Investigators Wiest and Halbert wanted to develop some leads on several U.S. Negro Soldiers who had drawn their weapons on MPs about two days ago, and the following day had cut an MP with a knife. Wiest had received some information that the suspects were known to frequent a bar and house of prostitution known as "So Chin Linda's." My reply to both of them was "No, I'm too short." I had been relieved as the OIC, of the Cam Ranh Bay field office, and was just finishing up things, so the new OIC, Rex Schulz, would not get stuck with anything. I was due to depart Vietnam within seven or eight days, and little did I know that it would be the last time I would see Agent Halbert alive.

When Criminal Investigators Wiest and Halbert got to "So Chin Linda's" bar, around 2225 hours, they found it to be closed, and Investigator Wiest asked the proprietor's daughter why they were closed and if there were any colored soldiers in the area. She replied that there were no soldiers in the area.

About five minutes later a two one half ton truck pulled in front of the bar, and approximately thirteen soldiers approached the bar, seven or nine were armed with M-16 rifles. One, a tall Negro soldier, approached the area where Investigators Wiest and Halbert were standing on the porch, walked up to them and said, "So you're the mother f......g CID, I've seen your ass around Cam Ranh Bay. I'm going to blow your shit away." At that point he swung the muzzle of his M-16 rifle into agent Wiest's stomach. Wiest grabbed the muzzle of the weapon with his right hand and the trigger housing with his left hand and swung the muzzle of the weapon away from his stomach. Three other Negro soldiers forced Investigator Wiest against the building. Wiest changed hands on the M-16, grabbing the muzzle with his left hand, and drew his .38 pistol with his right hand and shot the assailant, who fell to the floor, as did his M-16 rifle. Another Negro soldier had pointed an M-16 at Investigator Wiest and was retreating, still pointing the weapon at him, when Investigator Wiest shot him.

Investigator Halbert had become separated from Investigator Wiest and was about ten feet to his right against the wall. Three Negroes were struggling with him and one of them had seized

Investigator Halbert's .38 revolver, and another had leveled an M-16 rifle at his stomach. Wiest shot the one that had the weapon pointed at Investigator Halbert. The subject and Halbert fell to the ground and at this point the first subject, had gotten back on his feet and again was threatening Wiest who shot him once again. He fell to the ground and remained there. The others managed to escape.

Criminal Investigator Wiest tried to get several Vietnamese nationals to assist him in placing Investigator Halbert in his jeep but they refused. Wiest flagged down a GI in a jeep and they placed Halbert in his jeep and the subject in Wiest's jeep. As Wiest was transporting the Subject to the USAF hospital in Cam Ranh Bay, he still attempted to struggle with him. Wiest had made a quick search for Halbert's .38 revolver, at the scene, but was unable to recover it. Later we learned that a Vietnamese had stolen the weapon as well as Halbert's wallet, so much for our allies. Criminal Investigator Halbert died 30 minutes later, of massive brain injuries, after arriving at the hospital and the subject died forty five minutes later. Another subject, whom Wiest had wounded, was picked up by USAF ambulance and taken to the hospital.

I (the author) still remember going to the signal company's compound, the unit the assailants belonged to, with a couple of investigators. The unit's first sergeant came to the gate and asked me for a little additional time because some still had their M-16 rifles in their possession and the first sergeant wanted to disarm all of them and secure the weapons in the arms racks. I readily agreed, not being suicidal, and we later returned to the unit and the company was stood in formation while Investigator Wiest walked down the ranks and identified some whom he recognized as having been at So Chin. It was a sad New Year's beginning.

The sad beginning would continue, as I later found out, because another CID investigator, Criminal Investigator James T. Abbott, was murdered ten days later. On 11 January 1971, at Camp Evans, Thua Thien Province, Vietnam, a SSG of the 158th Aiation Battalion, 101st Airborn Division, threatened his commanding officer and his first sergeant. He then climbed an observation tower, firing one round from his M-16, and threatened to shoot and throw an Specialist four (E4) from the tower. Approximately two hours later, when Criminal Investigator Abbott attempted to apprehend the Staff

Sergeant he shot agent Abbott with his M-16 rifle. Indeed a sad beginning for the new year.

About Jul or Aug 01, while viewing the miniature "Vietnam Wall" at Travis Air Force Base, California, I looked up Criminal Investigator Leroy Halbert's name on the wall, and as I looked at it I got a sick feeling to my stomach. I remembered the moment when Wiest and Halbert had asked me "Herb, you want to go with us….." and I had replied "No, I'm too short", had I gone it could easily been my name on that wall.

Attempted Murder-Fragging, Negligent Homicide-Vehicular, and Two Drug Cases Interviewing and or Interrogating two hundred twelve Persons in Three Days

The case I am most proud of also occurred while I was assigned to Cam Ranh Bay. The Cam Ranh Bay field office also covered Phan Thiet, Bao Loc, and Phan Rang air base. It was my turn to go to Bao Loc, and the only way was by aircraft, either C-123, C-130, or helicopter. I went to Bao Loc where a negligent homicide (vehicular), two drug cases and a "fragging" awaited me. I quickly took care of the negligent homicide and drug cases and then worked on the fragging. One evening, after dark, a staff sergeant was urinating at the "tube" and when he had finished, he observed flames on the sandbags in the area of the first sergeants room. He started to walk towards the flames, and luckily for him the grenade exploded before he got close. The first sergeant (the intended victim) was not in the room, but his roommate, a black platoon sergeant was. The platoon sergeant normally slept with his head toward the wall, but for some reason had turned his bed around that night, which saved his life. He was hospitalized for six weeks with wounds to his feet, with one foot being messed up pretty badly. For the four investigations I interviewed and interrogated a total of two hundred twelve persons in a three-day period. Needless to say, I did not get much sleep. I developed a suspect and for some reason established rapport with this soldier. I interrogated him but he would not confess. However he agreed to take a polygraph test. All polygraph examinations were conducted at Long Binh, so it always took considerable time from the day a suspect agreed to take the test to the day it actually was conducted. In this case it took three months.

I believe the polygrapher was Theodore Ponticelli, a former USMC CID agent. The subject ran "dirty" (CID slang for showing deception) and was interrogated by the polygrapher for about half an hour, with me in the observation room. The polygrapher came to me and said, "You want to give it a try," and I did. After fifteen minutes the subject confessed but never told me why he wanted to kill his first sergeant. The U.S. Army engineers were building Highway #1 (North — South) in Vietnam and the Compound at Bao Loc was occupied by the egineer battalion headquarters and two companies. Two platoons were always out in the gravel pit. While in the gravel pit the subject took a hand grenade, placed thirty two rubber bands around it and gave them a twist, placing the other thirty two rings over the grenade handle. This gave him sixty four rings and he then put a few drops of lighter fluid on the rubber band rings opposite the twist, pulled the pin and lit the fluid. He timed the period it took from the time he lit the lighter fluid until the grenade exploded, it took twenty one seconds, including the internal four seconds of the grenade. He also ran from the first sergeant's hooch (slang for troop buildings in Vietnam and Korea) to his hooch, which took eight seconds. So he was well prepared when he repeated this act in earnest.

The Subject did not want to give me his Real Name
But we had ways of convincing him to disclose his real Identity

My funniest case occurred at Cam Ranh Bay. A sergeant was apprehended by the MPs for apparently being AWOL and involved in illegal activities. A search of his personal belongings disclosed he had several ID cards and ration cards, with different names on them and also a substantial amount of money (about ten thousand dollars).

I was assigned the case, and investigation disclosed that the good sergeant had used these ID and Ration cards to purchase cameras and other high-value black market items. His total purchases were in excess of twelve thousand dollars. When I first interviewed him, he would not give me his true name. I fingerprinted him (which was SOP) and we quickly came up with an idea that would instill in him the desire to give me his true identity. The CID office at Cam Ranh Bay was in a quonset Hut, as was the PMO/MP station next door to us.

The MP station only had three cells, so on the exterior next to the PMO/MP Station, there were three or four Conex containers with slits burned into the sides for light and ventilation. A tin roof had been built over the Conex containers to shade them from the sun, but believe me it still got plenty hot inside them. The Conex jails were primarily used to detain the many prostitutes the MPs would pick up during the evening and at night.

Now these "ladies" had a bad habit of urinating in the Conex jails, and the MPs would hose down the container in the morning. So in went my suspect without the usual hosing down of the Conex. After the second day I talked to my suspect, and he still would not give me his true identity. I informed him that I would send his fingerprints to the FBI in Washington, DC, and that they would without a doubt inform me of his true identity. However; it would take about three months to get the answer, and he would remain in the Conex jail until I received my answer from the FBI.

After the third day in the Conex jail, I, and everyone in the office, could hear him yell "Mr. Marlow, I want to talk to you." I talked to him, got his true identity and unit, took a statement, and called the unit (a helicopter unit at Long Binh). A helicopter from his unit arrived that afternoon, picked up the good sergeant, who was a deserter, and deposited him in the stockade at Long Binh.

Now remember I said "What goes around comes around". One day, while I was the OIC of the Cam Ranh Bay field office, my clerk said to me "Chief, there is a Mr. Whitecliff (remember my assignment to Korea in chapter four) on the phone, he is at the 21st Replacement Battalion, and would like to talk to you" and I said to the clerk "Tell him to get screwed." You see, it was the policy of the Cam Ranh Bay field office to pick up all newly arriving CID criminal investigators at the replacement battalion, because that was not a nice place to be. They had stacked bunk beds, mandatory formations etc. Yes, Mr. Whitecliff sat at the replacement battalion for five days and was then sent to Long Binh. I talked to him on the phone, on business matters, a couple of times, and always in a friendly but business-like manner.

One other interesting thing that occurred at Cam Ranh Bay was when I arrived. Criminal Investigator Jackson Smith, with whom I had served at Pusan, Korea, was there and said to me "You never guess who is over here." He then told me that Sergeant Lee from the Korean CID, who had been assigned to our office at Pusan was there with the CID of the Korean White Horse Division, we had many happy celebrations recalling our days at Pusan. Also Criminal Investigator Carl D. Coleman, with whom I had served in Germany. It just shows you how small this world is. Also, during 1971, at Cam Ranh Bay Matt Moriarty and I would once again see our old CO from the 142nd MP Company (Service) days, First Lieutenant and Captain James D. Smith, by now a Lieutenant Colonel.

Cam Ranh Bay

Criminal Investigators Robert A. Cappuccio and Carl D. Coleman
Was it a case of Fragging?

It was 1970, Criminal Investigators Bob Cappuccio and Carl D. Coleman were based at the Cam Ranh Bay field office (as was the author), but this did not mean that they would only work cases on Cam Ranh Bay, because the field office covered half of the Vietnamese II Corps area.

Investigator Cappuccio was the unlucky guy on duty when he was notified that an apparent grenade explosion at Prelin Mountain outside the city of Dalat had killed five U.S. soldiers.

It was the policy that an investigator would never travel alone to the outer areas of Cam Ranh Bay and so it was that Criminal Investigator Carl Coleman was picked to go with Cappuccio. Cappuccio was thinking about what possibly happened that five GI's were killed apparently by a grenade. Was it a fragging? (a term used in Vietnam indicating that a hand grenade had been used by a U.S. soldier to murder a fellow soldier, normally an none commissioned officer or an officer).

After Investigators Cappuccio and Coleman arrived at Prelin Mountain, the first thing Cappuccio did was to have the army explosives ordnance detachment (commonly referred to as EOD) check the room. Since EOD personnel were the experts in explosive matters, this was a wise move because the possibility existed that rigged and unexploded grenades were still in the room. A careful check disclosed this not to be the case, but it also disclosed numerous unexploded grenades in the room. EOD personnel told Cappuccio and Coleman that just one grenade had done all the carnage and damage in the room.

Investigators Cappuccio and Coleman began to interview members of the victims unit and soon determined that the room had not been booby-trapped. They soon learned that one of the deceased soldiers, Specialist four (E4) Harry Fowler, liked to play with grenades and it seemed he also was a prankster, except that his idea of fun was extreme and dangerous. By interviewing witnesses and going through photos and tapes made by Fowler, they learned that Fowler was known to play around with hand grenades. He would take the fuses out and then put the hand grenade in someone's hand and pull the pin, letting his fellow soldier think the grenade still had the fuse in it and if he released the handle it would blow up. He was also known to be even more extreme, by placing a hand grenade in a fellow soldier's hand, *without* removing the fuse and then pull the pin. A very sick sense of humor. His ill humor had backfired on him and not only cost him his own life but also killed four fellow soldiers. Sadly, one of the fellow soldiers killed was supposed to go home two weeks prior to the incident, but was unable to get off the mountain (transportation problem). His wife had just given birth to a baby. Investigators Bob Cappuccio and Carl Coleman were stuck on Prelin Mountain for five days doing the investigation. One night, while on the mountain, Carl Coleman saved Cappuccio from harm, when they were both sleeping during a mortar attack. Carl awakened and immediately grabbed Bob, as he rolled out of his bed, and pulled him down to cover. Another job well done by two CID investigators.

Saigon

Criminal Investigator Frank A. Chiusano
Knowing how General Custer felt, but being Luckier

During the period Mar 68 to Mar 69, Criminal Investigator Frank Chiusano was assigned to Detachment B. 8th MP Group, Saigon, South Vietnam. A big problem at the time was the theft of U.S. Army five ton trucks, loaded with building materials destined for U.S. installations for the purpose of building living and office space for U.S. troops. Vietnamese civilians, hired by the Ford Motor Company, drove these trucks for the U.S. Army. The convoy would pick up the material in the Saigon area and then head in the direction of the big U. S. Military base Long Binh. Our "allies" the South Vietnamese managed to steal trucks right out of convoys, even though the convoy had an MP escort at the front and rear. It got so bad that a helicopter was covering a convoy and, believe it or not, the South Vietnamese still managed to steal a truck.

Now Frank Chiusano was fortunate in that he had a South Vietnamese informant, who kept his eyes open for Frank. It seemed the trucks that disappeared would show up at a police station in Saigon which was located adjacent to the Ton So Nut Air Base. The good police chief, a major, was using the building material for his own purposes and enrichment.

One-day Investigator Chiusano's informant called him and told him that a truck full of building material was parked at the police station, and like any good investigator Frank proceeded to that police station. Little did he know of the surprise our "ally" had in store for him. Chiusano arrived at the police station and got started with his investigation by taking photographs of the stolen five ton U.S. Army truck loaded with roofing and siding building material. Chiusano's activities did not go unnoticed, in particular since he was Caucasian, and stuck out like a sore thumb amongst all the oriental males. Suddenly an agitated Vietnamese police major and ten policeman surrounded Frank, all armed with M-16 rifles, compliments of the U.S. Government, and all pointing their M-16's at Investigator Frank Chuisano. Frank thought his final hour had come. He now knew how General Custer felt when the indians surrounded him, but at the time it happened it was not so funny. Frank had no Vietnamese interpreter with him but was fortunate that the very hostile police major spoke English.

The good major obviously did not like the idea of being caught red-handed with stolen U.S. Government property and neither did he want to lose his treasure. One bad word from the major and Investigator Frank Chiusano's name would have been on the Vietnam Wall Memorial today. Frank determined that the major was the chief of police of the station and immediately flipped his badge and credentials at him, letting him know "I'm one of you, I'm an American cop." This did not seem to impress the chief and so Chiusano used procedure two and told him that he realized the major had recovered the stolen truck and material, and had not had the chance to let the CID know about it. Frank knew the truck and material would have disappeared in another hour. In Korea we used to say that "slicky boy" (thief) could steal a radio and leave the sound behind. Frank knew the Vietnamese were just as talented.

Investigator Chiusano had his photos and agreed with the police major to leave the truck and material in his custody. As soon as he got back to his office, he contacted the CID group commander and informed him of the incident. The group commander, a lieutenant colonel, used his powers and the truck was returned to U.S. Army custody. Frank was luckier than General Custer. He managed to keep his scalp and will always remember our friendly "allies" the South Vietnamese.

CHAPTER FOURTEEN

USMC CID

This chapter is dedicated to our brother investigators in the USMC, who, with the exception of short periods when they attended the OSI (Office of Special Investigations, USAF) School, for years have attended the US Army CID School. The author had four marines in his class and all were of great character. One of my marine classmates later came to the army CID where he was sworn in as a CID warrant officer.

Before I relate criminal investigations conducted by USMC criminal investigators, let me give a little background information on the USMC CID.

Marine Corps investigators conducted criminal investigations (including felonies) prior to 1968, however the official military occupation series (MOS 0111) title was investigator. The Marine Corps did not adopt the criminal investigator (5821) MOS for enlisted personnel and criminal investigation officer (5805) MOS for officers until 1968.

Investigators in the USMC then became known as criminal investigators, just as our army special agents used to be called criminal investigators prior to the creation of the United States Army Criminal Investigation Command (USACIDC). When the army title changed from criminal investigator to special agent, the USMC continued to use the title criminal investigator. It gets a bit more confusing. When a USMC criminal investigator transfers to the Naval Criminal Investigative Service (NCIS), his title changes to special agent and his authority increases. NCIS has primary jurisdiction over investigating felony crimes in the U.S. Navy (USN) and the USMC, making the USMC CID subordinate to NCIS.

The USMC CID became more centralized, but by no means to the extent of the Army CID. You also have to realize that in the army the military police and CID are not under one command, but the USMC CID and military police are. USMC CID investigators suffered from their own form of *"Maglinism"* (Remember the grief Colonel and then Major General Maglin brought to the CID, see Chapter Twelve) in that it all depended on who the boss was, in this case always the local provost marshal (PM). Some PM's would allow their investigators to wear civilian attire, others would not; some would permit them to carry a concealed weapon, others made them carry it in their briefcase. Some PM's would insist that the investigator always identify himself by his rank (hello, Maglin) and some would permit them to identify themselves as an investigator. Another problem the USMC CID investigators had to contend with was the contamination of the criminal Investigator's job. He had add-on jobs such as the additional duties of accident investigator, claims investigator (of the claims division, legal office), fireman, and even, get this, "dog catcher" at a base where criminal activities were low. Now army CID Agents also investigate accidents, but the difference is that they investigate only "fatal traffic accidents."

The criminal investigators in the USMC CID had an MOS (military occupational specialty) of criminal investigator, and were permitted to wear civilian attire, carry a concealed weapon, but still used the title criminal investigator. They also drew a civilian clothing allowance and were much more centralized. Those add-on jobs of accident investigator, claims investigator, and dog catcher were prohibited by the USMC, and just like the army CID the USMC CID criminal investigators investigated only fatal traffic accidents. The last word seems to indicate that the USMC will be retaining its CID. The criminal investigators the USMC has will be assigned to NCIS, which is responsible for investigating felony crimes involving USMC personnel. It appears the USMC will only have military police investigators for the investigation of misdemeanor crimes on Marine Corps camps and stations.

Marine Corps Base, Twenty Nine Palms, California

Criminal Investigator James B. Benson, Jr.

A Rifle Theft Investigation that led to Bigger Things
Don't hassle us — Not a Smart Thing to say to either a
USMC or Army Investigator

While serving at a three-man office, at the Marine Corps base, Twenty Nine Palms, California, with the chief investigator, Peter Koslowski and Criminal Investigator Charles Quail, Criminal Investigators Koslowski, Quail and Benson solved an interesting case. The MP desk sergeant informed them that a marine had reported he had observed two marines steal M1 rifles from the rifle racks in the barracks, place them in the trunk of their car and head off base. Benson, Koslowski and Quail interviewed witnesses at the barracks and obtained a description of the subjects and their car. It was reported to them that the car had been parked in the soft sand next to the barracks. A check of the crime scene disclosed tire tracks and Criminal Investigators Benson and Koslowski obtained plaster casts and photos of the tire tracks. Benson and his two fellow investigators headed for Twenty Nine Palms, in uniform and unarmed to search for the suspects. In less than one hour they spotted the suspects next to their car at an auto repair shop.

Benson, Koslowski and Quail identified themselves as USMC CID Criminal Investigators to the suspects, and asked them for their identification. They told them they were civilians and "Don't hassle us," not a good way to talk to any CID Investigator, Army or USMC. Criminal Investigator Quail went to a nearby telephone and summoned the sheriff's department for assistance, who arrived in less than five minutes. Sheriff's officers requested identification and it was disclosed that they had several ID cards with different names. At that point the sheriff's officers asked to look into the trunk of the suspect's vehicle, which disclosed four M1 rifles. Both suspects (now subjects) were arrested, patted down and transported to the local sheriff's office and their vehicle was impounded.

At the sheriff's office it was determined that both subjects were in fact members of the USMC, and all agreed that this was a matter for USMC CID jurisdiction. The suspects and weapons were turned over to Criminal Investigator Benson and his fellow investigators who returned them to the base. At the CID office the three criminal investigators took turns interrogating the suspects. Then came a shocker. During the interrogation one of the subjects stated, in a joking manner, "By the way, I am armed and the sheriff's search never discovered the weapon." With that he slowly reached into the crotch area of his trousers and pulled out a loaded derringer, and handed it over to Criminal Investigator Quail. Believe me, it was no joking matter to them, but a good lesson.

As a result of good interrogations it was determined that the two subjects had not only stolen the four rifles, but were involved in numerous felony crimes, some local, some national, and some international, a matter of "gun-running" which of course made it a matter for FBI jurisdiction. The local FBI office was more than happy to take the case (old story, of course "known subjects").

Because of the good investigative job Criminal Investigators Benson, Koslowski and Quail did, all three were awarded commendations, at a meritorious mast (to appear before the general and be presented the commendation), by Brigadier General Lewis Fields, the commanding general of the Twenty Nine Palms USMC base.

Criminal Investigator Benson retired from the USMC CID on 1 December 1966, and went to work for the Bank of America (BOA) on 2 December 1966. He was assigned to the delinquent loan department as a skiptracer/investigator later to be called a delinquent loan officer. The biggest part of the job involved locating and recovering cars of delinquent customers. Investigator Benson made a name for himself with BOA, and received commendations, for recovering on average three hundred cars per year during his eighteen-year career with BOA. As I always say, once a CID criminal investigator (USMC) or agent (Army), always a CID criminal investigator/agent. This applies to agents of the Army and USMC.

Investigator Benson caused much grief to Dennis Montgomery, a twenty-year-old carnival worker and resident of Downey, California, when he repossessed his 1968 camper for failure to make payments. While searching through the vehicle to remove the personal property of Montgomery, to be returned to him, Investigator Benson discovered a shopping bag filled with nineteen plastic bags of marijuana. Benson called the Downey police department and informed them of his find. Montgomery made the big mistake of calling the police department and reporting his camper stolen, which made his arrest a cinch. Additional marijuana was found in Montgomery's apartment. Another job well done.

Jim retired from Bank of America in 1985. He had attended and graduated from the U.S. Army CID school, Fort Gordon, Georgia, on 6 November 1958, after already having served over seven years as an USMC CID criminal investigator. He is also the author of the book *Marine Corps Detectives.*

Marine Corps Station El Toro, CA

Investigator Bart Immings
Every Service has a Dumb Criminal

It was 1962, and Corporal Bart Immings had been awarded the military occupational specialty (MOS) 0111, which officially made him an investigator in the USMC. This of course did not give him automatic experience and like all of us, he started out as an OJT (on the job trainee). Bart was assigned to the office of the provost marshal and had to endure what all aspiring investigators suffered, namely getting stuck investigating petty barracks larcenies and other minor cases. In other words those cases the experienced investigators, or as Immings called them "the old salts", didn't want to be bothered with. Someone had to do the job and it was Immings's turn.

One of those cases was the "Coca Cola Caper" which baffled Immings. On base, as in all military installations, there were numerous vending machines, specifically coin operated Coca Cola machines. It seems that the coke machines were not producing profits compared to the merchandise sold. In other words, the coin boxes did not contain the number of coins they should have in connection with the merchandise sold. Someone was "ripping off" the machines, but who? Was it the vendor? Who was the thief? The coin boxes showed no signs of forced entry indicating an inside job. The shortages continued for several months, to the dismay of the exchange officer, and Immings had not the faintest idea who the thief was. Immings, being an OJT, desperately wanted to solve this case and

302

one day his lucky break came. Criminal Investigators Guillermo Tovar and Dick Ringler, two experienced investigators assigned to the narcotics detail, or two of the "old salts" as Immings called them, informed him that they had a "snitch" (informant) who was willing to help solve the coin box case. The informant provided Immings with the name of a young marine, Private Jones (not his real name), who committed the biggest sin a thief can commit: he bragged to other marines in the barracks that he was in possession of keys to the Coca Cola machines. This bragging would be his downfall. Immings snatched up Private Jones and put him through the mill, applying all of the skills he had learned in his short period as an investigator, interrogating the young man for a lengthy period. He was not getting anywhere. The suspected thief would not confess, but appeared to be cooperating. Immings obtained the consent of Private Jones to search his wall and footlockers. A search of both disclosed absolutely no clues and there seemed to be no physical evidence whatsoever. Back to the office and further interrogation, Immings was not ready to give up, and his stamina paid off. After a very lengthy interrogation the young thief "copped out" (confessed). Immings determined that while on leave in Chicago, Illinois, (his home town) the young man had obtained a total of five keys from a friend, which he determined would fit most of the vending machines in the barracks at Marine Corps Station El Toro. After his confession Private Jones took Investigator Bart Immings to his barracks and removed a box of laundry soap from his wall locker. Immings had thoroughly searched the wall locker but had not completely checked out the box of soap powder. Inside the soap box Private Jones had concealed the keys to the Coca Cola vending machines. Immings developed a nasty habit from this experience, every time he conducted a search of a wall or footlocker, containing a box of soap he would empty the contents of the box on the suspect's bunk. The thief's commanding officer took a dim view of Private Jones's activities and after spending several months in the base brig (jail) he found himself back in Chicago with a dishonorable discharge.

Investigator Bart Immings was in the first group of five enlisted investigators to be selected for warrant officer with the new MOS (5805) criminal investigations officer. He later was selected as a limited duty officer and retired as a captain in 1978. Bart Immings final duty station prior to retirement was Marine Corps Air Station El

Toro, California where he was assigned as a special agent with the Naval Investigative Service.

Marine Corps Air Station, El Toro, California
Special Agent Bart Immings

Bart's Sixth Sense kicked in — The Witness became the Subject

It was around 1976, and Immings was assigned to the Marine Corps Air Station, El Toro, when it was his turn as the weekend duty investigator. He was assigned to the Naval Investigative Service (NIS — today called the Naval Criminal Investigative Service) and his title, while assigned to NIS was special agent. It was Immings's turn as the weekend duty investigator, and it was not going to be a quiet weekend. Special Agent Immings was notified by the duty officer of the 3rd Marine Aircraft Wing that an A4 Skyhawk aircraft, which is a very fast close air/ground support jet, had been "fodded" with .22 caliber cartridge casings in the engine intake. The term "fodded" is a marine slang term for debris on the runway or around a jet engine intake, which can be extremely dangerous and cause the crash of an aircraft. Preliminary investigation by Immings disclosed that Private Sharp had reported discovering the "fodded" aircraft while on flight line duty, and had reported this to the duty officer. So far so good. Special Agent Immings after checking the crime scene and securing the cartridge casings as evidence took Private Sharp, who had discovered the crime, to the NIS office to interview him as a witness.

During the interview Special Agent Immings had a feeling that something just was not right. He had met Sharp before when a larceny had occurred and had solved that crime after interrogating Sharp and determining that it was Sharp who had stolen funds from the squadron coffee mess fund. Sharp in that instance had confessed to the theft, and as a result was posted to guard duty on the flight line, awaiting punishment for the theft case. Special Agent Immings had eyeball to eyeball contact with Sharp and detected a nervousness in his behavior. It seems he could not take the eye to eye contact and would look away at times. Additionally he started to breathe heavier and at times was searching for answers. Bart being a graduate of the U.S. Army CID school, and by now an experienced agent, used some of the tricks of the trade. He advised Sharp that he was suspected of attempted willful damaging of government property, and of his rights to have an attorney present. Sharp declined to have an attorney present, and agreed to be interviewed (interrogated). Agent Immings told Sharp "I think you are the one who, fodded, the aircraft and you might as well tell me the truth, because I still have your fingerprints from the theft case on file." He told Sharp that he had also found some fingerprints on some of the cartridge casings (he had not), and that he was going to submit his fingerprints and the cartridge casings with the fingerprints to the crime lab. So it would only be a matter of time before his fingerprints would be matched to those on the casings identifying him (Sharp) as the person who had committed the crime. After being confronted with this strong (non-existent) evidence Sharp "copped out" (confessed) and provided Special Agent Immings with a written statement.

Private Sharp told Special Agent Immings that he had "fodded" the aircraft because he wanted to be a hero by showing how well he performed his guard duty, in that he discovered the "fodding" of the aircraft and thus possibly saved a pilot from danger. Some "hero" he was. Immings never had to attend Sharp's court-martial because he apparently entered a guilty plea to the charges, the larceny as well as the attempted destruction of government property charges, and Immings's testimony was not required. Case solved, and once again the long time experience of a seasoned criminal investigator paid off.

After retiring from the Marine Corps, Bart was selected as chief of police and security operations at the Naval Weapons Center, China Lake, California, and later as chief of the department of defense police at Pearl Harbor, Hawaii. During the late 1980s he served as the anti/counter terrorism officer for the commander in chief, United States Pacific Fleet.

Camp Pendleton, CA

Criminal Investigator Robert L. Ruble
His desire was to become an officer and a gentleman

It was 1972, Criminal Investigator Bob Ruble was assigned to the CID office at Camp Pendleton, California, and the Vietnam War was still in full progress. Camp Pendleton was a place that would keep any investigator busy due to the large number of marines assigned there. It was Bob's misfortune to be the duty investigator and it did not take long before he was informed that a crime had occurred.

The military police desk sergeant informed Investigator Ruble that a theft of a substantial amount of money had occurred at an infantry training regiment on base. Ruble wasted no time and proceeded to the crime scene, one of those luxurious billets the Marine Corps provided to its marines, commonly referred to as a "quonset hut." Upon arrival at the unit, Investigator Ruble noticed that the non-commissioned officer in charge, a gunny sergeant (E7) had done his job and assembled all of the marines, a total of seventeen, assigned to that quonset hut, which also was the scene of the crime.

It was a gorgeous day to say the least, one of those days when the temperature just seemed to be perfect, not too hot and not too cool. Investigator Ruble was wondering why one of the fifteen marines, Private first class (E3) Harry Greenwald was sweating profusely. Did he have a fever and should maybe see the doctor? *No, that was not the reason*, Ruble thought, because Private first class Greenwald was not only sweating profusely, but was also extremely nervous. This was a good reason for Investigator Ruble to zero in on this young lad, and he did. At first Private first class Greenwald told Ruble "I'm always nervous around a person of authority," not a good trait for someone who wanted to be an officer. Now Greenwald was going to skip becoming a non-commissioned officer and go straight for a commission. He now told Investigator Ruble that he had applied for, and had been accepted, to attend officer candidate school (OCS), and that he had a great desire to become a Marine corps commissioned officer. These were magic words to the ears of Bob Ruble, because he thought a little psychology might work here. Ruble looked Private first class Greenwald straight in the eyes and said to him, "You know that Marine Corps officers are noted for their honesty, regardless of the consequences." Having said that, Ruble thought it prudent to advise Greenwald of his legal rights now, and advise him at the same time that he was suspected of larceny, namely the theft of the money. So the first question Investigator Ruble asked young Greenwald, who had not forgotten the words of wisdom that Marine Corps officers were noted for their honesty, was, "Greenwald, wouldn't you feel much better if you returned the money, so that you can live by the standards of the Marine Corps officers?" To Ruble's surprise he replied "yes," and without hesitation, went to his wall locker, got the stolen money (one hundred five dollars) and handed it to Investigator Ruble. When asked why he had stolen the money he replied, "It was visible in an unlocked and open wall locker, so I just took it." Case solved as a result of an experienced criminal investigator's knowledge and intuition.

Investigator Ruble obtained a sworn statement from the subject reflecting the details of the theft and when he was finished with him he turned him over to his gunny sergeant. As the gunny sergeant led the young thief away, he stopped momentarily, looked at Ruble, and said, "Do you think this will screw up my chances of going to OCS and becoming a Marine officer?

Bob Ruble looked at the young marine, gave him a friendly smile, and replied "I think you need to discuss this with your commanding officer, but just be honest with him as you were with me." His commanding officer restricted him to his barracks pending the convening of a special court-martial.

DaNang, Vietnam

Criminal Investigator Robert L. Ruble
The Fragging of a Lifer

It was just before Christmas 1970, and Criminal Investigator Bob Ruble took his turn in Vietnam. He was assigned to the CID Office of the famous division from WWII days, the 1st Marine Division. One night he was the duty investigator and when he went to bed he thought *I hope it will be a quiet night, so I can get some sleep.* It was not to be, because at 0200 hrs (2:00 A.M.), the telephone rang and the Chief Investigator, Joe Sanchez answered. He informed Investigator Ruble, who had been awakened by the ringing of the telephone and the talking of Sanchez, that a fragging (military slang used by all military services investigators, meaning someone had used a hand grenade to kill or cause harm to one of his own soldiers) had occurred in one of the 1st Division units. Chief Investigator Sanchez, Bob Ruble and two other unfortunate criminal investigators, not on duty, were dressed and ready to go in thirty minutes. It is the policy of all CID units, army and USMC, that if a very serious incident occurs all will pitch in, and murder was certainly a serious incident.

Travelling during the middle of the night in Vietnam was a dangerous undertaking at any time. Some areas were more dangerous than others were and it seemed the marines were always in the thick of it. The four investigators arrived at the crime scene about one hour after leaving the office, and they split up into two teams, to expedite matters, interviewing members of the unit to which the victim, a young sergeant only twenty years of age, belonged.

Sergeant Daniel Noble had been sleeping in a bunker when someone had dropped a hand grenade through the gun port, causing it to fall between his legs and explode, killing him instantly. Noble was obviously a good marine and NCO, considering that he was only twenty years of age and had already attained the rank of sergeant. This clearly indicated that he must have had good leadership qualities that got him promoted to sergeant, which apparently had been a thorn in someone's side.

Investigator Bob Ruble was interviewing one marine and by asking skillful questions was informed by this marine that one member of his unit, Private First Class (PFC) Henry Jones, had been acting very nervously after the fragging had occurred. Ruble finished his interview with the marine and then headed straight for Jones, a nineteen year old marine.

The other marine was right, Jones was extremely nervous when Investigator Ruble started to talk to him. It seemed he had a hard time looking Ruble straight in the face, was breathing a little heavier than normal and his jugular vain was about ready to pop out, meaning his heart was beating really fast. Investigator Ruble took no chances and advised Jones of his rights to an attorney and that he was suspected of the offense of murder. Immediately after advising Jones of his rights, Ruble asked him "If you were the perpetrator, why would you kill a young sergeant, like Sergeant Noble?" to which he replied, "Because I don't like lifers (meaning someone who entered the Marine Corps and intended to make it his career). Investigator Ruble then asked him "Where did you get the grenade" and he replied "It was on the stage where they used it for classes and USO shows." It was getting interesting and Private first class Jones certainly had said some incriminating things, but he had not come out directly and said that he had thrown the hand grenade that had killed Sergeant Noble. Ruble called Chief Investigator Joe Sanchez to where he was, and they both began to interrogate Private first class Jones. Jones never came right out and admitted that he had thrown the grenade that killed Sergeant Noble, but he intimated that he had and then he told the two investigators that he wanted to see a lawyer. Ruble and Sanchez had no choice now, they had to stop interrogating Jones or they would create a problem for themselves. The least they would do was to ruin the chances of prosecution due to illegal behavior by an investigator. The next move was to take Jones and the crime scene under close scrutiny, which they did. This resulted in the discovery of a smudge of red paint on the side of an ammunition box, found just outside the gun port through which the grenade had been dropped, that seemed to align with a smudge of red paint on the boots Private first class Jones was wearing. Investigators Ruble and Sanchez placed Jones under arrest for the murder of Sergeant Noble, confiscated his boots and obtained some paint chips from the ammo box as evidence. Examination of the ground also disclosed boot prints leading up to the gun port or scene of the crime. Ruble and Sanchez made plaster casts of the boot prints. After completing the interviews of members of the unit, and finishing off the crime scene, informed the unit commander of their preliminary findings and then returned to the CID office.

The next day the evidence was properly packed and sent to the U.S. Army Criminal Investigation Laboratory, Fort Gordon, Georgia (now located at Fort Gillem, Georgia), for analysis. It took a little while for the evidence to be processed and returned to the USMC CID office with a laboratory report of findings. The Crime Lab determined that the paint found on Jones's boot was similar in color and texture to the chips of paint removed from the ammo box at the crime scene. Also that the soles on the boots, confiscated from Jones, were similar in size and print to the plaster cast made at the scene of the crime. Although Private first class Jones never came right out and admitted to dropping the hand grenade into the gun port of Sergeant Noble's bunker, he gave enough incriminating information which in combination with the laboratory findings resulted in his being given a general court-martial. Private first class Jones was incarcerated in the 1st Division stockade immediately after his arrest. His parents had hired a civilian attorney to defend him, to no avail. A general courts-martial found him guilty of the charge of murder, and he was given a dishonorable discharge, sentenced to life imprisonment without parole at Leavenworth, and he was reduced in rank to Private (E1) with forfeiture of all pay and allowances. All this because "He hated Lifers."

Jones, when asked later, as to why he had dropped the grenade into Sergeant Noble's gun port, said the "lifer sergeant" had found him sleeping on duty and had given him a real bad "ass chewing," which proved that Sergeant Noble was a good NCO.

Criminal Investigator Robert L. Ruble, using the pen name of Bobby Ruble, is the author of *Have No Mercy* and *The Mysterious Farm Girl*, books he wrote after his retirement from a successful career as a criminal investigator with the USMC CID.

Japan
Marine Corps Air Station

Criminal Investigators Roy M. Winters and Jim Walton
Problems a Twelve Months Pregnancy Caused

Investigator Winters was the chief investigator of the USMC CID office at a Marine Corps Air Station in Japan. One fine day he was informed by his boss, Major John Andre, the provost marshal (PM), that the base commander, Colonel Matt McGruder had had dinner with the commander of a base about twenty miles from the Marine Corps air station. The commander, Brigadier General William White, was giving Colonel McGruder the needle by telling him that one of his men, a Staff Sergeant (E6), had been on his base in a state of intoxication. General White told Colonel McGruder that he had been informed this Staff Sergeant had tried to steal an aircraft, and in the process damaged the aircraft and then attempted to bribe the guard. Brigadier General White told Colonel McGruder that he had not received a detailed report on the matter but that the company which handled aircraft security was in the process of preparing one.

Major Andre was interested in getting to the bottom of the matter, which of course was in his best interest since he worked for Colonel McGruder, and so he called Investigator Winters and instructed him to look into this matter. Investigator Winters informed his partner, Criminal Investigator Jim Walton, that he was going to assist him with the investigation. Walton was not to thrilled about this news because he was a "short timer" due to leave the base and report to his new duty station in the United States.

Prior to leaving their base Investigators Winters and Walton checked around the base to see if anyone knew Staff Sergeant Paul Penny the alleged perpetrator of the crime. They determined that Penny had been distraught and drinking heavily after receiving a letter from his wife informing him that he was the proud father of a baby girl.

Investigators Winters and Walton proceeded to the base of the incident and went straight to General White's office. The general was one of those impressive officers, straight as a ramrod, with distinguished looking gray hair, steely eyed, and when he talked you listened, in other words an ideal officer. Brigadier General White informed them that he had not received a report from the PM or CID, but that the guard company was preparing an incident report and that he considered the matter serious.

After obtaining permission from the general to visit the security guard company Investigators Winters and Walton proceeded to the guard company but were unable to find the commander or first sergeant. They did find Corporal Fred Johnson who, as it turned out, had apprehended Staff Sergeant Penny, the suspected offender. Corporal Johnson informed Investigators Winters and Walton that Staff Sergeant Penny had been near this one particular aircraft and had remarked to him that if he could fly this plane he could fly back to the United States and have it out with his wife. Now the funny part about all of this is the fact that the airplane in question was a motorized, radio-controlled aircraft. It was part of a group of several model aircraft, which were going to participate in the base hobby aircraft show. These model airplanes were being guarded against theft and no one had bothered to inform General White that the aircraft involved in the incident was a model aircraft. Corporal Johnson related that Staff Sergeant Penny had told him his wife had informed him that he was the proud father of a new baby girl. There was however a twist to this "being a proud father" in that Penny had been overseas, without a leave to the United States, for twelve months and had never heard of a "twelve months pregnancy." To the contrary he not only became very angry when he received the news, but got quite drunk. While messing around with this one particular model aircraft, which he had picked up in his drunken stupor, he managed to damage one of the wings. Staff Sergeant Penny told Johnson that he would pay for the damages caused to the aircraft and tried to give Johnson some money. Johnson, of course, looked at this as an attempt to bribe him to keep his mouth shut.

Investigator Winters and Walton returned to General White's office and briefed him on their findings. Needles to say General White was quite surprised when they told him that the damaged aircraft involved was a model aircraft. No one had bothered to inform General White of this and someone certainly would take some heat on this. Winters informed the general that it was apparent Staff Sergeant Penny was quite drunk when he went to the model aircraft area and slightly damaged the wing on one model, and that he had no business being in that area. Winters also told the general of the underlying cause of Staff Sergeant Penny's intoxication, and this obviously touched a spot of compassion in the general, because Winters then asked him if this matter could be handled by Staff Sergeant Penny's command (Colonel McGruder) and the general readily agreed to that. Winters told the General if there were any damages to be paid for the repair of the damaged model aircraft, he would take care of it, but the general said that he would take care of that matter within his command.

Investigators Winters and Walton returned to their base and prepared a report, providing a copy to Major Andre and one to Colonel McGruder. Colonel McGruder obviously had the last laugh when he found out General White had thought it was a real aircraft that had been damaged and was then informed it was a model aircraft. About two weeks later, while on their way to lunch, Winters and Walton ran into Staff Sergeant Penny, who of course was sober and dressed, like a sharp marine should be. Penny informed Winters and Walton that he knew his "goose was cooked" when he found out that the CID was investigating his "airplane caper" and he immediately envisioned himself behind bars for a considerable time. He then told the two investigators that he really appreciated the fairness CID had shown in their conduct of this investigation. He told them, that as a result of his actions, he had been given a reprimand when he was administered a "captain's mast," USMC and USN lingo (Article 15 in army talk). He also told them that he had been given assistance, through counseling, as to how to straighten out his life. His parting words were "I am going to make the marines my career," at this Walton gave Winters the "thumbs up," which means alright in the U.S. but "go to hell" in Japan.

Japan
Marine Corps Air Station

Criminal Investigators Roy M. Winters and Jim Walton
Hold for Investigation

It was during the Fall of 1956 and Investigators Roy M. Winters and Jim Walton were stationed at a Marine Corps air station in Japan and would have contact with marines stationed in Korea. Korea has many church sponsored orphanages and quite often nuns take care of these orphans. One early morning Winters received a call from Staff Sergeant Robert A. Rocke, who was stationed at the K-3 air base in Korea. He was someone Winters had known for some time. Rocke was an aerologist (weatherman), and he and his wife were unable to have children of their own and for that reason had adopted several children. Staff Sergeant Rocke told Investigator Winters that he was in the process of adopting a three-year-old Korean girl and his orders were to return to the United States and that he needed a couple more weeks to complete the paper work, so he could take his new daughter with him. Now someone had told Staff Sergeant Rocke that the best way to beat all the paper work was to have an "Hold for Investigation" placed on him long enough to get everything done. Rocke told Investigator Winters that since they knew each other, he thought he would call him and see what he could do for him in this matter. Winters told him he really did not know what could be done, but he would check on it and let him know. Investigator Winters related the story to his partner Jim Walton, who was still trying to get ready to return to the United States. Now Walton was a combat marine, had been awarded the Purple Heart, and was well read and an experienced investigator. Walton also had a dry wit, bordering on sarcasm, and said to Winters "Isn't there something in the SOP (standard operating procedure) on this?" Knowing full well there wasn't. Investigator Winters called Technical Sergeant Ken Swanson, in G-1 (Personnel), and told him about Staff Sergeant Rocke's problem and that he would like to help him but really did not know how to go about it. He asked him what kind of upheaval would be caused if an "Hold for Investigation" were placed on Rocke. Technical Sergeant Swanson told him, "Don't worry about it. That's an easy thing to do." Three weeks went by and Investigator Winters heard nothing further about this matter. Then the phone rang and it was Staff Sergeant Rocke, who informed him that he had all the adoption paperwork taken care of and that he was on his way to Yokuska, Japan, for his return by ship to the United States. Staff Sergeant Rocke told Investigator Winters that he needed the "Hold for Investigation" lifted, and that he had another problem in that he was assigned to take his new daughter on board a troopship, and did not think this was right. He said to Investigator Winters "See what you can do." Then Investigator Winters received a call from Technical Sergeant Swanson who told him "Hey, we have a problem." I received four dispatches from HQ, Marine Corps wanting to know where Staff Sergeant Rocke was." The reason for the big interest was the fact that the USMC did not have very many aerologists. HQ Marine Corps demanded to know if Staff Sergeant Rocke was being prosecuted for some incident, or found innocent, or where he was. Investigator Winters said to Tech Sergeant Swanson "You mean you put a "Hold for Investigation" on him?" and Swanson replied "Well, didn't you want one?" Winters told Swanson, "You'd better take it off because he is ready to go to Yokuska, and you'd better inform HQ Marine Corps that he is on his way." Investigator Winters next thought of how he could get better-suited transportation for Staff Sergeant Rocke and his new daughter. Somehow he managed to get him and his new daughter on a ship taking Army dependents back to the United States. Several months later Investigator Winters received a photo from a marine friend, taken by a newspaper in Miami, Florida, showing Staff Sergeant Rocke with his four adopted children, all five of them wearing Mickey Mouse hats and watching Mickey Mouse on TV.

Staff Sergeant Rocke was well known for going to an orphanage, taking off his dog-tags, and then placing them around the neck of a child he had chosen for adoption and saying "I claim this child." This was photographed on many occasions and written about in the Armed Forces newspaper and gave a certain fame to Rocke.

East Camp, Atsugi, Japan

Criminal Investigator Roy M. Winters
The theft of the Chaplains Chalice

East Camp, Atsugi, Japan, middle 1950s, Criminal Investigator Roy M. Winters and two of his fellow investigators were having a critique regarding Roy's court testimony at a general court-martial. At the time any investigator being between assignments, and for that reason not having a caseload, was required to attend any court-martial at which a fellow agent had to testify, and then to critique the testimony given by his fellow agent. Criminal Investigator Roy M. Winters was the chief investigator and was the one who gave those instructions, because he thought it was a good learning tool for new and old investigators. Criminal Investigator Jim Walton was getting ready to depart from Japan, and the discussion was getting somewhat heated when there was a knock on the door and it was none other than Father Timothy Powers, the Catholic chaplain for East Camp, Atsugi, Japan. The good padre was a very soft-spoken individual but had the grip of a bear and could break your fingers at will. Father Powers said in an apologetic manner "I'm sorry to bother you gentlemen, but someone stole my chalice during the night and until I get another chalice I can't perform communion service." Winters told the good priest that he would take the case. Winters got all the basic information from Father Powers and then he, Walton and Sergeant Paul Day, another investigator, proceeded to the scene of the crime, the camp chapel. The chapel had two offices, one for the Catholic chaplain, and one for the Protestant chaplain, which had an extra desk in it for the Jewish chaplain since the Jewish congregation was very small. The investigators checked the crime scene but did not observe any obvious signs of a break-in, but all noticed that the Catholic chaplain's assistant, Corporal Henry Jones (Not his real name), who was present, appeared to be very nervous and uncomfortable in the presence of the three investigators. Winters and his two fellow investigators departed the chapel and returned to the

CID office. It did not take long for Investigator Winters and his fellow investigators to come to the conclusion that Jones was a likely suspect, due to the nervousness he had displayed in their presence. Winters conjured up a scheme that he figured might soften up the apparent culprit prior to being interrogated. He instructed Investigator Day to return to the chapel and dust for fingerprints, also to be extremely generous with the use of the fingerprint powder and lifting tape. He was to be sure that Corporal Jones observed his activities, then return to the CID office before the MPs were dispatched. Winters then called the MP station and requested that they send over two of the biggest MPs on duty, which they did. The two "bully" MPs were briefed by Winters, who instructed them to handcuff Jones, advise him of his rights, and bring him to the CID office. The MPs then proceeded to the Chapel and promptly placed Jones under arrest, advised him of his rights and informed him that he was suspected of having stolen the chaplain's chalice.

After the MP's delivered Jones to the CID office, Investigator Roy Winters took him into an interrogation room, once again advised him of his rights and the fact that he was suspected of having stolen the chaplain's chalice. He then, in a very soft spoken manner, you might say in a "fatherly mode" as if he was having a fireside chat, started a conversation with Jones, which in reality was the beginning of the interrogation. Roy had also placed some of the lifted fingerprints on his desk, in plain view of Jones, and then pointing to the lifted fingerprints and asked Jones "What do you think this means?" To which he replied "I think it means you caught me." It did not take Investigator Winters very long and he had convinced Jones, who after all was the chaplain's assistant, and presumed to be religious and knowledgeable of the Commandment which says, "Thou Shall Not Steal," to unburden his soul, confess, and provide Investigator Winters with a sworn statement outlining the theft of the chalice.

Jones told Winters what he had done with the stolen chalice, and shortly thereafter he and Winters proceeded to a house of ill repute at Yamato, Japan. There they found a lady of the night, who when told by Jones that he came for the cup, without hesitation produced the stolen chalice from an old magnesium roller skating box. She handed the chalice over to Investigator Winters and told him that Jones had pawned the chalice with the madam of the house of ill-repute, so that he could gain her freedom for the day and take her to the beach.

Investigator Winters noticed a powdery substance in the bottom of the chalice, which raised his investigative curiosity, so he took his fingers and stuck them in the bottom of the cup and retrieved some of the powdery substance, intending to sniff it. At the time it did not dawn on Winters that it could be residue from the communion wafers. While in the process of raising his fingers to his nose, Jones apparently remembered that he was a chaplains assistant and promptly knocked Investigator Winters hand away from the chalice and said "Don't do that, that chalice is holy." which seemed a funny comment for him to make considering where and under what circumstances the chalice had ended up in the house of ill-repute. Jones was promptly given a special court-martial and convicted of the theft of the chalice which was made of sterling silver and gold plated, and valued at about one hundred and fifty dollars, a lot of money during the 1950s. At the time of the court-martial Father Powers himself became forgetful of the words in the bible, which state "Forgive thy enemy" because he did not forgive Jones for betraying his faith in him and resented his liaison with a lady of the night. The chalice was not government property but belonged to Father Powers, who explained that the chaplains had to provide their own chalice for communion. The amazing thing was the fact that Investigator Winters and his marine team, consisting of the investigators and MPs, managed to solve the case, recover the chalice and return it to Father Powers in less than five hours, and just in time for church service and communion. About two weeks after the court-martial Winters ran into Father Powers who made it a point to inform Roy that he had forgiven Jones. Winters left the USMC after ten years of service and had a successful career, as a detective with the Police Department, Elmhurst, Illinois, from which he retired as a sergeant.

CHAPTER FIFTEEN

Munford, Inc and Defense Investigative Service (DIS)

From Corporate Investigator to Special Agent
The Author's Career after CID

Johnny Bagwell, at the time vice president, Munford, Inc security department, Atlanta, Georgia, came to me at the Fort Gordon field office shortly before my retirement and asked me to come and work for him as an investigator. I retired from the army on a Friday, and on the Monday I was on my way to Atlanta to start my civilian career as an investigator for Munford, Inc. Munford owned Majic Market Stores, Handy Andy, an ice cream factory, Munford Institute of Polygraphy, and the security department which conducted polygraph examinations for Munford as well as for other businesses, doing pre-employment polygraphs, and polygraphs in case of thefts or missing monies. My job was to check Majic Market stores for compliance with company rules and investigate thefts and inventory shortages. After about six months, Munford ran into some financial problems and sold off its Handy Andy stores, the ice cream factory and reduced the investigator force from five to one. That meant I would have been out of a job, except Johnny Bagwell recommended that they send me to their polygraph school, since at that time Munford was making good money conducting polygraph examinations for other companies. I already had my application in for employment with the Defense Investigative Service (DIS), and Johnny Bagwell knew that he was going to quit his job with Munford and go into business for himself. Johnny did this for me because he knew I would continue to draw my salary while attending polygraph school. There were two polygrapher jobs open and neither appealed to me, and Johnny knew I would turn both of them down. I attended and graduated from Munford Institute of Polygraphy during June 1977, run by none other than Homer Tank, D.R. Jones and, Johnny Bagwell, all former instructors at the CID polygraph school, Fort Gordon, Georgia, now called the DOD Polygraph Institute and no longer located on a military installation. Johnny Bagwell had gone into business for himself by then, and so I worked for him conducting polygraph exams until I received a call from DIS asking if I was still interested in working for them. I told them that I was still interested.

Over Twenty Years with the Chicago DIS Field Office

For the next twenty and one half years I worked as a special agent for DIS out of the Chicago office, conducting background investigations for security clearance applicants, until I retired for good on 03 January 1998. I moved to California and have been here ever since. The reason for moving to California was that two of my sons reside in California and one in Oregon.

While working for DIS, a couple of funny incidents happened. This was during the time when all agents were overloaded with work, and it was not uncommon to be working until 1900 hrs before heading home. I interviewed a neighbor, a reference listed by a young man who was in the USAF and needed a security clearance, and he informed me that the young man had worked for this one neighbor, who would be a good reference. I knocked on the door and identified myself by showing him my credentials and stating "I'm Special Agent Marlow, with the Defense Investigative Service, Department of Defense. "I informed him that I was conducting a background investigation on so and so, and he replied "Good, I'll call you when we have a war," and slammed the door shut. Needless to say I thought he was joking and after a couple of minutes knocked on his door again. He came back and was a little hostile, to say the least, and told me "I was getting ready to eat supper," to which I replied "You are lucky I won't get home for another two hours," and how could I know he was getting ready to eat. I told him he did not have to be rude, that I did not need the security clearance but the kid did, and if he did not give a damn why should I. He calmed down and we completed the interview.

Another time I got out of my car and was just getting ready to walk to the front door of a house, on the south side of Chicago, in a predominantly black area. A very pretty black lady walked up to me and asked me if I was looking for a girlfriend, I flipped my badge at her and said "I don't think so," boy did she disappear in a hurry.

Military and Civilian Training/Schools:

1. Basic training from 23 April 1956 to 23 June 1956, at Fort Leonard Wood, Missouri.
2. Advanced military police training, from June 1956 to September 1956, U.S. Army military police school, Fort Gordon, Georgia.
3. Traffic accident prevention course, 03 June 1956 to 18 June 1956 (Honor Graduate), U.S. Army Intelligence, military police and special weapons school, Oberammergau, Germany.
4. Wheel and tracked vehicle mechanics school, from 21 October 1960 to 10 February 1961, U.S. Army Ordnance School, Aberdeen Proving Grounds, Maryland.
5. Basic CID Course, from 10 Mar 64 to 04 May 64, U.S. Army military police school, Fort Gordon, Georgia.
6. Drug Investigation Seminar #3, March 1967, U.S. Army military police school, Fort Gordon, Georgia.
7. Munford Institute of Polygraphy, from April 1977 to June 1977, Graduated, Augusta, Georgia.
8. USAF special investigations school, security investigators course (DIS), from 12 September 1977 to 23 September 1977, Washington, D.C.

Promotions:
1. To Private First Class (E3), 30 October 1956.
2. To Specialsit Three (E4), 30 April 1957.
3. To Sergeant (E5), 16 April 1962.
4. To Specialist Six (E6), 03 June 1966.
5. To Warrant Officer (W1), 12 July 1966.
6. To Chief Warrant Officer (W2), 01 December 1967.

7. To Chief Warrant Officer (W3), 13 August 1971.

Awards:
Good Conduct Medal (3rd Award).
National Defense Service Medal.
Army Commendation Medal.
Vietnam Campaign Medal.
Vietnam Service Medal with three Bronze Service Stars.
Vietnam Cross of Gallantry with Palm.
Armed Forces Reserve Medal.
Bronze Star Medal.
Meritorious Service Medal.

In Conclusion:

I am proud that as an immigrant American I was able to serve my country for twenty years in the military and I am proud of being able to say "I was a CID Agent." The next most treasured thing is probably being a member of the CIDAA. I served as a board member/director for four years in the past and am currently on the board of directors. I was the first chairperson of the ways and means committee for six and one half years, and this gave me the chance of obtaining and having created all of the items presently for sale. It was always my aim that we only have quality merchandise and one item in particular, the CID badges. I wanted to be sure that they looked authentic and could be proudly displayed in a shadow box. Presently I enjoy contributing by writing the "Someone You Should Know" articles. It is funny how that came into being. I had written an article by that title on our CIDAA chaplain, Father Charly Grico, and was then asked by the editor, Paul Haubner and the Chairperson of the Membership Committee, Louise "Mickey" Head, if I would not be willing to make it a regular feature of the newsletter, so I did.

Lastly, I am proud that I was a co-founder of the Chicago area CIDAA Group, along with Joey Thurman. Little did I know that Joey, at the time an ATF agent, would volunteer for an assignment with Interpol in France shortly after the group was formed, and that I would get stuck leading the group for almost ten years until I moved to California. During July 1993, Roy Winters, who now heads the Chicago area CIDAA group informed me that Francis "Ace" Arciaga, USMC CID (Retired) (one of two USMC CID full CIDAA members left, the other being Roy Winters) was in town (as he would be every two or three years). I told Roy "Why don't we surprise him and present him with a CIDAA membership certificate?" and Roy readily agreed. Normally when Ace came to town, about three of us would meet with him (Roy, Ken Swinson, and I) at a restaurant for dinner. When I arrived at the restaurant the entire Chicago group was present. I thought they all came to be there when I presented the CIDAA membership certificate to Ace, but Ace turned the tables on me. After I presented him with the certificate (which came as a surprise to him), he presented me with a USMC CID honorary badge, which reads on the back "Camaraderie" 1993, Hubert Marlow USA/CID. I was informed that I was only the fourth person, in USMC CID history, and the only U.S. army CID agent to be so honored. The other three recipients included one USMC commandant, one marine and one navy man. Yes, I am very proud of that distinctive honor.

After arriving in California I noticed that there were many retired, former and reserve CID agents, and so I started the group here in Northern California. I once asked several of the group why they had not formed a group long before, having so many CID types in the area, and they replied "We needed someone like you." Gee, it's nice to be needed. I believe I have, and am still serving the CIDAA well, as one of the current directors.

Now I am fully retired and am enjoying life. I feel very lucky to be able to live in the greatest country of the world. The United States is far from perfect but it is far better to live in than any other country in the world. Count your blessings and be happy.